The Massachusetts Constitution of 1780

A Social Compact   *Ronald M. Peters, Jr.*

The University of Massachusetts Press   Amherst 1978

Copyright © 1974 by Ronald M. Peters, Jr.
Originally copyrighted as "The Political Theory of the
Massachusetts Constitution of 1780"
All rights reserved
Library of Congress Catalog Card Number 77–90730
ISBN 0–87023–143–X
Printed in the United States of America
Designed by Mary Mendell
Library of Congress Cataloging in Publication Data
Peters, Ronald M.
The Massachusetts constitution of 1780.
Includes bibliographical references and index.
1. Massachusetts—Constitutional history.
2. Social contract.   I. Title.
JK3125 1780.P47   342'.744'029   77–90730
ISBN 0–87023–143–X

Contents

To Mother and Father

Acknowledgments

The political theory of the Massachusetts Constitution of 1780 would have remained undiscovered had I not had the support and assistance of many people. The book began as a doctoral dissertation, and my largest debt arising from the dissertation is to the chairman of my research committee, Tim Tilton. His shrewd criticisms of the developing manuscript wrought many improvements in both the argument and the style of the essay. He has been an inspiration, an example, and a friend to me, and for all of these reasons I am greatly indebted to him. Among other members of my research committee, I am grateful to both Lynton Caldwell and Bernard Sheehan for their thoughtful reading of the manuscript. Larry Hill came late to the project, but he was a major source of support and advice as I struggled to turn the dissertation into a book. Numerous persons helped in the research and preparation of the manuscript at various stages of its development. Connie Bolte, Ronald M. Peters, Sr., and Helene L. Peters were able research assistants; Helene Peters, in particular, received a second education in the history of her birthplace. Several members of my family were kind enough to house me during a summer of research on the East Coast: Mrs. Dorothy Loughlin, of Worcester, Massachusetts; Ted and Virginia Peters, of North Andover, Massachusetts; Cameron Peters, of Boston; George and Mary Jane Mastapeter, of Martinsville, New Jersey; and Mrs. Rose Mastapeter, recently departed, of Bound Brook, New Jersey. My debt to Glenda May Peters cannot be calculated; she changed her name, but she never changed. Pam Hussen, Geri Rowden, and Betty Anderson were faithful typists, each of whom corrected many of my errors and none of whom rubbed them into my face.

Librarians from Boston to New York gave me an education in the mechanics of serious research. I would like especially to extend a grateful thanks to Ms. Gertrude Fisher of the Massachusetts Historical Society, and to Mr. and Mrs. Leo Flaherty, of the Massachusetts Division of Archives. I must also acknowledge with appreciation the many people who were of help to me in the Boston Public Library, the Massachusetts State Library, the Boston University Library, the American Antiquarian Society, the New York City Public Library, the Indiana University Library, and the Lilly Library. I would not have been able to travel to these places and meet these people, however, without the generous support of the Earhart Foundation of Ann Arbor, Michigan, for which I extend my deepest appreciation.

Finally, a word about Charles S. Hyneman. During the time when this book was researched and written, Charles Hyneman was the source of whatever wisdom I obtained. He struggled for years to shape my mind and he ended up getting at my character as well. He led me to the serious study of politics and showed me how to do it. Charles Hyneman, more than any other person except myself, is responsible for what follows. But if it does not do him justice, the fault is mine and not his.

Preface

This book is an interpretation of the political theory of the Massachusetts Constitution of 1780. The focus is upon the relationship between the individual and the demos, as that relationship is defined by the Constitution. This is the central problem of social contract theory, as defined by Hobbes, Locke, and Rousseau. The Massachusetts Constitution of 1780 was adopted by a political society that was schooled in social contract theory, and was explicitly predicated upon a social contract. In order to understand that social contract, I found it necessary to reconstruct the theoretical basis of the Constitution. This reconstruction rests upon an exegesis of the political literature produced in Massachusetts between 1774, the year of the Continental Congress, and 1780. I attempt to develop the theoretical implications of this literature and bring them to bear upon the task of interpreting the theoretical foundations of the Constitution.[1]

Although the study falls within the broad area of the history of ideas, I enter the field with the perspective of the political theorist. Thus, my interest is in attaining theoretical insight into fundamental political questions, such as the proper relationship between the individual and the demos, questions that have implications that extend beyond the politics of Massachusetts during the Revolution. In developing and adopting the Constitution of 1780, the people of Massachusetts were compelled to deal with political fundamentals, and in the process they engaged in a theoretical discourse from which we may learn. Therefore, my interest in the political debates of this period does not run merely to a description of what was said, or to an explanation of what was said in terms of the political and economic conditions

1. For a discussion of the concept of "reconstructed logic" see Abraham Kaplan, *The Conduct of Inquiry* (San Francisco: Chandler Publishing Company, 1964), p. 8.

of the time. Instead, I analyze the literature in order to assess the political arguments it contains. Since the study necessarily impinges upon matters of concern to historians, some comments about my approach are in order.

The historiographic literature focuses upon the question of whether ideas can be properly understood in isolation from the context in which they arose. One school of thought affirms that this can be done, another denies it. In my opinion, neither point of view is acceptable when taken to an extreme. It would be difficult to assess the thought of John Adams, for example, if one knew nothing about his life or his times; it would be impossible to assess his thought if one knew only about his life and his times. Somewhere between these two extremes lies the proper balance between the weight that should be given to what a person said and the weight that should be given to the circumstances in which he said it. To err in one direction involves a naive acceptance of the notion that people say what they really mean; to err in the other direction may lead to a false imputation of meaning to what people say.

Precisely where the balance is to be struck may depend upon the sort of understanding one is seeking. For example, we know that John Adams said "it is certain, in theory, that the only moral foundation of government is, the consent of the people," but we still face the task of deciding what he meant. Since we cannot interview him, we must find some other basis upon which to interpret his statement. Six bases seem possible: (1) an analysis of the expression without recourse to other evidence bearing upon it; (2) a search through Adams's writing for other evidence of his views on consent; (3) the discovery of what persons privy to his thinking reported about his views on consent; (4) an exploration of what others had to say about consent at the time; (5) a study of Adams's life situation and behavior; and (6) an examination of the social, political, and economic environment of the period. Now what weight are we to give to each of these factors in attempting to determine Adams's meaning? In part, an answer depends upon our reason for asking the question. If we are primarily interested in Adams's views on consent in relation to the causes of the American Revolution, we may choose to lay great stress upon bases five and six, and much less upon bases one through four. Yet if we are most interested in engaging in a theoretical analysis of the meaning of the concept of government by consent, we may well wish to stress bases one, then two, three, and four, and consider bases five and six as secondarily important.

This study seeks to understand what the Massachusetts experience can teach us about a number of questions that have always been central to political theory. Is popular consent the only legitimate basis of government? If so, how can the consent of the people be secured? Do individuals possess natural rights? If so, what are they? What justifies rule by the majority? Under what circumstances should majority rule be limited? These questions go to the heart of politics, and cut across generations. I believe that the Massachusetts experience can inform our understanding of political theory today because of the unique circumstances that obtained at the time, and in spite of the fact that that time differed from our own.

Thus, I stand with those who argue for the possibility of the study of ideas independent from the study of the context in which they were spawned. One may legitimately investigate the relationship between political circumstances and the theoretical perspectives that arise within them, but one may also address the logic, coherence, and tenability of those perspectives. While I do not ignore the history of the period, the focus of this book is upon the ideas that it produced. I take cognizance of historical events only insofar as is necessary to provide a general background for the theoretical topics addressed. I try to avoid making inferences from historical contexts to the meaning of arguments, except to point out where a commonly accepted practice (such as taxing people to support religion) suggests a theoretical issue (such as the meaning of the right of conscience). This book is not a political history of the period.

Among those who accept the autonomy of ideas, however, the question of context is still an important issue. A prominent school of thought argues that utterances must be interpreted in terms of meanings which were available to those who did the uttering. Since the range of available meanings of words (and the concepts they embody) is determined by the environment of thought at the period of time in which the words were expressed, one must define that range of meaning by a thorough examination of that environment. Here, the assertion is that ideas must be understood in context, but that context is one of meaning, and not a social, political, or economic context. This point of view has its most powerful statement in the work of Quentin Skinner, and is most prominently exemplified in the area of revolutionary American political thought by the work of Gordon Wood.[2] I do not accept Skinner's historiographic principles. By his canons of interpretation it would be impossible to conclude that John Adams ever had an original idea, since we must interpret everything Adams said in terms of meanings already established at the time. Beyond this, I reject the notion that all ideas are historically specific to the period of time in which they were expressed. I would, however, accept the proposition that the words by which they were expressed might mean different things at different periods of time.

This seems to me to be the real contribution of Gordon Wood. In *The Creation of the American Republic*, Wood stresses the need for the researcher to "steep" himself in "the political literature of the period," in order to ascertain the meaning of the vocabulary by which political concepts were expressed. Many words, he notes, did not mean the same thing in the eighteenth century that they do now. "Although the vocabulary of the period was familiar, I found the meaning of much of that vocabulary strange and peculiar, and I learned that words such as 'liberty,' 'democracy,' 'virtue,' or 'republicanism' did not possess a timeless application."[3] Wood suggests that one must seek to understand the political writers of revolutionary Massachusetts as they understood themselves, and in this sentiment I fully concur. The interpretation this book provides is based upon an examination of every available political pamphlet, sermon, and newspaper essay published in Massachusetts between 1774 and 1780, and a study of private correspondences, broadsides, town meeting records, town returns, and Massachusetts laws for the same period. Having steeped myself in this literature, I found that it was possible to understand it. Wood goes too far when

2. Quentin Skinner, "Meaning and Understanding in the History of Ideas," *History and Theory* 8 (1969): 3–53; Gordon Wood, *The Creation of the American Republic, 1776–1787* (New York: W. W. Norton and Company, Inc., 1969). Skinner's work was assessed by political theorists in a symposium in *Political Theory* 2, no.3 (August 1974). For a discussion of Wood's impact upon the study of the political thought of the Revolution see Robert E. Shalhope, "Toward a Republican Synthesis: The Emergence of an Understanding of Republicanism in American Historiography," *William and Mary Quarterly* 20, no. 1 (January 1972): 49–80. For related discussions of historiography see: J. G. A. Pocock, *Politics, Language, and Time* (New York: Atheneum, 1971); Gene Wise, *American Historical Explanations* (Homewood, Ill.: The Dorsey Press, 1973).
3. Wood, *Creation*, p. viii.

he speaks of "the irretrievability and differentness of the eight-
eenth-century world." It was different, but that difference is
retrievable. If it were not, there would be little purpose in writing books on the subject.

It is on the question of the correct method of interpretation
that I part company with the historians of ideas. As a political
theorist, I am not entirely satisfied with the interpretations of
ideas provided by historians. Generally, they attempt to describe
what was thought and said during particular periods in history.
They often employ textual exegesis as a technique for present-
ing their interpretations, but the quotations they string together
are usually fragmentary, and sometimes they seem to be intended to convey atmosphere, rather than to provide evidence. Since
Wood's *The Creation of the American Republic* represents the
best work in this field, we may again consider it by way of illus-
tration. *The Creation* is marked by four difficulties which are
common to this genre of writing. First, Wood takes quotation
fragments out of the context in which they were uttered and
weaves them into a new context of description. This can lead
to a misrepresentation of the connotation and the denotation of
the fragmentary quotes within their original contexts. Second,
quotation fragments from diverse sources and varying contexts
are combined to make the same point; at least Wood's presumption is that they do, in fact, make the same point. Unfortunately, the reader is not in a position to judge unless he has read all
of the primary sources from which the quotation fragments are
taken. Third, Wood usually makes no attempt to establish other
evidence or cite further sources substantiating the same point.
Fourth, Wood often describes ideas without analyzing the arguments in which he found them. These techniques lead him into
misinterpretations of the literature (as I point out in several
places in this book), and leave the reader uncertain, even in
those cases where Wood's interpretation appears correct.

In order to avoid these difficulties, I have chosen to proceed
differently. I summarize and quote arguments at length and analyze them for their theoretical implications. This procedure en-
ables the reader to evaluate my exegesis, since the summaries
provide a basis for evaluating the interpretations. I take a wide
range of theoretical statements and arrange their implications
in a conceptual order. In order to substantiate my thesis, I cite
numerous sources in support of key points of interpretation.
Where evidence contrary to my thesis exists, I try to face it

squarely and provide my interpretation of it. And throughout, I keep my attention fixed upon the theoretical issue in which I am interested. This book is, above all, an exercise in social contract theory.

The conclusions of this study are restricted to my interpretation of the political theory of the Constitution of 1780. Some may question whether it makes any sense to speak of a constitution as embodying a political theory. Others, such as Eric Voegelin, argue that the evolution of political theory can be explained in terms of the attempts of peoples to symbolize their political beliefs by adopting fundamental law.[4] I do not employ Voegelin's framework of analysis in this book, but I do accept the Aristotelian dictum that a demos expresses a theoretical understanding of itself and of politics in general when it undertakes to draw up the rules governing its political life. Amid the political conflicts by which constitutions are shaped, parties to the debate are compelled to offer theoretical explanations and justifications of their positions. The constitution that emerges will reflect this theoretical debate, and can be interpreted in terms of it. While not all people will subscribe to all aspects of the constitution, the constitution must reflect consensus on the fundamental principles of political life shared by the demos if it is to serve effectively as the basic law of the community. It is for these fundamental principles of political theory, and the reasoning that supports them, that this study searches.

As to the question of the implications of this study for our understanding of the American Revolution, I say only this. There is some reason to believe that Massachusetts differed from other states by virtue of its Puritan heritage, although the extent of this difference remains to be clarified. Therefore, it would not be proper, and I do not attempt, to generalize from

4. Eric Voegelin, *The New Science of Politics* (Chicago: The University of Chicago Press, 1952); idem, *Order and History*, 4 vols. out of 5 (Baton Rouge: Louisiana State University Press, 1956-). For an application of Voegelin's theory to important documents in the American political tradition see Willmoore Kendall and George Carey, *Basic Symbols of the American Political Tradition* (Baton Rouge: Louisiana State University Press, 1970). The analysis of documents is an important first step in understanding the political self-conception of a people; it is not, however, sufficient. I apply Kendall and Carey's technique of textual analysis to the Constitution of 1780 to raise questions, but not to answer them.

the Massachusetts case. However, when the Massachusetts experience has been clarified, so has a large part of the political theory of the Revolution. In that sense, this study may serve to enhance our understanding of the political theory of that era.

The body-politic is formed by a voluntary association of individuals: It is a social compact, by which the whole people covenants with each citizen, and each citizen with the whole people, that all shall be governed by certain laws for the common good.—from the Preamble to the Massachusetts Constitution of 1780

I

The Massachusetts Constitution of 1780

The Theoretical Problem

The American Revolution was fought in order to achieve liberty. This at least is what we have always been taught. But for the revolutionaries the word liberty had two meanings. The primary objective of the Revolution was to achieve the liberty of self-government. The right of a free people to set up whatever form of government they wish and to choose the men who will rule over them was for many the very definition of liberty itself. Having achieved this liberty, the right to govern themselves, the new Americans were immediately confronted with the problem of deciding how to go about excercising it. In trying to solve this problem they had to confront liberty in the second of its two senses, the liberty of each individual to enjoy his alienable and unalienable natural rights. In order to keep these two notions of liberty distinct, let us call them by different names. The concept of liberty as self-government we shall call the concept of popular sovereignty. The concept of individual liberty we shall term the concept of individual autonomy. The concept of popular sovereignty holds simply that in a society organized for political action, the will of the people as a whole is the only right standard of political action. The concept of individual autonomy holds that each individual is endowed with rights that either cannot be taken from him under any circumstances (unalienable rights) or that can be taken from him only with his own consent (alienable rights).

The duality between these two concepts is strikingly evidenced in the most famous passage of the Declaration of Independence.

> We hold these truths to be self-evident, that all men are created equal, that they are endowed by their Creator with certain unalienable Rights, that among these are Life, Liberty, and the pursuit of Happiness; That to secure these rights, Governments are instituted among Men, deriving

their just powers from the consent of the governed; That whenever any Form of Government becomes destructive of these ends, it is the Right of the People to alter or to abolish it, and to institute new Government, laying its foundation on such principles and organizing its powers in such form, as to them shall seem most likely to effect their Safety and Happiness.

In what must be regarded as a masterly stroke of rhetoric, the Declaration moves from premises based on the concept of individual autonomy to a conclusion that presupposes the concept of popular sovereignty. While each individual has an equal unalienable right to life, liberty, and happiness, among other rights, only the people collectively have the right to alter or abolish a government that denies those rights to one or more persons. And only the people collectively have the right to establish a new government, which may be organized according to their collective taste.

It is evident that these two concepts are at least potentially inconsistent with each other. If the people are free to organize a government on whatever principles they wish, they presumably may choose to operate on the basis of principles that can and may be used to abridge the rights of individuals. And if an already established government chooses to abridge the rights of individuals, only the people collectively can act to restore those rights. Just government, according to the Declaration, must be based on the consent of the governed. But does this mean that the consent of each individual is necessary, or does it mean that the collective consent of the people is necessary? In other words, is just government based upon the concept of individual autonomy or the concept of popular sovereignty? The possible inconsistencies between the two concepts in the Declaration seem so apparent that one is led to wonder if the framers of the Declaration, and by extension the people of revolutionary America, may have had a much different understanding of individual rights and popular sovereignty, and of the relationship between them, than the text of the Declaration suggests to the contemporary reader. Or, if their understanding of these concepts was the same as that of the present generation, one may wonder which one would have been of higher priority for the revolutionaries when the potential conflicts between them became realized.

The text of the Declaration provides no answers to these questions. It is not, after all, the function of a declaration of principles to elucidate the reasoning behind them. The precise meaning of and relationship between these two concepts, as they were understood by those people who advanced and endorsed them during the American Revolution, can only be ascertained by examining the way in which they were implemented by those people. This implementation took place in the process of establishing new governments under new constitutions in the years immediately following the separation from England. As recent scholarship has revealed, this period of constitution-making was a time of searching political debate in America.[1] Arising out of this debate were two packages of principles, each of which can be identified with a corrresponding concept of liberty, and both of which were primary legacies of the Revolution to the history of American political thought.

One group of principles surrounded the concept of popular sovereignty. Included in it were the principles of collective consent, majority rule, and the common good. The concept of popular sovereignty recommended political institutions that would reflect as accurately as possible the will of the people, and the principles that formed this package all tended in the direction of accomplishing this end. The other group of principles surrounded the concept of individual autonomy. Among these principles were individual consent, individual rights, and self-interest. All of these principles furthered the objective of achieving the maximum of individual autonomy. Both of these packages of principles were derived from the same contractarian view of the nature of the state and they were often mixed together, although in various combinations, by the political writers of the Revolution. Indeed, there were so many permutations of the contract view of the state, and there were so many different admixtures of these two packages of principles, that a general conclusion about the regard in which each package was held

1. See Bernard Bailyn, *The Ideological Origins of the American Revolution* (Cambridge: Harvard University Press, Belknap Press, 1967); Elisha Douglass, *Rebels and Democrats* (Chicago: Quadrangle Books, 1955); Jack R. Pole, *Political Representation in England and the Origins of the American Republic* (Berkeley and Los Angeles: University of California Press, 1966); Clinton Rossiter, *Seedtime of the Republic* (New York: Harcourt, Brace and Company, 1953); Gordon Wood, *The Creation of the American Republic, 1776-1787* (New York: W. W. Norton and Company, Inc., 1969).

may be very difficult to reach. To the extent that the weight of the evidence can be determined to favor one concept at the expense of the other, however, the implications are important for a correct understanding of our political heritage. For at the heart of this question lies the problem of the proper relationship between the individual and the society of which he is a part, a problem as germane for America today as it was in 1776. And in trying to deal with this problem within the context of American political life today, it is a useful first step to understand the way in which it was viewed at the time when America's basic political institutions were being shaped.

A recognition of the distinction between these two divergent sets of principles is evident in the secondary literature on the subject of revolutionary American political thought, and it may be said that until very recently the question of their relative priority has been consistently answered in favor of the concept of individual autonomy and its concomitants. An excellent example of the unquestioning homage paid to individual autonomy is Clinton Rossiter's *Seedtime of the Republic*. Rossiter starts from the assumption that "the men who made the Revolution held a philosophy of ethical, ordered liberty that the American people still cherish as their most precious intellectual possession." Given this rather firm expectation, it is not surprising that Rossiter should arrive at the conclusion that one of the six major characteristics of revolutionary political thought was "individualism, since it placed man rather than the community at the center of political speculation, emphasizing his rights, his happiness, and his power to make and unmake government." There would appear to be some difficulty with this formulation, unless Rossiter intends that each individual had the "power to make and unmake government," which is an unlikely proposition.[2]

Rossiter is consistently insensitive to such tensions. In discussing the principle of popular sovereignty he reveals just how willing he is to ignore the plain meaning of the passages he cites when they do not correspond with the assumption he wishes to prove.

A corollary of the contractual origin of government was the doctrine of popular sovereignty, a very simple solution

2. Rossiter, *Seedtime*, pp. 1, 448. The other characteristics of revolutionary thought that Rossiter identifies were idealism, conservatism, optimism, toughmindedness, and pragmatism.

to a very complex problem. . . . In a proclamation dated January 23, 1776, the General Court of Massachusetts announced:

It is a maxim that in every government there must exist, somewhere, a supreme, sovereign, absolute, and uncontrolable power; but this power resides always in the body of the people; and it never was, or can be delegated to one man, or a few; the great Creator having never given to men a right to vest others with authority over them unlimited either in duration or degree.

Having done his duty in mentioning popular sovereignty Rossiter continues, without pause, to extract the true meaning from this passage from the General Court's proclamation. "The Americans . . . were speaking of *political* sovereignty, of the ultimate source from which all legitimate power must be derived. . . . All of them agreed that even the sovereign people were to be guided and restricted by the laws of nature in exercising their original sovereignty. Political sovereignty was 'supreme, irresistable, uncontrolled' only within the sphere assigned to it in the great plan of nature." On Rossiter's interpretation of this passage the phrase "supreme, sovereign, absolute and uncontrolable power" expresses a "limited political sovereignty." Just how something that is absolute and uncontrollable can in any sense be limited is a problem that Rossiter does not appear to notice. It is evident that his interpretation can only be true if it is the case that the word "men" in the quoted passage from the proclamation means "each individual" rather than the collectivity of men which is the people. If this is what had been intended, one may wonder why the General Court did not choose the word "man" to signify man qua man (i.e., each individual man).[3]

Rossiter also ignores the evident collective meaning of collective noun phrases. The proclamation of the General Court contends in the paragraph preceding the one quoted by Rossiter that "the Happiness of the People (alone) is the sole End of Government," and the subject of the proper ends of government is the next topic which Rossiter addresses. Although he does not quote the General Court, Rossiter provides a list of ten quotations in support of his contention that the end of government was thought by the "colonial theorists" to be the good of the individual. Of these, the first four speak of such ends as

3. Ibid., pp. 408–409.

"the Protection of Property," "personal liberty, personal security, and private property," and the enjoyment of "our own." The last six quotations mention such ends as these: "the benefit of the community," "the Salus populi," "the welfare of mankind," "the happiness of the governed," "the happiness of the people governed," and finally, "the Good, Safety and Happiness of the People." The first four quotations which focus upon individual ends would appear to be inconsistent with the last six quotations which deal with collective ends. Rossiter, however, does not perceive this distinction. "Colonial theorists," he says, "agreed almost unanimously that government existed only for the benefit of the men who had submitted to it. Even when they used such collective phrases as 'the welfare of mankind,' 'the public good,' and 'the benefit of the community,' they were thinking in terms of the welfare, good, or benefit of each individual." Just what the colonial theorists might have thought about a case in which the welfare, good, or benefit of two individuals came into conflict, Rossiter does not say. And he offers no argument or evidence in support of his contention that the collective phrases require an individualistic interpretation. The prima facie meaning of these collective phrases is clearly collective. In the absence of evidence to the contrary, it would seem only reasonable to suppose that what appears to be so is in fact the case. Rossiter's arbitrary treatment of this issue renders his argument unconvincing.[4]

Rossiter lays great stress upon natural rights. These rights were, according to him, viewed as "inherent, universal, unalterable, inestimable, sacred, indefeasible, fundamental, imprescriptible, divine, God-given, hereditary, and indelible." But, he asks, "what were these rights which man possessed as man and could never surrender?" While many such rights are to be found in the polemical literature, the truly theoretical works stressed five specific natural rights above all others: "life, liberty, property, conscience, and happiness." Unfortunately, the agreement which Rossiter finds in the literature in regard to these five natural rights is not matched by a corresponding precision in defining them. What, we may ask, does it mean to say that the natural

4. "Proclamation of the General Court, January 23, 1776," in Oscar and Mary Handlin, eds., *The Popular Sources of Political Authority: Documents on the Massachusetts Constitution of 1780* (Cambridge: Harvard University Press, Belknap Press, 1966), p. 65; Rossiter, *Seedtime*, pp. 409–411.

right of liberty is "inherent, universal, and unalterable"? What especially could it have meant to slaveholding society? Does not one forfeit such rights as he may have to liberty when he commits a crime? If so, then in what sense may they be held to be "unalterable"? And what of the natural right of property? This right was "universally acclaimed in the literature of the Revolution," according to Rossiter, and was notoriously illustrated by the problem of taxation without representation. Here, Rossiter quotes from the resolve of the town of Newburyport, Massachusetts in 1765: "That a People should be taxed at the Will of another, whether of one Man or many, without their own Consent in Person or by Representative, is *rank* Slavery." Does this imply that a people taxed by the consent of their representatives are perfectly in possession of their natural right of property? How far could the legislature go in taxing the people before representation shaded into slavery? If the literature provides answers for these and other similar questions, Rossiter has not found them.[5]

The uncritical acceptance of the predominance of the concept of individual autonomy, illustrated by the work of Clinton Rossiter, has been brought into question only in the very recent past. In 1967 Bernard Bailyn published *The Ideological Origins of the American Revolution*, a book that was immediately recognized as a milestone in the study of the Revolution. Bailyn argues that Americans distinguished sharply between the "sphere of power" and the "sphere of liberty." They were, he believes, anxious to protect the latter against the encroaching nature of the former. But what did they mean by "liberty"? According to Bailyn, liberty was understood by the Americans to be the excercise of natural rights under the limits set by law. He quotes John Allen in support of this conception. Liberty, said Allen in 1774, was "a power of acting agreeable to the laws which are made and enacted by the consent of the PEOPLE, and in no ways inconsistent with the natural rights of a single person, or the good of the society." Allen's definition is clearly replete with the tensions we have found to exist in the Declaration of Independence and in the work of Clinton Rossiter. And Bailyn, like Rossiter, wonders "what were these all-important 'natural rights'?" His answer to this question, however, differs significantly from that of Rossiter. Whereas Rossiter thought it pos-

5. Rossiter, *Seedtime*, pp. 375, 377, 379.

sible to present a list of the inherent rights of man, Bailyn finds the literature less clear. "They were," he says, "defined in a significantly ambiguous way." This ambiguity, according to Bailyn, may be traced to the concurrent influence on colonial thinking of the English common law, and that of the natural law philosophers. Their notion of natural rights was an odd conglomeration of common law precepts and natural law rhetoric. But, Bailyn notes, these two sources of natural rights were less compatible than the colonists at first believed because the common law of England was distinctly positive law while the natural rights of man were supposed to be antecedent to all political authority. Even if the English law were regarded as a mere expression of natural law, it sustained its authority from being determinate and specified, but natural rights were necessarily indeterminate and unspecified. Therefore, the ideal of natural law and natural rights transcended the English common law tradition. This distinction was precisely the grounds upon which the American view of natural rights later came to differ from that of the English. Nevertheless, even though the Americans denied that the content of natural law was entirely captured in the precepts of the common law, it was only to the common law that the Americans could look for specific tenets of natural law and specific natural rights. Therefore, they located the concrete manifestations of natural rights only in the common law.[6]

This is confirmed when Bailyn returns to the subject of natural rights in relationship to the topic of constitutional government. He says that "the *rights* that the constitutions existed to protect were understood in the early years of the period . . . to be at once the unalienable, indefeasible rights inherent in all people by virtue of their humanity, and the concrete provisions of English law as expressed in statutes, charters, and court decisions; it was assumed that the 'constitution' in its normal workings would specify and protect the unalienable rights of man." Bailyn then goes on to stress the importance that the concept of natural rights had for the colonists in terms of their understanding of the nature and function of written constitutions. Constitutions, properly understood, were nothing other than embodiments of natural rights. According to Bailyn, "the entire legitimacy of positive law and legal rights must be under-

6. John Allen, *The Watchman's Alarm to Lord North* (Salem, Mass., 1774), quoted in Bailyn, *Ideological Origins*, p. 77; ibid., pp. 77–79.

stood to rest on the degree to which they conformed to the abstract universals of natural rights." Now this interpretation may be true, but Bailyn's ambivalence on the specification of natural rights is evident. He speaks of natural rights as "abstract universals" and as "unalienable and indefeasible rights inherent in all people by virtue of their humanity," yet he finds them specified only in the English law. He does not attempt to search for a list of the universal rights, nor does he trace the implications of the conclusion that such rights are in a practical sense coextensive with the English law.[7]

Bailyn's discussion of natural rights and written constitutions occupies a place between his discussion of representation and consent, and his discussion of sovereignty. In discussing representation Bailyn contends that the American rejection of the theory of virtual representation "led to a recovery and elaboration of conceptions of government by the active and continuous consent of the governed. . . . The view of representation developing in America implied, if it did not state that direct consent of the people in government was not restricted, as Locke would have had it, to those climatic moments when government was overthrown by the people in a last final effort to defend their rights, nor even to those repeated, benign moments when a government was peaceably dissolved and another chosen in its place. Where government was such an accurate mirror of the people, sensitively reflecting their desires and feelings, consent was a continuous, everyday process." Sometimes, of course, the people have desires and feelings that may run contrary to the desires, feelings, and natural rights of some among them. What then is the proper relationship between the theory of government by consent and the theory of constitutional government based on individual natural rights? Bailyn provides no analysis of this issue.[8]

As important as the concepts of representation, consent, rights, and constitutions were, it was the concept of sovereignty, Bailyn tells us, over which the Revolution finally was fought. Sovereignty he defines as "final, unqualified, indivisable, power" which, he says, was properly located in the people, in the American view. It was to establish the principle of popular as opposed to parliamentary sovereignty that the Americans rebelled. Since

7. Ibid., pp. 184–185, 188.
8. Ibid., pp. 172-173.

sovereignty was indivisable, it must either rest in England or in
America; between these two alternatives the Americans really
had no difficulty in choosing. Oddly, Bailyn never discusses the
relationship between sovereignty and the other concepts that he
covers in this chapter. The issue of sovereignty appears to have
been more significant in his view to the later development of
the federal system in 1787, than it was in relation to the establishment of the state governments during the Revolution. Although he notes that it was in establishing these new governments that the Americans asserted their sovereignty, he takes no
note of the fact that this was accomplished specifically through
establishing written constitutions. In view of the fact that he
had just finished characterizing constitutions as embodiments
of principles of natural law, it would have been useful for him
to have considered the relationship between natural rights and
sovereignty, and the role that consent plays in relation to both.[9]

The Ideological Origins was clearly the most significant contribution to the study of the political thought of the American
Revolution up to the year of its publication, 1967. Two years
later, however, it was transcended by Gordon Wood's *The Creation of the American Republic, 1776-1787*. *The Creation*
picks up where *The Ideological Origins* had left off in describing
the development of American political thought during the period of the Revolution and founding. It is a massive piece of scholarship, based upon an examination of virtually all of the political
writing that was published during the Revolution, and much
that is available today only in private collections. Wood comes
full circle from Rossiter on the subject of natural rights. The index to *Seedtime of the Republic* lists thirty-two references under
the heading of "rights, natural," whereas the index of *The Creation* reveals only three entries under the heading of "rights and
nature." Interestingly, on none of the three cited pages does the
phrase "natural rights" appear. That Wood could have devoted
615 pages to an examination of the political thought of the
Revolution and founding period without once using the phrase
"natural rights" suggests the extent of the divergence between
his analysis and Rossiter's. But the ambiguities which we have
found in the interpretations of both Rossiter and Bailyn are to
be found in Wood also.[10]

9. Ibid., p. 198.
10. Rossiter, *Seedtime*, p. 554; Wood, *Creation*, p. 649.

One of the principal themes of *The Creation* is the development of popular sovereignty during the period of the Revolution. The English theory of legislative sovereignty was supplanted, according to Wood, by the pure concept of popular sovereignty, in which sovereignty rested in "the people-at-large outside of all governmental institutions." The "transferral of sovereignty" as Wood describes it effected a "radical redistribution of the powers of society within the government," and beyond that, "a shattering of the categories of government that had dominated Western thinking for centuries." This emphasis upon the importance of popular sovereignty, which parallels Bailyn's analysis, is obviously an important departure from the devotion Rossiter displays toward the concept of individual autonomy. But Wood stresses individual autonomy also in developing a second of his major themes, the fundamentality of written constitutions. According to Wood, the differentiation between constitutionality and legality was a principal development in revolutionary political thinking. Throughout this period the Americans were continually trying to distinguish between what was fundamental and what was not, and they eventually came to the conclusion that fundamental rights and principles should be demarcated in a written constitution and set above the ordinary operation of law and government. "Many Americans," says Wood, "were determined to provide for the protection of these fundamental rights and moved . . . toward a definition of a constitution as something different from and superior to the entire government including the legislative representatives of the people."[11]

Here again, we face the key question: What were these "fundamental rights"? Rossiter attempts to present a list of them. Bailyn identifies them with the rights recognized under the English Constitution. Wood provides no explicit answer at all. Are these fundamental rights superior to the sovereignty of the people? Wood contends that during the early years of the Revolution Americans laid less emphasis upon "the private rights of individuals against the general will" than they did upon "the public rights of the collective people against the supposed privileged interests of their rulers." They did so because they believed that "there could be no real sense of conflict between public and personal liberty." Indeed, it was perceived at that time, according to Wood, that "the people were the best asy-

11. Wood, *Creation*, pp. 383, 385, 266.

lum for individual rights." "In the Whig conception of politics," he says, "a tyranny by the people was theoretically inconceivable, because the power held by the people was liberty, whose abuse could only be licentiousness or anarchy, not tyranny." It was only after the Revolution was consumated, in the 1780s, that Americans came to see that even a democracy could be tyrannical.[12]

Wood's analysis of this theoretical problem is ingenious. While recognizing the tension in ideas, he circumvents the need for assessing it by asserting that the Americans did not recognize the implicit contradiction in their own thinking. Is this interpretation tenable? A complete answer to this question must await the full presentation of the argument of this book. As a preliminary gloss on the matter, however, we may note that, if it were the case that the tension between the rights of individuals and the authority of the people was one of which the Americans were not aware, then we should not expect to find the issue raised in the literature of that period. If the issue were raised, then it can hardly be held that it was one of which they were unaware, and if they were aware of it, we will have to search further than did Wood in order to find out if, and how, they resolved it. Such a search is the objective of this inquiry into the philosophical foundations of one of the most significant documents of the revolutionary period, the Massachusetts Constitution of 1780.

When Americans today contemplate their heritage and the principal symbols of it, they typically and understandably arrive early at a consideration of such documents as the Declaration of Independence, the Articles of Confederation, the Constitution of the United States of America, and the Bill of Rights. Few are aware of the importance of the revolutionary state constitutions as cornerstones of the new republic. Indeed, only within the past twenty-odd years has the scholarly community taken the sort of notice of these basic documents in our political tradition that they deserve. In the decade following the adoption of the Declaration of Independence, new constitutions were adopted in all of the former colonies except Rhode Island and Connecticut, each of which chose to retain its colonial charter until well into the nineteenth century. Three states, South Carolina, Vermont, and New Hampshire, each wrote two

12. Ibid., pp. 61, 62.

constitutions during the first decade after independence, bringing to fifteen the total of new constitutions written prior to 1787. Of these, thirteen were written down between 1776 and 1780. In the framing of these new constitutions, the principles that germinated during the early years of the Revolution became expressed in concrete form. It is to these documents that one must look to understand the views on government that prevailed during the period of the founding of the republic.

The Massachusetts Constitution of 1780 is, on any fair assessment, the most significant of these early state constitutions, and it is arguably deserving of a place along side the Declaration of Independence, the Constitution of the United States, the Bill of Rights, and the *Federalist*, as one of the five most important documents of the revolutionary era. This is a weighty claim, but consider for a moment the merits of the case. In the modern meaning of the term, these early state constitutions were the first written constitutions in the history of the world. Among them, the Massachusetts Constitution was the first one written by a special convention assembled for the sole purpose of framing a constitution. Among them, it was the first one submitted to the people for approval before ratification by the convention that framed it. Among them, it was the only one that has survived until today under the same rubric. In most of its essentials, it has not changed significantly in almost two hundred years. In sum, it can be seen that this constitution was among the first written constitutions in the world, was the first written constitution ever based upon the fully developed concept of a constitutional convention, and was the first written constitution ever expressly approved by the people over whom it was to operate. It stands today as the oldest written constitution in the world.

The principal architect of the Constitution was John Adams, who was by all accounts the most influential figure in the shaping of the new governments. According to Elisha Douglass, Adams's famous pamphlet *Thoughts on Government* was the "paramount guide" in at least five states, including Massachusetts. There can be little doubt that Adams was the most important political theorist of the revolutionary years. Even Jefferson, author of the Declaration of Independence and *Notes on Virginia*, was not as highly regarded during the Revolution as was Adams. In the words of George Dutcher: "The real author of this constitution was none other than John Adams who more than any other individual was responsible for launching and steering the movement for constitution-making and whose ideas, more than those of any other single person, guided and pervaded the movement which established republican government in America and therefore in the modern world."[13]

The fact of Adams's prominence is not as significant in relation to his role in the framing of the Constitution, however, as the ability and flair for expression he brought to the task. Perhaps because of his philosophic bent and flowing literary style, the Massachusetts Constitution is the most eloquent of all American constitutions. Indeed, it may be advanced with confidence that, at least upon this occasion, Adams's prolixity was an undisguised blessing. The Constitution stands in sharp contrast to the Federal Constitution of 1787, by virtue of the depth of its exposition. Where the Federal Constitution settles for a word or a phrase, the Massachusetts Constitution takes up a sentence or even a paragraph. Disdaining the spare writing style which earned Gouverneur Morris his reputation in 1787 as the draftsman of the Federal Constitution, Adams chose to develop in his draft of the Massachusetts Constitution the reasoning behind many of its provisions and to include in it a preface in which he developed the theoretical premises underlying the act of forming a government. It is this very attention to explanation, as well as the classic form and the completeness of the Massachusetts Constitution, that distinguishes it among other American constitutions, and commends it to the attention of scholars.

For all of these reasons, the Massachusetts Constitution was the most influential of the early state constitutions, according to much testimony. Adams himself, in his more cantankerous years, was able to claim, "I made a Constitution for Massachusetts, which finally made the Constitution of the United States." While Adams's ego may have led him to oversimplify the case, his boast contains more than the veneer of truth. According to Douglass, "the state constitutions—particulary that of Massachusetts—were the greatest single influence on the Federal Constitution," and Gordon Wood eulogizes the Massachusetts Constitution in these terms.

It was the Massachusetts Constitution of 1780 . . . that eventually came to stand for the reconsidered ideal of a

13. Douglass, *Rebels and Democrats*, p. 32; George M. Dutcher, "The Rise of Republican Government in the United States," *Political Science Quarterly* 55 (1940): 211.

"perfect constitution." . . . The Constitution seemed to
many to have recaptured some of the best elements of
the British constitution that had been forgotten in the ex-
citement of 1776. It alone of all the American constitutions had happily found the true mixture. . . .The Massachusetts Constitution of 1780 not only had a direct influence on the New Hampshire Constitution adopted in 1784
but it seemed to many in the 1780's to climax the second
wave of state constitution construction. In its structure at
least, it came to represent much of what reformers in other
states desired for their own constitutions.[14]

The Massachusetts Constitution of 1780 is, then, a historically prominent document and worthy of attention for that reason
alone. But it is also an interesting subject for theoretical analysis
precisely because of the unique circumstances of its adoption.
Rarely in the history of the republic has there been a more thorough, or a more thoroughly documented, public debate of basic
political principles. Periods of great public debate tell us about
the ideas that shaped public thinking and policy during times
past; they also may uncover truth in the philosophical sense,
since they necessarily reveal the complex interplay between
theory and practice out of which political truth is apt to emerge.
The focus of this investigation, then, will be upon the theoretical
underpinnings of the Massachusetts Constitution of 1780, as
those underpinnings were revealed in the public debates and en-
actments, and the private correspondence of the politically active members of the society. In examining this literature, our
attention will be fixed upon the key theoretical tension between
the concepts of popular sovereignty and individual autonomy.
In order to determine the relative priority of these concepts
it will be necessary to reconstruct the logic of the thinking
which motivated the people of Massachusetts in adopting the
Constitution of 1780. This reconstruction will begin with a
consideration of the text of the Constitution in chapter 2.
Before undertaking that task, however, it will be useful to consider the historical context within which the Constitution was
framed and adopted, and the personalities and issues that influenced its final shape.

14. John Adams to Mercy Warren, July 28, 1807, in "The Adams-Warren
Letters," *Collections of the Massachusetts Historical Society* 73 (1925):
375; Douglass, *Rebels and Democrats*, p. 32; Wood, *Creation*, pp. 434-435.

The Events

One of the most remarkable aspects of the American Revolution was the way in which political continuity was maintained amid the strife of the war and the economic and social disruption that it caused.[15] In Massachusetts, the move toward independence formally began on June 17, 1774, with the dissolution of the General Court. During the following summer, conventions were held in most of the counties in the province, and the outcome of these conventions was a consensus on two points: one, that a Provincial Congress should be called for the following fall, and two, that each county should assume responsibility for its own internal government. The events of the summer of 1774 were the culmination of years of conflict between the House of Representatives and the royal governors. The House of Representatives was dominated by the colonial majority, and it continually asserted its independence of the Crown and the governor. The governor, as the agent of the king, was able to effectively control policy in the colony through his domination of the court system and the governor's council. Through his power of appointing judges and his power of vetoing choices for the council, the governor was able to fill these agencies with sympathizers of the Crown. During the administration of Governor Hutchinson, the principal battle between the House and the governor was over the right to pay the judges.[16] The House contended that by controlling the salaries of the judges, Hutchinson also controlled the decisions that they made. The House was the eventual winner in this struggle, at least to the extent that there could have been a winner. The judges who accepted salaries from the Crown were intimidated and an effort was made to impeach Chief Justice Oliver, a Hutchinson crony, when he accepted his salary. The upshot of these tactics was

15. This account of the events leading up to the adoption of the Constitution of 1780 is based on the following sources: Harry A. Cushing, "The Transition from Provincial to Commonwealth Government in Massachusetts," *Columbia University Studies on History, Economics and Public Law* 7, no. 1 (1896): 281; Fred E. Haynes, "The Struggle for the Constitution of 1780 in Massachusetts" (Dissertation, Harvard University Archives, 1891); Samuel E. Morison, "The Struggle Over the Adoption of the Constitution of Massachusetts, 1780," *Proceedings of the Massachusetts Historical Society* 50 (May 1917): 353–411.
16. Hutchinson was governor from 1771 to 1774; Gage was governor from 1774 to 1775.

that the courts were effectively closed throughout the colony. Upon the replacement of Hutchinson by General Gage, the focus of the struggle shifted to the council. Gage insisted upon vetoing the appointment of any colonial sympathizer to its membership. The makeup of the council was important because of the veto power which the governor and council exercised over the House. When the House continued to send up councilors whom Gage would not accept, it became clear that the government of the colony was at an impasse. It was at this point that the General Court was dissolved in 1774, and the colonists moved toward ad hoc government.

Gage issued new writs of election on September 1, 1774, but it became apparent to him that he could not hope to control the council, and therefore the General Court, if a new session were to meet. He therefore dissolved the General Court on September 28, 1774. On October 5, 1774, ninety of its members showed up at Salem, where the court was supposed to meet, and on October 7, 1774, they resolved themselves into a Provincial Congress. The Provincial Congresses were to rule Massachusetts during the period from October 5, 1774, to July 19, 1775. In all, there were three Provincial Congresses during this period.[17] The power of these congresses was limited by circumstances. During this time the town of Boston was occupied, and the interior affairs of the state were under the direction of the county conventions and local committees of safety. The courts remained closed and the need for a statewide government based upon some more permanent foundation was widely recognized. On May 16, 1775, the Second Provincial Congress resolved to petition the Continental Congress for its advice on the subject of establishing a government. Although John Adams, as a delegate to the Continental Congress from Massachusetts, argued strongly that the recommendation of that body should call for the drafting of new constitutions in each province, other members of the Continental Congress were more cautious and the resulting reply to Massachusetts was a suggestion that the Province resume its colonial charter, with the Council acting in place of the governor as the executive agency. The Third Provincial Congress acted upon this suggestion and on July 19, 1775, the

17. The First Provincial Congress met from October 5, 1774 to December 10, 1774; the Second Provinical Congress met from February 1, 1775 to May 29, 1775; the Third Provincial Congress met from May 31, 1775 to July 19, 1775.

House of Representatives met under the resumed charter of 1691. Two days later the House chose twenty-eight men to serve as councilors, and the Council met on July 26, 1775, for the first time. The Council sat as the executive power in continuous session from July 28, 1775, until the inauguration of Governor Hancock under the Constitution of 1780 on October, 25, 1780.

During the years from 1775 to 1780 there were three movements toward establishing a new constitution for the state. During the spring and summer of 1776 the House of Representatives had the question under consideration but no action was taken until September 17, 1776, when in a resolution, the House requested permission from the freeholders of the state to frame a constitution. Through the months of October and November the returns of the towns filtered in, and they were largely negative. There were two principal objections to this proposal. The first was that the times were not ripe for such a serious undertaking because of the exigencies of the war and the absence of many men who were away in the Continental Army. The second was that the General Court was an improper body to frame a constitution under which it would later have to function. Some degree of popular participation in the process of framing and adopting a new constitution was seen to be necessary in order to insure its fundamental character.

With the rejection of the resolution of September 17, 1776, the question of forming a new government was placed in abeyance by the General Court. Pressures for a new government continued to build, however, from out of doors. On May 5, 1777, the House tried again to obtain the authority to form a government. This time the tactic it employed was to seek new authority under the aegis of new elections. The towns were requested to empower their representatives at the next election with authority to form a constitution. In spite of the objection of Boston, the new General Court proceeded on June 17, 1777, to resolve itself into a constitutional convention, and appointed a committee to draft a new constitution. Meeting intermittenly as a constitutional convention during the next nine months, the General Court on February 28, 1778, produced the ill-fated Constitution of 1778. This constitution was presented to the towns for their approval or disapproval. According to the terms of the May 5 resolve, two-thirds of the freeholders of the state had to approve of the plan before it could be ratified by the

General Court, meeting again as a constitutional convention. This constitution was a relatively simple document. It possessed no preamble and did not include a bill of rights. Suffrage was granted to all freeholders, except for "negroes, Indians, and mulattoes." The suffrage for the House of Representatives was apportioned by town, according to the size of the town. Suffrage for the Senate was based upon special districts. Property qualifications for office were as follows: for representatives, £200; for senators, £400; for governor, £1,000. In each case, one-half of the specified amount was to be in real property, held within the geographic area represented. The governor, as a member of the Senate could vote in it, but he had no power to veto legislation passed by the General Court.

The Constitution of 1778 was opposed on a number of grounds. Many towns felt that the legislature, even convened as a constitutional convention, was an inappropriate body to frame a constitution. Others felt that the time was not yet ripe for adopting a new constitution, again citing the fact that many men were away in the war. But these general objections were not the only reasons for which the Constitution of 1778 was opposed. Many features of the Constitution were themselves objectionable. Perhaps the largest number of objections was lodged on the grounds that the plan contained no bill of rights. The Virginia Declaration of Rights of 1776 had created a precedent to which many thought Massachusetts should conform. The ratio of representation for the House of Representatives was also opposed on the grounds that the House would become too unwieldy. Some towns wished to simplify the government by doing away with the governor and lieutenant governor altogether, while others wanted a more distinct separation of powers and provisions for rotation in office.

The weight of these objections was sufficient to bring about the rejection of the Constitution of 1778. Although 129 towns gave no returns at all, there were still 9,972 nays counted against only 2,083 yeas. The rejection of the Constitution of 1778 did not bring about the termination of the demand for a constitution, however. Although throughout most of the state the ordinary operation of government had been restored, in dissident Berkshire County the courts were still prohibited from sitting. During the summer and fall of 1778 the towns of Berkshire County argued their case in opposing the courts on the grounds that there was no constitution to sanction the laws of the state.

So emphatic were the citizens of Berkshire County in their position that at one point they threatened to secede from the state should constitutional government not be established. The Berkshireans were for the most part alone in their stubborn opposition to the authority of the state. In spite of their failure to win the support of other counties, and in spite of the fact that many in the east might just as soon have seen Berkshire County leave the state, if only to silence it, the very fact of their resistance and the potential example it set for other counties created considerable pressure for a new effort to frame a constitution.

In a resolve dated February 20, 1779, the House of Representatives solicited the views of their constituents on two questions, which were as follows:

> *First*, whether they chuse at this Time to have a new Constitution of Form of Government made.
>
> *Second*, whether they will impower their Representatives for the next Year to vote for the calling of a State Convention, for the sole Purpose of forming a new Constitution, provided it will appear to them, on examination, that a major Part of the People present and voting at the Meetings called in the Manner and for the Purpose aforsaid, shall have answered the first question in the Affirmative.[18]

The vote on these questions was clearly in the affirmative. With 134 towns responding, the votes on the first question were 5,591 yea, 2,041 nay. The votes on the second question were generally either not given, or corresponded with those on the first question. The strongest support for these proposals came from Berkshire County, but the overall pattern of the vote reveals no significant geographic variation. Often towns within the same county cast opposite votes.

With this evidence of popular will in their hands, the members of the House of Representatives, on June 15, 1779, issued a call for a Constitutional Convention to convene on September 1, 1779, in Cambridge. The Convention met in four sessions over the period of the next nine months. The first session, which lasted from September 1 to September 7, was devoted to the certification of delegates, the determination of rules, and the selection of a drafting committee. The drafting committee

18. Handlin and Handlin, *Popular Sources*, p. 383.

consisted of thirty members of the Convention, and had the responsibility of developing a first draft of the Constitution for the purposes of discussion. This committee was composed of some of the most illustrious members of the Convention: from Suffolk County there were John Adams and James Bowdoin, who was also elected as president of the Convention; from Essex County, Theophilus Parsons and Jonathan Jackson; from Middlesex County, James Sullivan; from Bristol County, Robert Treat Paine and Samuel West; from Plymouth County, Gad Hitchcock; from Worcester County, Jedediah Foster and Joseph Dorr; and the at-large delegates were Samuel Adams, John Pickering, and Caleb Strong. From among the committee of thirty, a subcommittee composed of Samuel and John Adams and James Bowdoin was asked to develop a preliminary draft. John Adams assumed the burden of actually writing that draft.

Little is known of the deliberations within either the subcommittee of three or the committee of thirty. Adams's original draft was not preserved, and the only evidence of the committees' activities is the proposal which they eventually laid before the Convention. The reconvened Convention met in its second session from October 28 to November 12, 1779, to consider this proposal. During this session the principal focus of attention was the Declaration of Rights. Attendance was not good, due in part to the fact that many members of the Convention were also involved in the state government as members of the General Court and as judges in the several courts. Because of this, on November 12, 1779, another recess was taken until January 5, 1780, when the Convention met at Boston for its third session. This session too was marked by poor attendance, this time due to the severity of the winter weather. The session did not resume official business until February 27 and during most of it only about sixty delegates were present. The Frame of Government was extensively debated during this session, and the final form of it and the Declaration of Rights was determined. On March 2, 1780, 1,800 copies of the final draft were ordered to be printed and distributed to the towns. The fourth and final session of the Convention met from June 7 through June 16, 1780, and in this session the Constitution of 1780 was ratified and the date of its inauguration was set for October 25, 1780.

There is some question as to whether or not all articles of the Constitution received the required two-thirds approval from the voters in the towns. According to the rules adopted by the Convention, every town was to examine the Constitution and vote on each article of it separately. Having done so, the towns were to transmit the record of their votes to the Convention, along with any amendments that a town might wish to propose. The Convention would then tally the votes, and if it appeared that any article did not receive the approval of two-thirds of the voters, the Convention would amend it in order to bring it into line with the wishes of a two-thirds majority. The Convention was then to ratify the modified Constitution without distributing it to the people again. The problems created by this procedure are easy to imagine. Many towns objected to the same articles, but for different reasons, thus making it impossible to amend an article to the satisfaction of everyone. In addition, the Convention compounded the problem of assessing the popular will by the manner in which it chose to count the votes. Separate tallies were made for each article. In counting the votes on any given article, three distinct tallies were made. First, a tally was made of those who approved the article. Second, a tally was made of those who approved the article, if amended. Third, a list of those who opposed the article was made. In adding the yeas and nays for the article, the total of those who approved was added to the total of those who approved if amended. The result was that a large number of persons who must have opposed an article as it stood, were counted in favor of it. Samuel E. Morison contends that this practice jeopardized the legitimacy of the Constitution, since on certain of the more heavily opposed articles, especially Article III of the Declaration of Rights, these as-amended votes might have been enough to swing the vote against the article, or at least to deny it the two-thirds majority needed for approval.[19]

Unfortunately, the town returns are not reliable in testing this nor any other specific hypothesis that requires an exact counting of the votes. The returns of the towns were haphazardly collected and tabulated according to principles that were incapable of rendering an accurate count. At the town meetings, people wandered in and out, and abstained from some articles while voting on others. Towns are recorded as approving unanimously, with no mention of the number of voters. Towns voted against some articles on principles that ought to have entailed

19. Morison, "The Struggle," pp. 396–401.

their disapproval of other articles, of which they made no mention. It appears from the returns that a very large majority of the voters must have approved of almost all of the Constitution, yet there is no way to count the votes accurately. It is clear that Article III of the Declaration of Rights was opposed by more people than any other article in the Constitution. But that article received at least a majority of approving votes, even if it fell below the required two-thirds majority which the Convention had required. If any aspect of the town returns is worthy of comment, it is the nearly universal approbation that almost all of the articles in the Constitution received. If the level of approval for some of the more disputed articles fell toward the two-thirds mark, the fact itself would not seem to be of much theoretical interest.

The Personalities

It is almost literally true that John Adams had no sooner stepped from the deck of the ship *Sensible* upon his return from his first European sojourn, than he found himself appointed as Braintree's delegate to the Constitutional Convention that was to frame a new constitution for Massachusetts. The honor should have come as no surprise to Adams, who, by 1779, had established himself as the third most prominent American after Washington and Franklin. As the principal force in the Continental Congress, Adams served on scores of committees, including that which drafted the Declaration of Independence and that which planned the American efforts to make treaties with foreign countries. As the chairman of the Board of War and Ordnance he carried much of the responsibility for the logistics of the war, and he was acknowledged by all to be the most vociferous advocate of new governments for all of the states. He nominated George Washington for the post of commander of the Continental Army, and was delegated to help negotiate a treaty of alliance with France during the years from 1777 to 1779. To mention these accomplishments is, of course, to forego mention of his numerous activities prior to the Revolution, and the major honors of his life which were to come in the two decades following it.

John Adams's prominence and his key role in developing the original draft of the Constitution should not be allowed to obscure the quality of the other delegates to the Convention. Approximately 297 men actually participated in some phase of the Convention.[20] Among these were 138 who at some time in their lives served in the House of Representatives, 39 who at some time in their lives served in the Senate, and 7 who were to become governors of the Commonwealth. The future governors were Samuel Adams, John Hancock, Caleb Strong, James Sullivan, Levi Lincoln, James Bowdoin, and Increase Sumner. Several members of the Convention were to become distinguished jurists, among them John Lowell, William Cushing, Theophilus Parsons, Robert Treat Paine, and David Sewall. The quality of the assemblage is indicated by their collective occupational and educational statistics too. Fifty-four of the delegates had at least some higher education, and 38 had received degrees from Harvard. Broken down by occupation, the Convention could boast of 31 lawyers and judges, 39 merchants and businessmen, 22 farmers, 18 physicians, 21 clergymen, and 18 public officials.

The specific accomplishments represented by these individuals cannot be perceived in these gross figures. The names of John and Samuel Adams and John Hancock are familiar to everyone, and those of James Bowdoin, James Sullivan, Theophilus Parsons and Levi Lincoln will be recognized by anyone who is conversant in the history of this period. But consider for a moment some of the lesser known personalities.[21] Samuel Barrett, the secretary of the Convention, was a Clerk of the Market and Overseer of the Poor, who conducted a state lottery to raise money for the war. Later he was elected to the General Court. Judge Joseph Cushing was in and out of the General Court during his long career in the law. In addition to participating in the Massachusetts Constitutional Convention, he also took part in the state convention which ratified the Federal Constitution. William Cushing, apparently no relation to Joseph, was also a judge. After a long period on the Massachusetts bench he was appointed by President Washington to the first term of the United States Supreme Court. Jedediah Foster of Brookfield, eulogized as "a forgotten patriot" by Grinnel, was said to have been influential in the early drafting of the Consti-

20. These statistics are taken from C. B. Tillinsghast, "An Alphabetical List of Members of the Various Constitutional Conventions of Massachusetts, with Biography and Their Classifications 1780–1917," *Massachusetts Archives.*
21. These biographical sketches are taken from J. L. Sibley, ed., *Harvard Graduates* (Cambridge, Mass.: C. W. Stever, 1873).

tution of 1780.[22] A middle of the road Whig, he was one of the elected councilors vetoed by Governor Gage in 1774. Later he served on the state Supreme Court, and was a member of the Convention at the time of his death on October 19, 1779.

Daniel Noyes, a schoolmaster from Ipswich, was a postmaster and registrar of probate for Essex County for many years. He also served in the convention that ratified the Federal Constitution. Joseph Orne was a doctor. Said to have been a precocious child, he was more interested in art than in politics. His participation in the Convention was the only political activity of his life, and after being stricken with the palsy in 1781, he died in 1786. Samuel Allyne Otis was the brother of the famous James Otis. In spite of some early reading in the law, he disdained it, and became a merchant and trader. He was wily enough to marry the daughter of a major creditor, but such tactics did not prevent him from going bankrupt later in his life. He served Massachusetts in the United States Congress, and had the honor of holding the Bible for George Washington as he took the oath of office for the first time as President of the United States. Robert Treat Paine was an arrogant man. A lawyer and a one-time preacher, he once refused an appointment to the Superior Court because he did not wish to be the junior of the chief justice of that time, John Adams. A man of strong prejudices, his only close friend was said to be John Hancock. Oliver Wendell was a wealthy merchant and trader. He spent most of his life walking with a cane due to a youthful injury. He served on the Boston Board of Selectmen, and Committee of Correspondence, and was a delegate to the first and second Provincial Congresses. In 1792 he was elected to the state Senate, where he served for fourteen consecutive years. His grandson was Oliver Wendell Holmes, the essayist and father of the famous jurist.

These brief sketches serve to give some idea of the quality of the group of men who assembled to draft the Constitution of 1780. Of course, those who participated in the actual drafting of the Constitution were not the only ones who influenced its final shape. The political climate of Massachusetts during the years between the dissolution of government in 1774 and the adoption of the Constitution of 1780 was very active. Nowhere

22. Frank Washburn Grinnell, "A Forgotten Patriot: Jedediah Foster of Brookfield," *Proceedings of the Massachusetts Historical Society* 67 (February 1942): 128–134.

was this more apparent than in the newspaper debates of the period, and the people who took part in those debates must also be counted as a major source of influence on the Constitution. Unfortunately, it is not possible to provide biographical sketches for these debaters, because they chose to conceal their identities behind the shield of pseudonyms: Mentor, Benevolus, Verax, Tribunus, A Watchman, A Son of Liberty, Philadelphus, Cato Censorinus, A Freeman, Clitus, A Countryman, A By-Stander, Fiat Justitia, Democritus, Lycurgus, Philalutheros, Clericus, A True Patriot, Adolescentulus, A True Republican, Libertatis Amici, Eleatherus—the list could be extended indefinitely. These anonymous essayists, polemicists, and occasionally, theorists, were the vocal cords of the Revolution in all of its aspects. The practice of writing under pseudonyms, which was common during the Revolution, has fallen into disfavor in recent times. Today one who chooses to withhold his identity from a published letter or essay is presumed to have something to hide. A person of integrity, it is now believed, will not be afraid to stand behind his views. The result is that one, and sometimes both, of two evils frequently mark contemporary public debate: either the debate is inhibited because people do not wish to be associated with unpopular views; or the debate is uninhibited and irrational because ideas cannot be separated from the identity of their authors. The Americans of the revolutionary generation knew better. Because of the use of pseudonyms, ideas were able to stand on their own, independent of the reputation of those who espoused them. Consequently, public debate was vigorous and enlightened.

In addition to the newspaper debates, public dialogue was carried on in the pamphlet literature. Most prominent among the pamphlets were the published sermons. Among the revolutionary pamphleteers in Massachusetts, none had greater influence than the preachers. Some members of the clergy took a more direct role in politics, and as has been noted, twenty-one ministers took part in the Convention. At least two of these men published sermons. Gad Hitchcock, a minister from Hanson, was a prominent public speaker who was honored with a number of election sermons, the Dudley Lectures of 1779, and the Convention Sermon of 1787.[23] After he returned from the

23. The Dudley lectures were given each year and stressed the virtues of Protestantism.

Constitutional Convention he freed his slaves, although they refused to leave him. Elisha Fish, from Upton, offered the keynote sermon for the Worcester County Convention of 1775, and served on the local committees to consider the proposed Constitution of 1778.

Even if not a single minister had sat in the Convention, the influence of the clergy would have been reflected in the Constitution.[24] The most vocal preacher in Massachusetts was a rabid newspaper essayist, William Gordon of Roxbury. Having arrived in America at the outbreak of the Revolution, he was a relative newcomer, but he quickly established himself as an outspoken advocate of democratic reform. His advocacy of admitting Negroes, mulattoes, and Indians to the suffrage and his opposition to stringent property qualifications for voters labeled him a dangerous political thinker in the minds of many, and his practice of disdaining pseudonyms and subscribing his name to his essays earned him the scorn of most. Compared to other writers, Gordon was told, you stand "as the small dust of the balance to the Pyrenean mountains."[25]

Among other publishing preachers were Isaac Backus from Middleborough and Samuel Cooper, from Boston. Backus was the agent for the Baptist churches of Massachusetts and waged an incessant battle in the newspapers and in a number of pamphlets against the oppressive tactics of the Congregationalist majority.[26] He fought particularly hard against the concept of public support for the ministry, on the grounds that it tended to favor the Congregationalists. Cooper held degrees from Harvard, Yale, and Edinburgh, and served as vice-president of the American Academy of the Arts and Sciences upon its initiation in 1780. He was the Dudley Lecturer in 1773, and delivered several election sermons. He was honored by being chosen to

24. These biographical sketches are taken from: J. L. Sibley, ed., *Harvard Graduates*; Frederick L. Weis, *The Colonial Clergy and the Colonial Churches of New England* (Lancaster, Mass.: by the society of the descendents of the colonial clergy, 1936); Frank Moore, ed., *The Patriot Preachers of the American Revolution; with Biographical Sketches, 1766–1783* (New York: C. T. Evans, 1882).
25. Trenaeus [pseud.] , *Continental Journal*, May 25, 1780.
26. Alvah Hovey, *A Memoir of the Life and Times of the Rev. I. Backus, A. M.* (Boston: Gould and Lincoln, 1859); William G. McLaughlin, *Isaac Backus and the American Pietistic Tradition*, ed. Oscar Handlin (Boston: Little, Brown and Company, 1967).

deliver the sermon given on the day of the inauguration of the new government under the Constitution of 1780, on October 25, 1780.

Simeon Howard was one of the most widely published of all the Massachusetts clergy. A fellow of the American Academy of the Arts and Sciences, he delivered the Dudley Lectures in 1787, the Convention Sermon in 1790, and numerous election sermons. He preached in Boston for almost forty years. Nathaniel Niles was a peripatetic preacher. Born in Rhode Island and educated at Princeton and Dartmouth, he preached in a number of New England towns, although he was never formally ordained. Settling in Connecticut, he served in the state legislature there from 1779 to 1781 and then he moved to Vermont. In 1784 he became a judge of the state Supreme Court, where he served until 1788. He served in the United States Congress from 1791 to 1795. During his career he was at one time or another a preacher, inventor, politician, businessman, poet, physician, lawyer, judge, and member of the Massachusetts Historical Society. Samuel Stillman was born in Philadelphia and educated at the University of Pennsylvania, Harvard College, and Brown University, where he earned both an honorary A.M. and an S.T.D. He served as a trustee of Brown University from 1764 to 1807. Ordained in South Carolina, he preached in New Jersey before being installed in Boston in 1765, where he remained until his death in 1807. He was a member of the American Philosophical Society and delivered a number of election sermons.

Specific characterizations of these ministers could be considerably extended, but for the purposes of this discussion, a few general comments will suffice. They were well educated, most having more than one college degree. They were philosophers and political activists, as well as students of divinity. Many were members of literary and philosophical societies; many possessed honorary degrees; many had studied abroad. The very fact of their having been selected to deliver the sermons that were regularly published indicates the esteem in which they were held by and among their colleagues. In addition to those mentioned above, the roll call of these "patriot preachers" includes Phillips Payson of Chelsea, Samuel Webster of Salisbury, Samuel West of Boston, Peter Whitney of Northborough, and Samuel Williams of Bradford. The influence of these ministers on the political thinking of their fellow citizens was vast.

In addition to these individuals, there were two political factions in Massachusetts, each of which had a direct influence on the Constitution of 1780. One of these factions was the Berkshire Constitutionalists. It is not clear how the membership of this group should be defined, and it is perhaps as accurate as anything to describe the Constitutionalists as everyone in Berkshire County except the Tories. During the interim from 1775 to 1780, Berkshire County was under the domination of a "vast majority party." According to its most prominent historian, Berkshire County stood to the rest of the province as a "feudal Barony," and the majority of the county insisted upon maintaining the right of internal self-government for the county. The leader of this majority party of Constitutionalists, and the catalyst behind their opposition to province rule, was the Reverend Thomas Allen. Allen is described by a biographer as a "Jeffersonian Calvinist," and as a "religious Jacobin." He traveled the length and breadth of Berkshire County preaching the gospel of constitutional government. That he was illogical and shallow in his reasoning did not diminish his influence. Berkshire County was ripe for a radicalizing agent during the Revolution. Most of the people were debtors beholden to their absentee landlords, and abused by the colonial system of justice, which was often arbitrary in the sparsely populated western region.[27]

Allen and his followers have been described as key links in the development of American political thought. The fact that they were vocal advocates of constitutional government during a period in which the concept of constitutional government was becoming established lends credence to this reputation. It is not clear, however, that the facts justify the ascription of such a prominent role to the Constitutionalists. It must be remembered that they were at all times a minority, and indeed, a minority that was explicitly rejected by the rest of the province. The single issue for which they are remembered was their insistence upon the need for a political constitution as a foundation upon which government should stand. This issue, however, was not the particular province of the people of Berkshire County. They were not, in fact, the first to advance the point of view. The earliest known endorsement of the need for a constitution adopted by a special convention, to operate over the regular legislature,

27. J. E. A. Smith, *History of Pittsfield 1734-1800* (Boston: Lee and Shepard, 1869), p. 324; Richard D. Birdsall, "The Reverend Thomas Allen: Jeffersonian Calvinist," *New England Quarterly* 30, no. 2 (June 1957): 147-165.

came from the towns of Acton and Concord in the east.[28] On the question of the structure of government, the Constitutionalists had little to say. Indeed, the town of Pittsfield, the home of Allen and the center of Constitutionalist activity, unanimously approved the Constitution of 1778, even in the absence of a bill of rights, and voiced no objections to the Constitution of 1780.

The second major political faction in revolutionary Massachusetts was the Essex Junto.[29] This was a group of political conservatives from Essex County who played an important role in both state and national politics during the last quarter of the eighteenth century and the first quarter of the nineteenth century. They reached their pinnacle of prominence within the Federalist Party. Consisting principally of wealthy merchants and lawyers, the Junto was centered geographically in Newburyport and the surrounding area. The word "Junto" is perhaps a misnomer when applied to this group, in that it implies a much greater degree of regular interaction and cohesion than probably occurred. There is little doubt, however, that this group of individuals shared a common political outlook, and there can be no doubt of their collective political efficacy, particularly in respect to the establishment of constitutional government in Massachusetts.

The Junto surfaced as far back as 1775, when Essex County assumed the lead in opposing the prevailing system of representation in Massachusetts, which did not reward populous and prosperous Essex County for either its numerical weight or its tax burden. In 1778, the people of Essex County held a convention to determine their attitude on the proposed Constitution of 1778, and the convention rejected the plan. The results of these deliberations were published in the form of an extended essay on government that became known as "The Essex Result." This pamphlet was written by Theophilus Parsons, a young Newburyport lawyer who is customarily identified with the Junto. "The Essex Result" is widely regarded as a crucial factor in the defeat of the Constitution of 1778, and as a classic state-

28. Frank Washburn Grinnell, "The Resolution of the Town of Concord on October 22, 1776, and its Constitutional Significance," 1 *Massachusetts Law Quarterly* 60–65 (August 1928).
29. See David H. Fischer, "The Myth of the Essex Junto," *William and Mary Quarterly*, 3rd Ser., 21, no. 2 (April 1964): 191–235; Benjamin W. Larabee, *Patriots and Partisans: The Merchants of Newburyport, 1764–1850* (Cambridge: Harvard University Press, 1962).

ment of conservative republican political principles. The Junto
was well represented in the Constitutional Convention of 1779–
1780. Among the members of the Convention, the following
ten may be identified with the Junto: George Cabot, Benjamin
Goodhue, Benjamin Greenleaf, John Greenleaf, Jonathan Jackson, John Lowell, Daniel Noyes, Theophilus Parsons, John Pickering, and Nathaniel Tracy. The influence of the Junto in the
Convention is beyond doubt. One need only compare the discussion of representation in "The Essex Result" with the corresponding discussion in "The Address of the Convention" to
become convinced of this fact.[30]

The Issues

The most vitriolic political issue in Massachusetts during the Revolution was the public support of the ministry. The
issue was not new at that time, and indeed, it had been a hot
political issue during much of the colonial history of Massachusetts. In 1692 the General Court passed an act that required
every new town to support a minister, and it became common-
place that each town would be coterminous with its parish, thus
creating a geographic identity of church and state.[31] The way in

30. "The Essex Result" and "Address of the Convention, March 1780"
may be found in Handlin and Handlin, *Popular Sources*, pp. 324–365 and
pp. 434–440 respectively.
31. Morison says: "For readers not initiated into the mysteries of New
England ecclesiastical law and nomenclature, it may be well to explain
some of the phrases of Article III (of the Constitution of 1780), which had
a perfectly definite meaning in 1780, though vague today. A *parish* in Massachusetts was (1) a territorial unit, usually coterminous with the town-
ship, though many large townships were divided into two or more parishes,
which in this case were often called precincts; (2) a *corporation* consisting
of all those who lived within the territorial limits of the parish or precinct,
except those who formally joined a Baptist, Episcopal, or other dissenting
church. The term *religious society* was applied both to parishes in their
corporate sense, and to any other religious corporation. A *Church*, in Massachusetts, meant the body of communicants, or full-fledged church members of a religious society; and was never officially applied to the church
edifice, called the *meeting-house*. A *public teacher* of piety, religion, etc.,
was a modification of the old Puritan term, 'teaching elder,' meaning, minister of the gospel. He was, by a law of 1692, nominated by the Church
and confirmed by the parish; paragraph 3 of Article III was an innovation,
and produced such unexpectedly liberal results that it was compared to
the cockatrices egg. Both before and after 1780 a Congregational minister
had to be ordained by a council of his colleagues from other towns. In

which this act was implemented may be described briefly as follows. The members of the church would propose a teacher, who would then be voted upon by the members of the corporation. Thus the majority of persons in the parish (i.e., the town) would determine who was to be the teacher. Minority sects were not recognized under the law. In cases where a town was divided into more than one parish (which happened when towns became populous) the same procedure was followed within each parish. All citizens of the town or parish were liable to be taxed for the support of the teacher elected by the church and corporation. Therefore, minority sects were taxed for the support of ministers upon whose teachings they did not attend. The only way in which a minority sect could benefit under the law was by becoming a majority, either through proselytizing or by breaking away into a new parish. The latter method required the approval of the General Court.

The minorities struggled for tax exemptions under the law, and with some success. Under the developing case law, Anglicans, Quakers, and Baptists won abatements. Such victories were hard fought, however, and the minority denominations met with opposition from the majority Congregationalists at each step for the understandable reason that the more numerous the abatements were, the heavier the tax load would be for those who had to pay. During the period from 1775 to 1780, things came to a head. It was apparent to all that the disposition of the religious issue in the new constitution would determine the relationship between church and state in Massachusetts for years to come. Those in the Congregationalist majority insisted upon some provision for public support of the ministry. Those among the minority sects wished to take the teeth out of the proposal in order to assure their own religious and financial autonomy. The result was a compromise, but one which favored the majority point of view.

Article III of the Declaration of Rights proclaimed the right and the duty of the state to support the teaching of "piety, religion, and morality," on the grounds that these virtues were necessary for "the happiness of a people, and the good order

---

probably a majority of the towns, in 1780, the inhabitants were unaware of any distinction between parish and town, the affairs of both corporations being transacted in town meetings, and entered in the same book" ("The Struggle," p. 370n.).

and preservation of civil government." This right was to be institutionalized by requiring all "towns, parishes, precincts, and other bodies politic, or religious societies" to provide instruction in these virtues at public expense. Attendance upon such teachings was to be made mandatory where it was "conscientiously and conveniently" possible. As a sop to the minorities, it was also provided that any individual could stipulate that his money be paid to his own sect or denomination, if that sect or denomination were incorporated in his town. Otherwise his money had to go toward the teacher who was incorporated in his town, which was invariably the Congregationalist teacher. Additionally, the framers included in Article II of the Declaration of Rights a strong statement of the equality of all sects, in order to assuage the minorities even further.

The public support of religion was the subject of vigorous political debate in the newspapers during the entire period of the renewed charter (1775-1780). The leader of the minority opposition was Isaac Backus, the Baptist agent for the state. His legion of supporters in these debates included Philanthropos, Vox Populi, Milton, Mentor, and Libertatis Amici. Arrayed against this formidable group were such illustrious gladiators as Hieronymus, Swift, Trenaeus, and A Member of the Convention. The arguments against public support were comprehensive, and included the following points: (1) that the "happiness of a people, and the good order and preservation of civil government" did not, as a matter of historical fact, depend upon "piety, religion, and morality"; (2) that even were that assumption valid, it would not follow that the state had a right to meddle in religious affairs, since Christ's kingdom is not of this earth and does not require the support of the public law; (3) that the effect of Article III would be contrary to the right of conscience defined in Article II; (4) that because the state had the power to determine which religious societies would become incorporated, it had the effective power to create a religious establishment by allowing the incorporation of only Congregationalist churches; (5) that mandatory public support amounted to taxation without representation; (6) that the determination of whether or not an individual can "conscientiously and conveniently attend" upon the deliverance of a teacher would be left to a jury, thus involving the public authority of the state in a determination of conscience. The theoretical relationship between Article III and the right of conscience will be discussed in chapter 3. Here it must be noted that the immediate question for those who objected to Article III was, Who decides? Who decides when a religious society ought to be recognized and incorporated? Who decides if a minister is qualified to be a public teacher? These were the questions upon which Article III was eventually to founder.

Those in favor of the public support of the ministry, and in particular Article III, rested their case on one simple procedural principle—majority rule. According to its supporters, the objective of Article III was not to coerce consciences. Rather, it was intended to insure the stability of government. The problem was simply utilitarian. The purpose of government is to secure the public happiness, yet this cannot be achieved if individuals are unrestrained in the pursuit of their own interests. The sanctions that government can impose upon individuals are inadequate safeguards for the public good. Many individuals will act contrary to the public good in spite of legal sanctions, and this will be particularly true in situations where an individual believes that he is unlikely to get caught. In such a case, the internal restraints of conscience are the sole protection for the public interest, and these restraints presuppose "piety, religion, and morality." Only if an individual believes himself accountable to God for his actions will he restrain his behavior toward others. Its advocates held that the requirements of Article III did not invade the right of conscience, because no one was to be forced to believe anything. All that was required by the Constitution was that the opportunity for enlightenment be provided by the state, and all the state attempted to do was to encourage people to avail themselves of the opportunity. In assuming the right to establish these provisions, and in establishing them on the basis of majority preference, the people of Massachusetts were merely exercising their political sovereignty. In the words of Hieronymous, "it is incident to a state of society, that the majority should govern the whole."[32]

The second issue that dominated Massachusetts politics during the Revolution was the perpetual problem of representation. If for the people of Massachusetts the crucial political question was always, Who decides? then the establishment of the system of representation was the most important political decision they had to make. The theoretical aspects of the representation issue

32. Hieronymus [pseud.] , *Boston Gazette,* January 18, 1779.

will be discussed in chapter 4. In practical terms, the problem of representation reduced to three constitutional determinations. One, How will the representation be apportioned? Two, Who will be allowed to hold office? Three, Who will be allowed to participate in the suffrage?

In the Constitution of 1780, these three questions were answered in the following way. The legislature was divided into two chambers, a House of Representatives and a Senate. The House was to be apportioned by towns, with the ratio of representation tied to the population of each town. Every town of 150 rateable polls was to have one representative, each town with 375 rateable polls was to have two representatives, and so on, with an additional representative added for each additional 225 rateable polls.[33] All towns already incorporated would continue to be entitled to a representative, irrespective of their populations. The Senate was to be apportioned by specially drawn districts, with the ratio of representation determined on the basis of the relative tax burden of each district. Initially, each county was to be a separate district. There was a property qualification for all representatives, senators, and for the governor and lieutenant governor. Each representative was to possess £100 freehold or a rateable estate of £200 within his town.[34] Each senator was to possess £300 freehold, or a rateable estate of £600, within his district. The governor and lieutenant governor were required to possess a freehold of £1,000 within the state. Senators had to have resided in the state for five years, and they had to reside in their districts at the time of their election. Representatives had to have lived in their town for a year, and the governor and lieutenant governor had to have been residents of the state for seven years. The qualifications for suffrage were the same for the Senate, House, and executive offices. Each voter had to be twenty-one years old, a resident of the town or district in which he wished to vote, and possessed of a freehold within the town or district of £3 or a rateable estate of £60.

In settling upon these rules of representation, the people of Massachusetts were confronting another implicit question, one that was really the most basic of all. Who, or what, was the system of representation to represent? There were three candidates:

33. A rateable poll was a person who met the eligibility requirements for the suffrage.
34. A man's freehold was his real estate, or land holdings. His total rateable estate included all of his property.

persons, property, and the towns. The formula adopted by the Convention was based on a mixture of all three. In basing the ratio of representation in the Senate on the distribution of taxes, and in including property requirements for suffrage and office-holding, property was represented. In granting to every town that was already incorporated a representative, and in apportioning the representation for the House on the basis of towns, the towns were represented. And by basing the ratio of representation in the House according to the population of each town, persons were represented.

The question of representation harbors within it the problem of political equality. Political equality, in turn, involves the problem of income distribution. And income distribution in revolutionary America was in part a geographic phenomenon, since the farming communities of the west were both less populated and less wealthy on a per capita basis than were the towns of the east. These facts raise the question of whether the debates over representation reflected differences in theoretical perspective between economic classes and/or between geographic regions. Historians have stressed the geographic division between east and west during the Revolution, and have attempted to connect it with a corresponding difference in the economic base of the two regions. Elisha Douglass, for example, has interpreted the entire period during which these first state constitutions were adopted by the thirteen colonies in terms of a struggle between the radicals of the west and the conservatives of the east. He says in regard to Massachusetts, that "the great majority of towns calling for democratic reforms were in the interior or western part of the state," and in another place that "the basis of representation for the lower house produced wails of anguish from the West." Morison also recognizes the geographic division. He says that "no two subjects gave the Convention so much trouble as the basis of representation and the organization of the House of Representatives. . . . It was not hard . . . for the towns to pick flaws in Chapter I, Section III, Article II. . . . Criticism was particularly rife in the west." Jack Pole makes express the connection between geographic division and economic conditions. He says, "when questions of economic policy arose, it was the representation of the interior towns which collected the sense and interest of the farmers of the Commonwealth. Thus the agricultural interest found itself in a natural alliance with the corporation interest that was so deeply felt in the smaller towns."[35]

More recently, Steven Patterson has attempted to demonstrate that there was in revolutionary Massachusetts a rudimental political party system which reflected the division between east and west. The vote on the Constitution of 1780, he says, "produced more than an ideological split among the electorate, it produced a geographic split as well." The towns of the west were predominantly democratic while those in the east were for the most part conservative. While the theory upon which the Constitution of 1780 was based was "antipartisan," the reality out of which that theory emerged was strongly partisan. Patterson's interpretation raises the question of the relation between theory and practice. While there were without doubt differences of opinion over the specific provisions of the Constitution of 1780, it does not follow that all such differences of opinion represented disagreement on theoretical fundamentals. For example, the extent of the appointive power of the governor is not as central to the theory of the Constitution as is the extent of the suffrage. On theoretically fundamental issues, such as the suffrage, there appears to have been little disagreement. Patterson contends that the west was more "democratic" than the east, but on the suffrage issue, which appears sure to distinguish democrats from conservatives, there was not a significant regional variation in the vote. Seventy-three of the 99 towns in the three western counties supported the restricted suffrage, while 93 of 108 towns supported restricted suffrage in the eastern counties, according to Patterson's data. Thus, an overwhelming majority across the entire state supported restricted suffrage.[36]

35. Douglass, *Rebels and Democrats*, pp. 179, 210; Morison, "The Struggle," pp. 386, 387; Pole, *Political Representation*, p. 200.
36. Steven E. Patterson, *Political Parties in Revolutionary Massachusetts* (Madison, Wis.: University of Wisconsin Press, 1973), p. 235. Patterson's analysis of the town returns is presented in an appendix (pp. 269-281). His method is to tabulate the objections he finds in the town returns, then to categorize the towns as either democratic or conservative depending upon the number and nature of their objections. While Patterson's data reveal clearly that upon certain issues there were more objections in the west than in the east, we must view cautiously his conclusion that the west was more democratic than the east, for three reasons. First, all towns that were indifferent, or that gave the Constitution only a cursory examination, are arbitrarily categorized as conservative. It is impossible to determine

While some provisions of the Constitution occasioned more objections in the west than in the east, it is not clear that these provisions were as central to the theoretical base of the Constitution as were the many others which illicited few objections. The major issue that divided the west and the east was local control of government. It is not certain, however, that the desire in the west for local control represented a greater faith in democracy. Finally, it is apparent that the total number of objections laid against the Constitution were not great. By and large, the document was acceptable to a large majority of the towns, and it appears to have been accepted by a large majority of the voters. The fact of the matter is that during most of the revolutionary period, the debate over representation revolved primarily around the question of persons v. towns. This was an east-west issue insofar as the towns in the east were older and more populous than those in the west. But the small towns in the east were no less vociferous than those in the west in defending their right to independent representation. This issue was diffused once the demands of the small towns in the east and west were assuaged by granting to each town already incorporated a representative.

---

from a two sentence approval whether a town found the Constitution unobjectionable, or whether it was merely unconcerned about the matter. Second, Patterson assumes that the demand for local control was a demand for greater democracy. This may have been the case, but requires demonstration. Third, Patterson treats all objections equally. Yet in determining whether the towns were democratic or conservative, some objections would appear to be more revealing than others. For example, sixty-one of ninety-one towns labeled democratic by Patterson approved (or did not object to) the Constitution's restricted suffrage. By some standards, all such towns might be labeled undemocratic. Patterson's typology is less ambiguous on the other end of the continuum, however, for no town opposing restricted suffrage is labeled conservative. Therefore, it appears that to oppose restricted suffrage is a sufficient, but not a necessary, condition for being labeled democratic. Why this is so, Patterson does not say. Again, attempts to weaken the governor are regarded by Patterson as democratic. Yet the governor was to be annually elected and therefore subject to democratic control. Finally, even if Patterson is correct in finding more democratic sentiment in the west than in the east, it remains to be established that this represented a difference of opinion on the fundamental values underlying the Constitution. For other studies of western Massachusetts during the Revolution see: Robert Taylor, *Western Massachusetts During the Revolution* (Providence: Brown University Press, 1954); Lee N. Newcomer, *The Embattled Farmers* (New York: Columbia University Press, King's Crown Press, 1953).

Religion and representation were the dominant political issues in Massachusetts during the Revolution. Both harbored substantive implications, but both were ultimately reduced to procedural determinations. This fact may serve to underline the importance that procedural matters in general held for the people of Massachusetts. It was this very faith in procedure that caused them to be so cautious and meticulous in establishing their constitution, and this same concern for procedure is one of the most distinguishing characteristics of that constitution. But what principles guided the people of Massachusetts in deciding which procedures to adopt? What view did they have of the proper nature and function of the state? And what did their faith in procedure imply about the nature of government itself? In order to answer these questions we must begin by examining the document itself.

II

The Text of the Constitution

The General Arrangement

In trying to understand the Massachusetts Constitution of 1780 the chief source of evidence is, of course, the document itself. From the brief review of the events surrounding its adoption it has been learned that this constitution was as well and thoroughly considered a document as any in the history of the Republic. It is known that the debates over the Constitution during the seven months of the convention were lengthy and full, and even though we know little about the specifics of the debate, there is sufficient evidence to conclude that the framers were attentive to distinctions in phrasing, as well as to the problems of order and arrangement. Thus, at the outset of the examination, we are forewarned that the arrangement of the document, as well as the wording of its various declarations and clauses, is to be taken quite seriously as evidence of reasoned intent.

The title of the document, as submitted to the people, reads as follows: "A CONSTITUTION OR FRAME OF GOVERNMENT, Agreed upon by the Delegates of the People of the STATE OF MASSACHUSETTS-BAY,—In Convention,—Begun and held at Cambridge, on the First of September, 1779, and continued by Adjournments to the Second of March, 1780." While it may appear that there is nothing particularly striking about this title, it does appear that the framers thought it necessary to specify precisely the authors of the document, and in so doing they identified themselves as "the Delegates of the People of the STATE OF MASSACHUSETTS-BAY." Evidently, then, the formation of this constitution was a representative act of a given people, viz. the people of the state of Massachusetts-Bay. Let us proceed to consider what follows.

The Constitution is divided into three discrete parts. In the order in which they appear they are the Preamble, the Declaration of Rights, and the Frame of Government. The Preamble is devoted to an elaboration of a general theory of the nature and purposes of the state. The Declaration of Rights is a list of thirty articles which vary greatly in type, but which have in common the characteristic that they each make some descriptive, prescriptive, or proscriptive statement addressed to either individuals or to the collection body of the people. The Frame of Government contains the formal delineation of the various departments of the government, and the rules for carrying out the business of government.

From this arrangement, it may be inferred that the framers viewed the making of a constitution as a theoretically structured task. The actual frame of government, or what might be regarded as the constitution proper, is constructed on the foundations of an express theory of the state and a specific delineation of certain general rules.[1] These rules are presumably derived from that theory of the state and are to act as parameters within which the frame of government is to be established and is to operate. The extent to which these three parts of the document are theoretically integrated is a reflection of the extent to which the framers were guided by a theoretical conception. Assessing the degree of integration is a principal objective of this analysis.

The Preamble

Let us first turn our attention to the Preamble, assuming that our own understanding of the document must proceed along the same lines of reasoning that the framers pursued in making it. As the Preamble is quite brief, it is convenient to reproduce it in full.

> The end of the institution, maintenance and administration of government, is to secure the existence of the body-politic; to protect it; and to furnish the individuals who compose it, with the power of enjoying, in safety and tran-

1. The phrase "the theory of the state" and any variant of it, wherever it is used in this book, refers to the package of ideas and concepts that are necessary to explain the origin, nature, and extent of political authority, the setting up of government, and the dissolution of government (i.e., revolution). The phrase "the theory of government" and any variant of it, is intended to convey the idea of the package of principles upon which the organization of government is based.

quility, their natural rights, and the blessings of life: And whenever these great objects are not obtained, the people have a right to alter the government, and to take measures necessary for their safety, prosperity and happiness.

The body-politic is formed by a voluntary association of individuals: It is a social compact, by which the whole people covenants with each citizen, and each citizen with the whole people, that all shall be governed by certain laws for the common good. It is the duty of the people, therefore, in framing a Constitution of Government, to provide for an equitable mode of making laws, as well as for an impartial interpretation, and a faithful execution of them; that every man may, at all times, find his security in them.

We, therefore, the people of Massachusetts, acknowledging, with grateful hearts, the goodness of the Great Legislator of the Universe, in affording us, in the course of His providence, an opportunity, deliberately and peaceably, without fraud, violence or surprise, of entering into an original, explicit, and solemn compact with each other; and of forming a new Constitution of Civil Government, for ourselves and posterity; and devoutly imploring His direction in so interesting a design, DO agree upon, ordain and establish, the following Declaration of Rights, and Frame of Government, as the CONSTITUTION of the COMMONWEALTH OF MASSACHUSETTS.

The Preamble begins by proclaiming the ends for which governments in general (and by implication, this government) are established. Three specific ends are mentioned: to secure the existence of the body-politic, to protect the body-politic, and to furnish the individuals who compose it with a certain power, viz. the power to enjoy peaceably their natural rights and the blessings of life. We are not, at this point, told why these are the ends of government, nor are we told that they are the only ends of government. In fact, we are not even told if they are consistent with one another. This seems curious, since on the surface it would appear that there is at least a potential conflict between the obligation of government to protect the body-politic and its obligation to furnish individuals with the power to enjoy natural rights and the blessings of life. Does the power to do these things also involve a power to harm the body-politic? If not, what kind of power is it, and how does government go about furnishing it to individuals? This question becomes even more interesting in light of the next statement in the Preamble, which holds that if these three objects are not obtained, the people (and it is not clear if "the people" is here the body-politic or the individuals who compose it) have a right to change the government, and to do anything necessary for their safety, prosperity, and happiness. Depending on how the phrase "the people" is interpreted, this provision might take on quite distinct meanings. If "the people" refers to a collective entity then the right of revolution is one which can only apply to that entity. But if "the people" has as its referent a number of individuals, it might be held that one or several individuals may be possessed of the right to revolt.

Perhaps the answers to these questions would be easier to determine if more was known about this strange creature, the body-politic. Obligingly, the Preamble goes on to inform us further in this regard. "The body-politic," it is held, "is formed by a voluntary association of individuals: it is a social compact, by which the whole people covenants with each citizen, and each citizen with the whole people, that all shall be governed by certain laws for the common good." Now this is curious. The body-politic is formed by a voluntary association of individuals, yet it is a social act, to wit, a social compact. Furthermore, the individuals who undertake this act do not associate with each other directly, but they do so through the intermediary of a distinct party, the "whole people." And again, the individuals who do this associating are not merely individuals, they are citizens. Citizens of what? Clearly, this formulation implies some sort of ongoing social enterprise, or at least a viable social entity called "the people" which is capable of making binding moral agreements. Here, of course, we are reminded of the title to the document, which indicated it to be the act of the representatives of a certain people, and the reference to the people of Massachusetts in the last paragraph of the Preamble. These facts seem to suggest that the phrase "the people" wherever it is used, refers to a collectivity, the people who live in Massachusetts, rather than to any individual or group of individuals who are a part of it.

The Preamble indicates that the parties to this agreement agree upon something specific, that all individuals shall be governed by certain laws for the common good. This is the *only* substantive point of the agreement, and it seems to be susceptible to at least two interpretations. On the one hand, it may be taken to mean that the agreement to be governed by certain laws is in the common good. In this case the parties agree to only one thing. Or, on the other hand, it may be taken to mean that the agreement is to two things: first, that individuals will be governed by certain laws, and second, that they will be governed for the common good. In either case, if the common good may be taken to mean the good of the people (one party to the contract), then it appears that the only guarantee that the individuals are to gain from this bargain is that they will be governed by certain laws. This fact is confirmed by the next sentence of the Preamble which contends that the bargain implies, directly, three duties on the part of the people. The people must make provision for an equitable mode of making laws, an impartial interpretation of the laws, and a faithful execution of the laws. These are the only duties imposed on the people by the social compact and, if duties and rights are correlative, they imply the only three rights which individual citizens may claim on its authority. Although it is not explicitly stated it is inferred that these three duties (i.e., rights) are coextensive with, if not in fact the very definition of, certain laws. In making these observations, it should be remembered that these three duties are imposed so "that every man may, at all times, find his security in them." This implies at least two things: one, that for the individuals who voluntarily join the association, security is the primary motive; two, that the degree of security to which they are entitled is defined by these three procedural duties (i.e., rights).

In reviewing the analysis to this point, then, the following conclusions may be drawn relative to the teaching of the Preamble. First, "the people" is an entity distinct from the several individuals who are a part of it.[2] Second, the people who are

2. When the phrase "the people" is placed in quotations to stress the fact that it is the collectivity to which it refers, it will be used with a singular verb. In general, however, I intend to follow the practice of the Constitution of 1780, which is to use plural verbs with the phrase. This grammatical issue should not be allowed to obscure the point, which is that "the people" is used collectively. In contending that "the people" is an entity distinct from any individual, group of individuals, or even all individuals, I mean that this was what was meant by the phrase in the Constitution of 1780. An entity is a "thing that has real and individual existence, in reality or in the mind" according to Webster (*Webster's New World Dictionary of the American Language*, 2d ed., s.v. "entity"). The

involved in making this compact are the people of the state of Massachusetts-Bay. Third, the compact which is being made creates a new creature, the body-politic. This body-politic is to be called the Commonwealth of Massachusetts. Fourth, the compact that creates the body-politic is between the people and each individual. Fifth, this compact consists of an agreement that each individual consents to be governed according to certain laws, for the common good. Sixth, this agreement implies three specific duties on the part of the people, as they frame their government for the body-politic: they must provide for equity in the mode of making laws, impartiality in the interpretation of laws, and faithfulness in the execution of laws. Seventh, these duties imply three corresponding rights to which individuals are entitled.

In order to fulfill these three specific duties, the people are to create a government, but this government must, in addition, achieve three other ends. It must secure the existence of the body-politic, it must protect it, and it must secure to each individual in it the power to enjoy natural rights and the blessings of life. If the government fails to meet the procedural qualifications implied by the social compact, then the compact has presumably been violated and is void. If, however, the government fails to satisfy any or all of the ends for which it is established, then the social compact is still valid, but the people (one party to the compact) have a right to alter it and to establish a new government, which must still meet the three procedural qualifications, but must be better designed to satisfy the three substantive ends of government. In the case where the social compact is violated, individuals are *perhaps* free to consult their own good. We are not specifically informed on this point. In the case where the ends of government are not met, the right of making decisions falls to the people. In the former case, the violations are procedural; in the latter case, they involve the substantive notions of existence, protection, and natural rights.

While the Preamble has told us a great deal, it has raised a number of questions that it has failed to answer. Perhaps the foremost among these unanswered questions concerns the right of the people to alter the government when it does not satisfy

people of Massachusetts believed that an entity, "the people," had real existence and political relevance. This conception, whether valid or invalid, was central to their thinking. It must, therefore, be accepted and understood if their political principles are to be correctly interpreted.

the ends for which it was established. Not only are we not told what procedures are to be followed, in either deciding that the ends of government have not been satisfied, or in changing the government when that fact has been determined; we have not even been given any specific information concerning the ends of government. Under what conditions, for example, would the body-politic cease to exist? And what specifically are the natural rights of individuals? The concepts of existence, protection, and natural rights, as they are presented in the Preamble, are too general to be helpful. The meaning of natural rights is of special importance, since natural rights apply to each individual, rather than to the collectivity. Noticing that the framers saw fit to include "A Declaration of the Rights of the Inhabitants of the Commonwealth of Massachusetts," it is perhaps there that we should look for an answer to these crucial questions.

The Declaration of Rights

The Declaration of Rights, as has been noted above, consists of thirty articles which are so various as to almost defy any attempt to render an orderly account of them. Some are simple assertions: so for example, Article XIII reads, "In criminal prosecutions, the verification of facts in the vicinity where they happen, is one of the greatest securities of the life, liberty, and property of the citizen." Others are commands: so, in Article XII, "No subject shall be held to answer for any crime or offence, until the same is fully and plainly, substantially and formally, described to him." Still others appear to be recommendations. Article XVI reads: "The liberty of the press is essential to the security of freedom in a state: it ought not therefore, to be restrained in this Commonwealth." Some of the articles apply to individuals; others apply to the people. Some simply state that a right exists; others conjoin to the statement of the right a specific duty or prohibition.

In spite of the complexity of the Declaration of Rights, we must not be dissuaded from trying to come to some understanding of it, as such an understanding is essential to an understanding of the problem of the Constitution as a whole. This can be seen from the role the Declaration plays in the overall structure of the Constitution. If the Preamble is intended to develop a general theory of the state, including a statement of the general purposes for which government is to be erected; and if the Frame of Government is intended as the institutional embodiment of that theory; and if the ends of government are substantive and are predicated upon and circumscribed by some notion of natural rights; then a Declaration of Rights inserted between the two can be expected to be the place where the concrete manifestations of the ends of government are to be stated. And it is here where we must look for the answers to some of the questions raised by the analysis of the Preamble. In particular, it is here where we must look for an answer to the question, What does the Preamble mean by the natural rights of individuals?

In examining the Declaration of Rights, the first observation to be made is that the rights therein specified are not held to be the rights of man, or even the rights of the people of the state of Massachusetts-Bay. Rather, they are the rights of the inhabitants of the Commonwealth of Massachusetts (=the body-politic that is being created by the social compact embodied in this Constitution). Secondly, we must observe that the rights that are contained in the Declaration are not called natural rights, but are merely referred to as the rights of these individuals. Some of these rights may be natural rights, some are presumably not. Whether they are natural rights, or merely civil rights under the Constitution, the immediate source of their authority is the political majority that is creating the Constitution. Having made these observations, let us now consider the articles that compose the Declaration of Rights.

In Article I may be found the only mention of natural rights other than in the Preamble. In phrasing that strongly parallels that of the Declaration of Independence, we are told that all men are born free and equal, and that they have certain "natural, essential and unalienable rights." Three specific examples of these rights are listed: the right of enjoying and defending life and liberty; the right of acquiring, possessing and protecting property; and the right of seeking and obtaining safety and happiness. Are these the natural rights referred to in the Preamble? What other natural rights are there, and why are they not specified? Why are these rights called "essential" and "unalienable," as well as being called "natural?" And what relationship do these natural rights have to the other rights specified in the Declaration of Rights?

While we do not find the term "natural rights" used anywhere again in the document, we do find three of the specific instances of it mentioned in Article X, which reads as follows:

Each individual of the society has a right to be protected by it in the enjoyment of his life, liberty and property, according to standing laws. He is obliged, consequently, to contribute his share to the expense of this protection; to give his personal service, or an equivalent, when necessary: But no part of the property of any individual, can, with justice, be taken from him, or applied to public uses without his own consent, or that of the representative body of the people: In fine, the people of this Commonwealth are not controlable by any other laws, than those to which their constitutional representative body have given their consent. And whenever the public exigencies require, that the property of any individual should be appropriated to public uses, he shall receive a reasonable compensation therefor.

Is the statement in the first sentence of this article a logical derivative of the third purpose of government, as expressed in the Preamble, which imposes upon the government the obligation of enabling individuals to enjoy their natural rights? If so, then it would appear that society furnishes individuals with a *power* of enjoying their natural rights by protecting them in the enjoyment of them, a curious construction to say the least. Or perhaps this statement is a derivative of the conditions imposed by the social compact, where it is stated that individuals are entitled to be governed by certain (i.e., standing) laws. Taken in this sense, the emphasis in the first sentence of Article X should be placed on the provision for standing laws, rather than on the things the laws are to secure. But this too seems unsatisfactory, for if these rights are unalienable, as specified in Article I, then it would seem that society has a duty to protect them whether by standing laws or any other means. The emphasis must surely be placed on the substance of natural rights, rather than on any method to secure them. But if so, aren't these rights adequately secured by Article I, and in light of Article I, isn't this provision of Article X redundant?

Article X proceeds to connect the rights of life, liberty, and property with obligations for each individual in the body-politic. Each individual must contribute money to help pay the cost of this protection, and he must offer his service in helping to protect these rights, unless he can furnish some equivalent. This is surprising, and seemingly inconsistent, for in order to secure the natural rights of life, liberty, and property, they must to some extent be relinquished. To what extent, and upon what occasions? As if to allay our doubts about these questions, Article X goes on to assure us that, at least in respect to property (but not to life and liberty?), the forfeiture can only be made under one or both of two conditions: when the individual has consented to it, and/or when the representative body of the people has consented to it. Here we see that the concept of natural rights and the concept of consent bear some relation to each other, because consent is the sole authorizer of the forfeiture of a natural right. But aren't natural rights supposed to be unalienable? This is the express declaration of Article I. Yet if they are unalienable, how can they be forfeited under any circumstances? And, lurking beneath it all, why do the consent of an individual and the consent of the representative body of the people equally justify the forfeiture of a natural right? These questions cannot be answered immediately, and perhaps not at all on the sole evidence of the text.

Article X ends with two express statements about the limitations of authority over individuals. The only laws to which the people are obliged to submit are those to which their constitutional representatives have given their consent, and even where this is the case, individuals are entitled to a just compensation for the loss of any property appropriated to public use. These statements yield two implications. One, that the consent of the representative body of the people is a sufficient condition to compel the obedience of the citizens (in any matter?). Two, that in a case where the loss of property is involved the person who loses it is entitled to compensation, and therefore the representative body of the people presumably is obliged to provide such compensation. Thus, it appears that the representative body of the people is under some form of limitation in the exercise of the power of its consent. The specific nature of this limitation is very unclear, for "a reasonable compensation" is a very ambiguous concept indeed. Yet it is quite consistent with several other provisions of this article, and with the teaching of the Preamble. We have seen already that the social compact is an agreement that implies rights and duties, which is to say that it implies a contractual situation where obligations are created and balanced between two parties, in this case the people and individuals. Now, in Article X we see that rights and duties are again to be balanced, and that any shift in the balance creates an obligation to compensate for the difference. Thus, individuals must contribute to the expense of protection received; an individual must contribute personal service, or an equivalent; and society must provide reasonable compensation for property exacted for public purposes. There seems to be, underlying these various conditions, some concept of fair dealing that implies moral obligations as well as legal obligations under the Constitution. But the nature of this concept is not made express, and the procedures by which it is to be made operative are not specified. We are not able to examine this concept in any more depth at this time, other than to note that there is perhaps some relationship between it and the problem of what might be called "alienable, unalienable rights," and the relationship of this conceptual oddity to the idea and mechanisms of consent.

The dichotomy between the individual and the people is reflected throughout the Declaration of Rights. Of the thirty articles, numbers I, II, IX, XI, XII, XIII, XIV, XV, XVI, XXIV, XXV, XXVI, XXVII, and XXVIII, or a total of fourteen, assign rights primarily to individuals. Numbers IV, V, VI, VII, VIII, XVII, XVIII, XIX, XX, XXI, XXII, and XXIII, or a total of twelve, assign rights primarily to the people. Three articles, III, X, and XXIX, assign rights to both the people and to individuals, and Article XXX is apparently not directly related to an assignment of rights. Some pattern is revealed in the distribution of these rights. Of the fourteen articles which deal with the rights of the individual, eight (Articles XI, XII, XIII, XIV, XV, XXIV, XXV, and XXVIII) involve some aspect of the right of due process under the law. Of the twelve articles which deal with the rights of the people, six (Articles IV, V, VI, VII, VIII, and IX) deal directly with the right of self-government; the other six are derivatives of this right.

These observations encourage, if they do not demand, a conclusion that the Declaration of Rights is theoretically related to the theory of the state developed in the Preamble. The same duality between the individual and the people which forms the basis of the social compact is revealed in no less than twenty-nine of the thirty articles of the Declaration of Rights. The emphasis of the Declaration on the problem of due process of law reflects the concern of the Preamble for certain laws as the contractual right of individuals. The emphasis of the Declaration on the right of self-government reflects the idea of the social compact as expressed in the Preamble, and the related concern with the common good. The inference to which we are being drawn is that the Preamble and the Declaration of Rights are together a part of a developing theoretical point of view, which involves a conscious and distinct differentiation between the right of individuals to be governed by certain laws, and the right of the people to make the laws by which the individuals are to be governed. Are these two fundamental precepts of the Constitution of 1780 theoretically and operationally consistent with each other? And if they are not and are capable of coming into conflict with each other, which of the two is of higher priority?

Although a full understanding of this problem will require a deeper examination of the thought underlying the Constitution, the answer to these questions is suggested within the Declaration of Rights itself. As noted above, three of the articles in the Declaration deal with both the individual and the people (Articles III, X, and XXIX) and perhaps here, where these two parties are placed side by side, we may discover something about the relation between them. Having already discussed Article X at some length, let us now focus attention on the other two.

After initiating the Declaration of Rights with a ringing affirmation of the natural rights of man in Article I, the framers saw fit to turn their attention immediately to the great right of conscience. Article II declares in no uncertain terms the right and the duty of each individual to worship God according to his own conscience. Article II reads as follows:

> It is the right as well as the duty of all men in society, publicly, and at stated seasons, to worship the SUPREME BEING, the great creator and preserver of the universe. And no subject shall be hurt, molested, or restrained, in his person, liberty, or estate, for worshipping GOD in the manner and season most agreeable to the dictates of his own conscience; or for his religious profession or sentiments; provided he doth not disturb the public peace, or obstruct others in their religious worship.

It is interesting to note that the framers thought it proper to assign this as a right *and as a duty*, for it implies that whatever the freedom of conscience is taken to be, there is no such thing as the freedom to be unconscientious. It is also interesting to note that, unlike Article I, Article II refers only to the rights of men *in society*. There is no suggestion that the right of conscience is prior to society, i.e., there is no suggestion that this is a natural right. And in fact, this right of conscience was excluded from the list of natural rights in Article I. And in society, this right of conscience is limited in two ways. The right of conscience does not legitimate any actions that disturb the public peace, nor does it legitimate any actions that have the effect of disturbing others in their exercise of the right of conscience.

These facts suggest strongly that society itself has some rights in the matter of conscience, and here again, as if anticipating the analysis, the framers go on immediately to a consideration of these rights of the people in Article III, here reproduced in part.

> As the happiness of a people, and the good order and preservation of civil government, essentially depend upon piety, religion and morality; and as these cannot be generally diffused through a community, but by the institution of the public worship of GOD, and of public instructions in piety, religion and morality: Therefore, to promote their happiness and to secure the good order and preservation of their government, the people of this Commonwealth have a right to invest their legislature with power to authorize and require, and the legislature shall, from time to time, authorize and require, the several towns, parishes, precincts, and other bodies-politic, or religious societies, to make suitable provision, at their own expense, for the institution of the public worship of GOD, and for the support and maintenance of public protestant teachers of piety, religion and morality, in all cases where such provision shall not be made voluntarily.
>
> And the people of this Commonwealth have also a right to, and do, invest their legislature with authority to enjoin upon all the subjects an attendance upon the instructions of the public teachers aforesaid, at stated times and seasons, if there be any on whose instructions they can conscientiously and conveniently attend. . . .

This part of Article III may be translated into a syllogism in the following form:

Premise 1: The happiness of a people and the good order and preservation of civil government ought to be achieved.

Premise 2: The happiness of a people and the good order and preservation of civil government depend upon piety, religion, and morality.

Premise 3: Piety, religion, and morality cannot be generally diffused without, public worship of God and public instructions in piety, religion and morality.

Q.E.D.: The people have a right to invest their legislature with a power to authorize and require the institution of the public worship of God, and the support and maintenance of public Protestant ministers of piety, religion, and morality.

Q.E.D.: The people of this commonwealth have a right to invest their legislature with authority to enjoin upon all the subjects an attendence upon the instructions of the public teachers aforesaid.

From this argument, we are able to infer that the duty each individual has to worship God is derived from his obligation to support the social enterprise, and is related to the right society has to provide for ministers to help him worship. It should be noted that in the argument of Article III outlined above, the right of the people to provide for public instruction in religion and public support of ministers derives from two empirical propositions in conjunction with a single normative premise, viz. that the happiness of the people and the good order and preservation of civil government ought to be achieved. This entails that the people derive rights from the purposes or ends of the social enterprise, in addition to any that they might derive from the conditions of the social compact. And this suggests the possibility that the people have a right to do anything conducive to those ends.

But would this be true even in a case where, in pursuing the ends of society, the people transgressed the right of conscience of the individual? We have already seen in chapter 1 that Article III of the Declaration was objected to on precisely the grounds that it was inconsistent with the provisions for the right of individual conscience granted in Article II. Was this a valid objection? Underlying this problem are two related questions. First there is the question of whether or not the public support of ministers, according to the plan outlined in Article III, violates the right of conscience of the individual. Second is the question of whether or not, if this is the case, the people have an overriding right to do this. The only evidence the text provides in relation to the former question is the stark fact that the two articles were offered as a package, and therefore were presumably thought not to be inconsistent with each other. In regard to the question of priorities, it may be noted that the right of the individual in Article II is limited by a concern for the public peace and the rights of others, whereas the right of the people in Article III is not limited in any way. This observation pulls us in the direction of a conclusion that society can indeed transgress the rights of individuals, but the evidence is not clear and compelling, and it will perhaps be best to defer from drawing any conclusion at this time.

Articles II and III tell us something about the relationship between the individual and the people, but not in respect to the problem of due process of law. Article XXIX is directly related to this concern however.

> It is essential to the preservation of the rights of every individual, his life, liberty, property and character, that there be an impartial interpretation of the laws, and administration of justice. It is the right of every citizen to be tried by judges as free, impartial and independent as the lot of humanity will admit. It is therefore not only the best policy, but for the security of the rights of the people, and of every citizen, that the judges of the supreme judicial court should hold their offices as long as they behave themselves well; and that they should have honorable salaries ascertained and established by standing laws.

The third sentence of this article is of great significance. In it the two concepts that are at the heart of the problem are distinguished; the rights of the people, and the rights of every individual. We are told that both of these ends are served by the establishment of an independent judiciary, because an independent judiciary will secure an impartial interpretation and an impartial administration of the laws. We are not told that the rights of the people and the rights of every individual are the same thing. Quite the contrary, by mentioning both it is implied that they are different. All we are told is that they are equally served by the establishment of an independent judiciary. While instances of the rights of the people are not mentioned, certain of the rights of every individual are given: life, liberty, property, and character. Character is a new one, but the other three are old friends, the natural rights of man, as indicated in Articles I and X. These rights were specified in Article I, and certain obligations derivable from them were given in Article X. Now, in Article XXIX, certain procedural prerequisites of these natural rights are indicated. This is strongly reminiscent of the emphasis of both the Preamble and the other articles of the Declaration on the right of each individual to be governed by certain laws. Here we are informed that the institutional prerequisites for securing certain laws serve both the rights of the people and the rights of the individual. The rights of individuals and the rights of the people are evidently not mutually exclusive, but we still do not know if they may not, at some point, come into conflict. And we still do not know, if this should ever come to be the case, which one of the two will be given higher priority.

Two other observations need to be made before concluding the discussion of the Declaration of Rights. The first is that there does seem to be some sense of priority in the order in which the articles are presented. Article I deals with natural rights and Articles II and III deal with the right of conscience. The following six articles (the fourth through the ninth) deal with the right of self-government, and following these, the next six have something to do with due process of law. If this ordering is not thought to be a persuasive demonstration of preference, the terms in which the two types of rights are couched may be thought to be more so. Thus in regard to the rights of the people to self-government, we find in Article IV: "The people of this Commonwealth have the sole and exclusive right of governing themselves"; in Article V: "All power residing originally in the people and being derived from them"; in Article VII: "Government is instituted for the common good; for the protection, safety, prosperity and happiness of the people." These unequivocal phrases contrast sharply with the qualifications that are placed on the rights of the individual, as for example in Article II, where the right of conscience is limited by a concern for the public peace and the rights of others. Frequently, this limitation on the rights of individuals comes in the form of a requirement of legislative consent to justify any exception to a generally phrased right. We have already seen this in Article X, but it appears elsewhere, as for example in Article XXVII where the quartering of soldiers is forbidden except in time of war with the consent of the legislature, and in Article XXVIII where it is held that individuals cannot be subject to "law-martial" except by authority of the legislature. These passages, and others like them, suggest that the rights of the individual are not absolute, and that they are circumscribed directly and formally by the rights of the people to self-government through the mechanism of their representative assembly.

It appears that we must allow, however reluctantly, the suspicion that the Constitution subordinates the individual to the body of the people. We must now consider the Frame of Government in order to see if an analysis of it will serve to buttress this suspicion. If, as has been suggested, the framers had it as their conscious intention to proceed in a logical way in structuring the Constitution, we should expect to find in the Frame of Government evidence of the concerns that have been seen to dominate the Preamble and the Delaration of Rights. We should also expect that the several articles of the Declaration of Rights will be made operative in the Frame of Government.

The Frame of Government

Perhaps the analysis of this facet of the Constitution may best be advanced by briefly returning to the Declaration of Rights in order to try to make some inferences about what its provisions seem to entail in the way of governmental structure. Even the Preamble offers some constructive hints, for it requires that laws be made, interpreted, and executed, and this would seem to imply that some institutions have to be set up to accomplish these tasks. By distinguishing them, it also suggests that they might best be accomplished by three distinct agencies, although this may be no more than the prescience of hindsight.

The only two institutions specifically mentioned in the Declaration of Rights are the legislature and the supreme judicial court. The legislature is mentioned in several places and the supreme judicial court is mentioned in Article XXIX. That these two institutions are specified should be no surprise in light of the analysis to this point: one institution to represent the idea of self-government and one institution to represent the idea of government by law. We are also given some information about these two institutions: the legislature must assemble frequently; it is to be subject to close popular control, through free and equal elections and through the rights of instruction and petition for redress of grievances. We are also informed of certain powers of the legislature, as for examples the power to tax and the power to support religion. In regard to the supreme judicial court, we are told that it must be filled with independent judges who will serve during good behavior.

Perhaps the most important structural principle to be found

in the Declaration of Rights is that which is given in the famous "separation of powers" clause, Article XXX.

> In the government of the Commonwealth, the legislative department shall never exercise the executive and judicial powers, or either of them: The executive shall never exercise the legislative and judicial powers, or either of them: The judicial shall never exercise the legislative and executive powers, or either of them: to the end it may be a government of laws and not of men.

Here it is confirmed that the three duties of the people set down in the Preamble must be fulfilled by distinct departments of the government. Two features of Article XXX should be noted. One is the absolute terms in which the separation of powers is delineated. The phrase "shall never" is as clear as language can be, and it is used in relation to every possible permutation of the three powers of government. No account is given of how this separation will be effected, or even of what the principle might in theory be taken to entail. It may be assumed that the framers thought this to be self-evident or else unnecessary. Whatever they may have thought, we are left in a position of having only one place to look in order to find out what Article XXX in fact requires, and that is in the Frame of Government itself. The other fact which deserves notice is that the separation of powers is required for a specific purpose—that this government may be one of laws and not of men. How is the separation of powers, as described here, related to government by law? While this question cannot be answered on the basis of the text, it can and should be noted that Article XXX establishes a direct connection between one of the normative prerequisites of the government and a specific structural principle of it. If we are able to determine precisely what the Constitution means in Article XXX by this definite expression of the principle of separation of powers, we may be in a better position to understand the relationship between those obligations and rights derived from the nature of the state and the social compact given in the Preamble and the Declaration of Rights, and the structure of the government in the Frame of Government.

In addressing the Frame of Government we encounter something startling. It begins with the formal expression of the social compact described in the Preamble! "The people, inhabiting the territory formerly called the Province of Massachusetts-Bay, do hereby solemnly and mutually agree with each other, to form themselves into a free, sovereign, and independent body-politic or state, by the name of THE COMMONWEALTH OF MASSACHU-SETTS." Why does this statement of the compact appear in this place? It is logical that it must come after the Preamble, for it is in the Preamble that it is described and explained. But why should it not precede the Declaration of Rights? Two possible answers suggest themselves. It may be that the rights which are given in the Declaration of Rights are anterior to any political organization. But if this is the case, what is the source of their authority? Are they natural rights? If so, why are they not specified as such? And how can "the people of this commonwealth" (Article IV) have any rights prior to the initiation of the commonwealth? The other possibility is that this compact is intended to be a governmental compact, rather than a social compact. This would be consistent with the Lockean distinction between the three stages of political organization: the state of nature, civil society, and government. But if this is the case, why is there not also a formal expression of the social compact? And why is there not a separate discussion of two compacts in the Preamble?

Once again our analysis of the Constitution has raised questions which the Constitution does not seem to answer. We may hypothesize that, if there was a reason for placing this compact after the Declaration of Rights, it is implied that the rights described in that Declaration cannot be derived from, or authorized by, the compact itself. This in turn suggests that there must be some other source of authority for the rights specified in the Declaration. Two sources of authority seem to be possible: one, a concept of natural rights, existing prior to government and society; two, the people of the state of Massachusetts-Bay, who are mentioned in the title. If it is the former, the implication must be that the natural rights of individuals are of the greatest importance, since they are antecedent to the formation of the body-politic. If it is the latter, then it would appear that there is a residuary authority present in the people in the state of Massachusetts-Bay prior to this formal step of organizing themselves politically. And this would imply that any rights that are established on their authority are subject to their own revision. This problem is particularly distressing, because it would appear that depending upon how this dilemma is resolved, our earlier tentative conclusion that the Constitution subordinates the individual to the people may be called into question.

The Frame of Government establishes three departments of government, corresponding to the three functions of government mentioned in the Preamble; a legislature to make laws, a judiciary to interpret laws, and an executive to enforce laws. The legislature is the first department to be established. It is composed of two representative houses, each independent of the other in terms of their constituencies. One house, the House of Representatives, is based on a suffrage by the people apportioned according to the size of the towns. The other house, the Senate, is apportioned according to specially drawn districts. Property qualifications are assigned for both houses for both the right to vote and the right to serve. In both cases, the requisite amount of property is greater for the Senate than for the House.

Prior to establishing this structure, the framers saw fit to determine the scope of the authority of the legislature. In the process of doing that they provided a few surprises, in relation to the separation of powers. In the first place, the first substantive point to be established concerns not the legislature, but the executive! The executive is provided with a limited veto upon all the acts of the legislature, which can be overridden by a two-thirds vote by both houses of the legislature. That the Frame of Government should begin with a chapter on the legislature, and that this chapter should be initiated with a provision for a role for the governor in the legislative process is absolutely striking, in view of the fact that in the very last article of the Declaration of Rights it is required that the executive shall never exercise the legislative power. What are we to infer from this? It would seem that either the framers have involved themselves in a significant contradiction, or else they must have thought that an executive veto did not constitute an exercise of legislative power. But if this latter interpretation is correct, what must they have understood by the term "legislative power"?

The third article of the first section of Chapter I deals with the judiciary, or to be more precise, with the power of the legislature to erect a court system. It is unclear how this provision relates to the requirements of Article XXX, since the power to create the court system would seem also to imply the power to destroy it. Here, we must notice that whatever degree of separation of powers was intended by Article XXX, it must not have been the intention of the framers to bring it about by separate sources of authority, at least as applied to the relationship between the legislature and the judiciary.

The fourth article of the first section of Chapter I might be called the "plenary power" clause.

> And further, full power and authority are hereby given and granted to the said General Court, from time to time, to make, ordain, and establish, all manner of wholesome and reasonable orders, laws, statutes, and ordinances, directions and instructions, either with penalties or without; so as the same be not repugnant or contrary to this Constitution, as they shall judge to be for the good and welfare of this Commonwealth, and for the government and ordering thereof, and of the subjects of the same. . . .

Here the legislature is given the authority to pursue the public good. The only limitation placed on this power is that the laws passed by this authority should not be contrary to the Constitution. It must be immediately observed, however, that this important qualification can have little meaning by itself, for it is obviously the case that if laws are contrary to the Declaration of Rights they must be contrary to the Constitution. Yet, we have already become perplexed in trying to determine just what the Declaration of Rights actually requires. In a case where the provisions of the Declaration of Rights for the right of the people to govern themselves come into conflict with the provisions designed to secure the rights of each individual, we can not yet know whether or not any particular law might be contrary to the Constitution, precisely because we do not know where the constitutional priorities lie.

In light of this extraordinary grant of authority to the legislature, an extended discussion of the particular powers granted to it is not necessary in order to establish the wide scope of its power. It is interesting to note, however, that one power that appears to be judicial is assigned to the legislature: the power of impeachment. Impeachment involves the removal of public officials from office by a process of indictment (a bill of impeachment) and conviction at a trial for impeachment. These procedures are at least quasi-judicial. Impeachment historically has been a function of the legislative branch of government, and therefore may be regarded as a part of the legislative power. Even if it was understood to be so by the people of Massachusetts, however, the implications are significant, for this understanding would imply that, whatever the definitional characteristics of a particular power might be, they do not necessarily include the procedures by which it is exercised. We are thus able to distinguish another possible limitation of the concept of separation of powers as given in Article XXX. It does not include the notion of separate sources of authority (at least between the legislative and judicial branches of the government), and it does not necessarily include the procedures by which the power is exercised (again, at least as between the legislative and judiciary branches of the government).

The executive power seems to have required no general definition. In Chapter II, the Constitution states that there will be a supreme executive magistrate; it was not even thought necessary to say that his job is to execute the laws. The major specific grant of power is in Section VII, where the war powers of the governor are specified in no uncertain terms. This is quite understandable, considering that the war was in full force at the time, but even this large grant of power is "for the time being." The governor is given the power to grant pardons in all cases except impeachment, and he is given the power to make certain appointments (including judicial officers), with the advice and consent of his Council.[3] The governor is given the power to adjourn or prorogue the legislature upon certain occasions, and to call it into session in emergencies. He is also to have the sole power of authorizing all expenditures of public monies, where the money is to be spent as a matter of policy rather than in payment of debts already assumed, when such expenditures are pursuant to an act or resolve of the legislature. And, of course, he has the limited power of veto over the acts of the legislature.

How strong an office is that of chief executive? Why are these powers enumerated? What is the relationship of the executive to the other two branches of government? It would appear that the governor is to some extent to act as a control on the legislature and judiciary, as he has a power to overturn decisions of both branches in some cases (through the veto and pardon). He is also to referee anticipated conflicts between the two branches of the legislature, and to oversee the military functions

3. The Council was to be an advisory body to the governor. Nine members from those elected to be senators were chosen to sit on the Council by joint ballot of the Senate and House. In the absence of the governor and lieutenant governor, the Council was to act as executive.

of the state. Nothing is said, however, about his role in securing domestic tranquility. He may, with the council, "hold and keep a Council, for the ordering and directing the affairs of the Commonwealth, agreeably to the Constitution and the laws of the land." Does this imply a concept of prerogative? Does the power to authorize the expenditure of funds imply a power to refuse to do so? May he dissolve the legislature when he disagrees with what it is doing, or is about to do? And is not the power to dissolve the legislature, temporarily or permanently, a legislative power? In contrast to the provisions of Chapter I in specifying a wide grant of authority for the legislature, the scope of the executive power is not well defined at all.

The court system is to be established by the legislature, and the officers of the court are to be appointed by the executive. This leaves very little to be determined in a separate chapter on the courts, and indeed, the chapter on the judiciary (Chapter III) is very brief. The first article of this chapter reflects the demands of Article XXIX of the Declaration of Rights, in establishing good behavior as the tenure for all major judicial officers. (Article III makes an exception to this rule for justices of the peace, who serve for seven years, and Article IV states that certain of the courts will meet at fixed places and at fixed times.) The other two articles of Chapter III seem to subordinate the judicial branch to the legislature and executive. For it is required in Article II that the other branches of the government have the authority to require opinions of the justices of the supreme judicial court, without saying that they are necessarily bound by any opinion so solicited. This may have been assumed, but it seems probable that so important a provision as judicial participation would have been made explicit had it been intended to operate in the process of forming policy. And Article V removes from the jurisdiction of the courts cases of marriage, divorce, alimony, and all appeals in probate cases, and gives them to the governor and council, at least until the legislature decides it should be otherwise. What notion of separation of powers is involved here, and again, in relation to the judiciary?

Having briefly surveyed the provisions for each of the three types of power, we should be in a better position to understand the separation which is supposed to exist between them. Yet we are more befuddled than ever before. For contrary to any reasonable expectation we might have had, instead of separating the three powers, the Constitution seems to be much more concerned with running them together! But perhaps this is too strong a conclusion for the evidence to support. It is at least the case that the legislature is granted the power to make laws, and the executive and judiciary are not; and the executive is given the power to protect the commonwealth, and the legislative and the judiciary are not; and the judiciary is granted the power to hear most civil cases and all criminal cases, and at least most of the time the legislative and the executive are not. But if this is what is meant by "shall never" in Article XXX of the Declaration of Rights, then perhaps it was premature to say that those words were as clear as words can be.

Before leaving this question, Chapter VI should be considered. Here we find the matter of "incompatability of and exclusion from offices" discussed. In a lengthy clause (Article II), it is forbidden for almost every officer under the Constitution to hold any other constitutional office. This article may be described as a provision for "separation of persons."[4] Is the concept of separation of persons the same thing as that of separation of powers? If so, is this provision of Chapter VI all that was intended in the way of a structural embodiment of Article XXX? This seems unlikely for the simple reason that it is difficult to make the phrasing of Article XXX compatible with the idea of separation of persons only. Even if we interpret Article XXX to intend that, for example, the phrase "the legislative department shall never exercise the executive and judicial powers, or either of them" to be taken as meaning that the persons in the legislative department can never hold office in either of the other two branches of government, we must confront the fact that the words do not seem to say that. Rather, they say that the persons of one department shall not exercise the powers of the other departments. This may entail that they should not hold office in the other departments, but it suggests also some notion of power and its exercise, which transcends any definition in terms of the structure of the institutions. In other words, to assume that Article XXX calls only for a separation of persons, requires that the concept of the exercise of power be understood in purely institutional terms. This does not seem to make any

4. For the idea of "separation of persons" see below, chapter 4, pp. 164–168; see also Ellen E. Brennen, *Plural Office-Holding in Massachusetts, 1760–1780* (Chapel Hill: University of North Carolina Press, 1945); and M. J. C. Vile, *Constitutionalism and the Separation of Powers* (Oxford: The Clarendon Press, 1967), p. 17.

sense, for certainly the exercise of power is substantive and a particular *type* of power must be defined by the sphere of its operation, rather than by who exercises it. Or, at least, so it seems.

Although we appear to have come a long way, the journey has apparently been through the land of the Looking Glass, and we have not even the energy of the Red Queen; for the analysis has raised many more questions than it has answered, and all of our running has not been sufficient to keep us in place. We do not know what are the natural rights of man; we do not know who is "the people"; we do not understand the relationship between consent and natural rights; we do not know what Article XXX of the Declaration of Rights requires; we do not know how the requirements of Article XXX for the separation of powers are related to government by law; we do not know how they are to be made operative in the relationship between the three branches of the government; we do not know the relationship between government by law and self-government; and we are not sure if all of these problems are tied together in the way in which our analysis supposes that they are. Nevertheless, we have discerned enough of a theoretical structure to whet our curiosity. We have noticed elements of consistency as well as potential confusions. We have seen that, often, the Constitution seems to anticipate the questions which the analysis has raised. And in those cases where the meaning of the Constitution has appeared obscure, our difficulty in understanding it may perhaps be related to conceptual confusions. Sometimes the words of the Constitution do not seem to say what we think they should mean. Perhaps, then, the words they used might have been understood differently by the framers than by us. For all of these reasons, a deeper immersion into the thought underlying the Constitution is needed if an adequate understanding of its meaning is to be obtained.

III

The Theory of the State

The Social Compact Theory

It should come as no surprise that the revolutionaries were concerned with establishing the legitimacy of the new governments that they were creating after independence was declared. The logic of revolution leads inexorably to the logic of political organization in general, if it does not proceed from it, and in the process of developing a theoretical defense of their separation from Great Britain they were led to a general consideration of the legitimate foundations of government. Many wondered with Samuel Stillman, "How come the men whom we call magistrates, with any power at all over the people?" In attempting to answer this question the Americans were driven to trace political authority from its beginnings. "The times," said Peter Whitney in 1777, " have led to a free inquiry into the origin, nature and design of civil government." This free inquiry led to the notion of the social compact. "The body-politic is formed by a voluntary association of individuals," proclaimed the Constitution of 1780, "it is a social compact." A government formed by and for that body-politic should be based on a compact too. The town of Lexington described the origin of government in these terms: "A civil constitution or Form of Government is of the nature of a most sacred Covenant, or Contract, entered into by the Individuals, which form the Society." Some people wondered when any compact could be shown to have taken place. Thus the town of Pittsfield, in 1776: "We have heard much of Governments being founded in Compact. What Compact has been formed as the foundation of Government in this Province?" But for these skeptics, there was a ready reply. "This at least appears to be the most just and rational idea of government that is founded in compact," said Gad Hitchcock, "as . . . all governments, notwithstanding later usurpations, originally were; and if the compact, in early ages hath not always been expressed, yet it hath been necessarily implied, and understood, both by governors, and the governed, on their entering into society."[1]

As with any expression that becomes elevated to the rank of cliche, the phrase "social compact" was actually a symbol for a group of related concepts that, taken together, formed a coherent theory of the origin, nature, and extent of the legitimate authority of the state. The analytic structure of the social compact theory involves the division of the problem of political authority into four stages: the state of nature, civil society, constitutional government, and administration. The ultimate objective of this division is to explain the proper relationship between the individual and the state in the third and fourth stages, where political societies are operating according to known and established rules and procedures. In order to accomplish this, however, it is necessary to trace political authority through the first and second stages from its origins. In other words, the social compact theory views political authority in developmental terms, its conditions changing as it passes through each stage of the theory.

The first and second stages of the theory, which we may call the social stages, involve the creation of the society itself, and are symbolically represented by the metaphor of the social compact. The third and fourth stages of the social compact theory may be called the governmental stages, for they deal with the establishment and administration of the institutions of government under a written constitution. The essence of the governmental stages of the theory is to be found in the formation of a constitution of government, and in the choice of persons to hold office under it. This aspect of the social compact theory has sometimes been represented by the idea of a governmental

1. Samuel Stillman, *A Sermon Preached Before the Honorable Council and House of Representatives* . . . *May 26, 1779* (Boston, 1779), p. 7; Peter Whitney, *American Independence Vindicated* (Boston, 1777), p. 45; "The Return of the Town of Lexington on the Constitution of 1778," in Oscar and Mary Handlin, eds., *The Popular Sources of Political Authority* (Cambridge: Harvard University Press, Belknap Press, 1966), p. 317; "Pittsfield Petitions, May 29, 1776," ibid, p. 92; Gad Hitchcock, *A Sermon Preached Before His Excellency Thomas Gage, Esq.,* . . . *May 25th, 1774* (Boston, 1774), p. 7. For other examples of Hitchcock's point, see: Elisha Fish, *A Discourse Delivered at Worcester, March 28th, 1775* (Worcester, Mass., 1775), pp. 13-14; Joseph Warren, *An Oration, Delivered March 6th, 1775* (Boston, 1775), pp. 6, 12-13; Handlin and Handlin, *Popular Sources,* pp. 57, 65, 374.

compact. This distinction is most often associated with Locke. According to Laslett, the governmental contract was, for Locke, less legalistic than the social contract, more akin to a trust.

> In applying the word trust to the various political powers in the state, the constitution, Locke draws an important distinction for us, perhaps two of them. He divides off the process of compact, which creates a community, from the further process by which the community entrusts political power to a government; although they may take place at the same time, these two are distinct. This puts his system amongst those which distinguish the "contract of society" from the "contract of government", though in Locke this second process is not a contract at all. And this may be his second point; to underline the fact that the relation between government and governed is not contractual, for a trust is not a contract.[2]

It is true that, according to Locke, the people in a civil society choose to trust those who come to have political power over them, and this decision to trust, or rather to impose a trust, in governors is subsequent to the establishment of society through the social compact. It is not surprising that the people of Massachusetts, good Lockeans all, should have emulated Lockean theory in the process of erecting their own constitution. However, we must take note of the fact that the literature of revolutionary Massachusetts does not reveal that the distinction between the social and governmental compacts was much discussed. Indeed, the distinction between these two contractual ideas was obviously one about which they were confused. This can be seen quite clearly by considering the text of the Constitution along side of the "Address of the Convention" which accompanied it. In the Preamble to the Constitution, as we have seen, the social compact is explicitly described: "The body-politic is formed by a voluntary association of individuals: It is a social compact, by which the whole people covenants with each citizen, and each citizen with the whole people, that all shall be governed by certain laws for the common good." And in the Frame of Government, it is formally enacted: "The people, inhabiting the territory formerly called the Province of Massachu-

2. John Locke, *Two Treatises of Government*, ed. Peter Laslett (New York: The New American Library, 1965), pp. 126–127.

setts-Bay, do hereby solemnly and mutually agree with each other, to form themselves into a free, sovereign, and independent body-politic or state, by the name of THE COMMONWEALTH OF MASSACHUSETTS." Now the fact that this compact is formally enacted in the Constitution suggests that the people of Massachusetts thought they were emerging from a state of nature as they adopted the Constitution, or that they were enacting a governmental compact rather than a social compact in the Frame of Government, or else that the social compact stated in the Constitution was only meant to be pro forma, having been actually consummated at an earlier date. The first alternative is eliminated by the following passage from the "Address of the Convention": "You will observe that we have resolved, that Representation ought to be founded on the Principle of equality; but it cannot be understood thereby that each Town in the Commonwealth shall have Weight and importance in a just proportion to its Numbers and property. An exact Representation would be unpracticable even in a System of Government arising from the State of Nature, and much more so in a state already divided into nearly three hundred Corporations." The language of this passage will simply not allow the conclusion that the framers envisioned themselves to be arising from a state of nature by including the statement of the social compact in the Frame of Government. Either, then, they thought they were enacting a governmental compact or they thought that it would be useful to state the social compact formally. The former interpretation is suggested by the position which the enactment of the compact occupies, but the latter interpretation is supported by a passage from Blackstone's *Commentaries*.

> I proceed next to the duties incumbent on the king by our constitution; in consideration of which duties his dignity and prerogatives are established by the laws of the land: it being a maxim in the law, that protection and subjection are reciprocal. And these reciprocal duties are what, I apprehend, were meant by the convention in 1688, when they declared that King James had broken the original contract between king and people. But, however, as the terms of that original contract were in some measure disputed, being alleged to exist principally in theory, and to be only deducible by reason and the rules of natural law; in which deduction different understandings might very consider-

ably differ: it was, after the revolution, judged proper to declare these duties expressly, and to reduce that contract to a plain certainty. So that, whatever doubts might be formally raised by weak and scrupulous minds about the existence of such an original contract, they must now entirely cease.

Since there were people in Massachusetts who thought that they had been "driven into a state of nature," it would have behooved the framers to have included a statement of the compact for no other reason than to have alleviated the concern of the stubborn and vocal Constitutionalists of Berkshire County.[3]

In evaluating the explanation of the political theory underlying the Constitution in terms of a logic that stresses two distinct contractual arrangements and four distinct stages, the ambiguities of the text must be weighed against evidence offered by the literature of the period preceding its adoption. This chapter will consider the first two stages of the social compact theory, and examine the important changes that occur when a group of individuals in a state of nature unite to form a civil society. The following chapter will consider the problems that society faces in establishing and operating a government under a written constitution. The formation of a civil society from an unorganized state of nature forms the subject matter of what we shall call the theory of the state. Such a theory explains the origins, nature, and extent of the authority of society over the individuals who compose it. The theory of the state guiding the people of Massachusetts attempted to explain the origins of civil society by considering how such a society might have developed from a state of nature. Whether or not the state of nature was perceived by the people of Massachusetts historically, or merely metaphorically, cannot be determined. The historicity of the state of nature was not a major subject of debate among the publicists of revolutionary Massachusetts. The distinction between the state of nature and civil society was repeatedly articulated, however, and in order to perceive how the latter derives from the former, it is necessary to begin by examining the state of nature.

3. Handlin and Handlin, *Popular Sources*, p. 436; William Blackstone, *Commentaries on the Laws of England*, 4 vols. (New York: W. E. Dean, 1836), 1: 233; Phileleutherus [pseud.], *Independent Chronicle*, March 6, 1777.

The State of Nature

The state of nature is a condition in which individuals are bound by no formal political ties. The function of the concept of the state of nature within the social compact theory is to establish the conditions under which formal political ties are established in a community of individuals. Its defining characteristic is precisely the lack of such political ties, or in Locke's term, the absence of a common judge. Its descriptive features are crucial, however. For depending upon how a state of nature is viewed, one's opinion concerning the legitimate extent of political authority will vary. Thus the state of nature is a backdrop against which civil society is to be evaluated, and it must be understood on its own terms before its relationship to civil society can be established. As Locke had put it, "To understand Political Power right, and derive it from its Original, we must consider what State all Men are naturally in." Just what state were all men naturally in? There were, for Locke, two principal characteristics of the state of nature: freedom and equality. For all men, he says, the state of nature is "a state of perfect Freedom to order their Actions, and dispose of their Possessions, and Persons as they think fit, within the bounds of the Law of Nature, without asking leave, or depending upon the Will of any other Man. . . . A State also of Equality, wherein all the Power and Jurisdiction is reciprocal, no one having more than another." The people of Massachusetts shared with Locke this view of the state of nature. For them, as for Locke, the state of nature was a state of freedom and a state of equality.[4]

One of the most widely cited oracles on the subject of liberty was the Englishman Richard Price, whose pamphlet *Observations on the Nature of Civil Liberty* was published in Boston in 1776. Price divides the subject of liberty into four categories: physical liberty, moral liberty, religious liberty, and civil liberty. Physical liberty he defines as the "principle of Sponteniety, or Self-determination, which constitutes us as Agents," and moral liberty is described as "the power of following, in all circumstances, our sense of right and wrong." Similarly, religious liberty "signifies the power of exercising, without molestation, that mode of religion which we think best," and civil liberty "is the power of a Civil Society or State to govern itself by its own dis-

4. Locke, *Two Treatises*, p. 309.

cretion." It must be noticed that for Price, liberty is above all a *power,* a capability of acting in any and all situations according to free will. It is, in other words, a positive concept of liberty. He says, "It should be observed, that, according to these definitions of the different kinds of liberty, there is one general idea, that runs through them all; I mean, the idea of Self-direction."[5]

This positive concept of liberty as a power of self-direction was commonly accepted in Massachusetts during the Revolution. Perhaps the most complete analysis of the concept of natural liberty is to be found in a sermon of Gad Hitchcock, published in 1775. In his original state, says Hitchcock, man was endowed with natural liberty: "liberty is innate, and original; the plant of our heavenly Father," and "liberty is the right of nature confirmed to us by revelation, and essential to our happiness." Because man is free, because "liberty was an essential principle of his constitution, a natural quality, and a necessary spring, and incentive to all virtuous improvement," man could be regarded as morally responsible to God for his actions. "He was a moral agent, endowed as it is commonly expressed, with freedom of will, or a self-determining power, in regard to such volitions and actions as form the moral character, and begat a likeness to the divine purity, or the contrary." This freedom or liberty was seen by Hitchcock as a power of self-direction, and this power is described as a "right of nature." Its operation is particularly related to the sphere of moral decisions, where each individual is provided with the freedom to choose between right and wrong actions. But this moral prerogative implies the complete freedom to direct one's actions in all cases, and in respect to all worldly things. Indeed, worldly things are provided for man by God, with just this end in view, to provide for man the materials necessary to capitalize on this divine grant of liberty. "His right to use the things provided for the supply of his necessities, or convenience, was derived from the divine grant, either explicitly made, or discovered by the light of his own understanding, subject to no restraint, but the law of his nature, which was not only consistent with, but the perfection of Liberty; obligation to obey the laws of the Creator, being on-

5. Richard Price, *Observations on the Nature of Civil Liberty* (Boston, 1775), p. 4.

ly a check to licentiousness, and abuse." Hitchcock's view of liberty is thus fully consistent with both Locke and Price: liberty is a power of self-determination in respect to all things, being bounded only by the laws of nature and God. This view, which pervades the literature of the period, was accurately summarized by Samuel Stillman in 1779: men are by nature, says Stillman, "in a state of entire freedom. Whatever they possess is their own; to be disposed of solely agreeable to their own will."[6]

This view of natural liberty as a power of self-determination had as its direct corollary the concept of natural equality, which was defined as an equality *of liberty*. We live in an era, says Stillman, "in which the great principles of liberty are better understood. With us it is a first and fundamental principle, that God made all men equal." In his 1774 sermon, Gad Hitchcock had this to say about equality: "In a state of nature men are equal, exactly on a par in regard to authority; each one is a law to himself, having the law of God, the sole rule of conduct, written on his heart." Hitchcock and Stillman were not alone in these sentiments. Samuel West said of the state of nature in 1776 that "it is a state wherein all are equal, no one having a right to control another, or oppose him in what he does, unless it be in his own defence, or in the defence of those that, being injured, stand in need of his assistance." In 1778, Peter Powers affirmed that, "all men, indeed, are by nature equal: and all have, most certainly, an equal right to freedom and liberty by the great law of nature." Simeon Howard declared flatly in 1780 that, "in this state every one has an equal right to liberty, and to do what he thinks proper." And Samuel Cooper echoed those sentiments in the same year: "We want not, indeed, a special revelation from Heaven to teach us that men are born equal and free; that no man has a natural claim of dominion over his neighbours."[7]

6. Gad Hitchcock, *A Sermon Preached at Plymouth December 22d, 1774* (Boston, 1775), pp. 16, 39, 8; Samuel Stillman, *A Sermon*, pp. 8–9. For other references to natural liberty, see: Isaac Backus, *Government and Liberty Described* (Boston, 1778); *New-England Chronicle*, July 4, 1776; Handlin and Handlin, *Popular Sources*, p. 330.

7. Stillman, *A Sermon*, p. 8; Hitchcock, *A Sermon . . . May 25th, 1774*, p. 20; Samuel West, *A Sermon Preached before the Honorable Council, and the Honorable House of Representatives . . . May 29th, 1776* (Boston, 1776), in J. W. Thornton, ed., *The Pulpit of the American Revolution* (Boston: Gould and Lincoln, 1860), p. 270; Peter Powers, *Jesus Christ the True King* (Newburyport, Mass., 1778), p. 10; Simeon Howard, *A Sermon*

The equality of the state of nature was, in essence, political equality of the most basic sort: the equality of liberty that each individual would have in the absence of formal poltical ties. There is no suggestion that any other sort of equality typifies the state of nature. Indeed, as shall be seen, the extreme inequality that characterizes the state of nature in other respects is one of its most critical features. Are there no guidelines or standards for human behavior in the state of nature? Is it a state of licentiousness and anarchy? According to Hitchcock, individuals in the state of nature are obliged to obey the laws of God, as a check to licentiousness, and Locke speaks of the liberty of the state of nature being bounded by the law of nature. What is the law of nature, and how is it related to the law of God? In order to understand the state of nature completely it is necessary to understand natural law, and its relationship to divine law.

Twentieth-century scholarship has witnessed the contention that it was the intention and effect of the two principal seventeenth-century natural law philosophers (Hobbes and Locke) to drive a wedge between natural law and divine law. At least in the case of Locke, however, it is contended that it was also his intention to obscure the fact that natural law and divine law were incompatible, thereby to extend the appeal of his ideology to as many people as he possibly could. It is not necessary to enter here the lists of the debate concerning whether or not Locke had "one foot planted side by side with that of Saint Thomas." For the purposes of this discussion it suffices to say that for the people of Massachusetts in the 1770s, there was no incompatability between the law of nature and the law of God. Indeed, the law of nature was seen to be a part of the law of God.[8]

Preached Before the Honorable Council and the Honorable House of Representatives . . . *May 31, 1780,* in Thornton, *The Pulpit,* p. 362; Samuel Cooper, *A Sermon Preached Before His Excellency John Hancock, Esq.,* . . . *October 25, 1780* (Boston, 1780), p. 14. For other references to equality, see: John Murray, *Nehemiah, on the Struggle for Liberty* (Newbury, Mass., 1779), p. 6; Samuel Webster, *A Sermon Preached before the Honorable Council, and the Honorable House of Representatives* . . . *May 28, 1777* (Boston, 1777), p. 2; Handlin and Handlin, *Popular Sources,* pp. 329–331, 385, 411, 418, 429, 830.

8. Willmoore Kendall, "John Locke Revisited," in *Contra Mundum* (New Rochelle, N. Y.: Arlington House, 1971), pp. 420–421. See also: George Sabine, *A History of Political Theory* (New York: Henry Holt and Company, 1937), pp. 523–526; Leo Strauss, *Natural Right and History* (Chicago: University of Chicago Press, 1953), pp. 202–220, 228–230.

[74] The Theory of the State

The laws of God were revealed in scripture, and set a standard of morality for everyday living in the state of nature. Of this there was no doubt. According to Peter Powers, the state of nature was directed by "divine revelation, which gives us the most perfect rules for the conduct of mankind, in every station and condition" and "should be received as a perfect standard." Men were free, however, to choose whether or not to follow the divine guidance. This was the essence of liberty in the state of nature. In order to direct men to the divine moral standard, God provided them with a moral sense. "We are born with a sense of right and wrong, which grows quicker and stronger as we advance in age, unless weakened, corrupted and overborne by education and example." This moral sense is a gift from God. "God manifests his will by the operations of hands, as well as by the dictates of his word. Mankind in general shew the work of the law written on their hearts." This law, this moral sense, is the law of nature.

> In infinite wisdom, the creator fixed a law of nature to every species of Beings, animate and inanimate. And according to that is the system governed. Nature, or its fixed laws, is nothing without him who is the God of nature. . . . Law was given to man. The original law our Maker gave us, commonly called the law of nature, was not a blind law of instinct, but the eternal rule of righteousness, the moral law, agreeably to the nature of the divine perfections. The spirit of this was written on the heart of innocent man, for in the image of God made he them; and the great Creator positively enjoined his punctual obedience.

The law of nature is not only compatible with revealed law, it is only another way of knowing the will of God. They are perfectly the same. "The ten moral precepts are a brief summary of the whole moral law, the great law of nature. And the blessed bible gives us a perfect comment upon it."[9]

The law of nature was perceived to be general in type but specific in content. Whatever is dictated by the moral sense is a part of the law of nature, but there was widespread agreement on many of the specific tenets of natural law. Among these tenets are the natural rights of man. Natural rights are specifically

9. Powers, *Jesus Christ*, p. 13; Nathan Fiske, *The Importance of Righteousness* (Boston, 1774), p. 7; Powers, *Jesus Christ*, pp. 9, 29. See also: Philadelphus [pseud.], *Independent Chronicle*, April 17, 1777.

those rights that inhere to man as man, and were his possession in the state of nature. An individual's natural rights are the rights to perform actions required of him in his natural condition. In a state without government, each individual would be left to his own devices in supporting his existence, and in protecting it. He would be at liberty to make use of the bounty of nature in his attempt to achieve temporal happiness, and he would have a right to keep whatever wordly possessions he could claim on the basis of his own industry. These rights are confirmed to man by the law of nature, or natural reason, which is equivalent in its authority to the scriptures. "Now, whatever right reason requires as necessary to be done is as much the will and law of God as though it were enjoined us by an immediate revelation from heaven, or commanded in the sacred scriptures." The scope of natural rights is thus defined by natural law, and made known to man through it. It is reason that distinguishes man from other animate beings, and it was reason that was to guide man in the state of nature. Above all, natural rights were perceived in terms of freedom to act. If a man has a natural right to do something, then it is wrong for anyone to try to stop him. Even were he to be prevented from taking an action to which he had a natural right, his right to take that action remains inviolate. By providing this normative standard, natural rights establish the basis upon which rested the moral law of the state of nature.[10]

There are two types of natural rights: alienable natural rights and unalienable natural rights. As the birthright of each individual, natural rights establish normative claims which are the possession of each individual alike. In making the distinction between alienable and unalienable natural rights, the publicists of Massachusetts were motivated by a concern to lay the theoretical groundwork for their conception of political authority in civil society. Some of the natural freedom (i.e., rights) enjoyed by individuals in the state of nature had to be yielded upon entering civil society. Determining precisely how much of this freedom each individual had to relinquish was the theoretical problem. By distinguishing between rights that could be relinquished and those that could not be relinquished, criteria were established by which the legitimate extent of political authority could be determined. This explanation of the rationale

10. West, *A Sermon*, in Thornton, *The Pulpit*, p. 275.

behind the distinction between alienable and unalienable natural rights comports with much of the rhetoric of the revolutionary era, as well as with that of the scholarly literature of more recent times which has sought to interpret the political thought of that era. It is readily apparent, however, that a correct determination of the implications of the distinction between alienable and unalienable natural rights for the problem of political authority must hinge upon an understanding of the criteria employed in defining each category.

This problem is complex, and was perceived to be so in revolutionary Massachusetts. It is addressed by Theophilus Parsons in "The Essex Result" in the following terms: "All men are born equally free. The rights they possess at their births are equal, and of the same kind. Some of those rights are alienable, and may be parted with for an equivalent. Others are unalienable and inherent, and of that importance that no equivalent can be received in exchange." According to Parsons, individuals may choose to divest themselves of their natural rights only on the condition that they receive an equivalent in return. Where no equivalent can possibly be received for a particular right, the individual presumably is not free to give up the right, and it is therefore an unalienable right. This concept of equivalency between value lost in giving up the right, and value received in return for it bears the veneer of utilitarianism. The calculation could presumably be reduced to a simple preference schedule. This appearance is deceptive, however. Unalienable rights were thought to be beyond the reach of any utilitarian alternative not only because of their "importance," but also because of their "inherent" character. It might, after all, be the case that the individual would choose to give up one of his natural rights even though he could not receive any equivalent in return because of the importance of that right. Parsons was aware of this possibility, however. "Sometimes," he says, "we shall mention the surrendering of a power to controul our natural rights, which perhaps is speaking with more precision, than when we use the expression parting with natural rights—but the same thing is intended."[11]

By distinguishing between an individual's natural rights and the power to control those rights, Parsons suggests that the nor-

11. Theophilus Parsons, "The Essex Result," in Handlin and Handlin, *Popular Sources*, p. 330.

mative force of natural rights is not contingent upon the actual exercise of them. Since the individual is to forfeit, not his natural rights, but instead the power to control them, it would appear that the notion of "importance" as a definitional characteristic of an unalienable natural right must refer to this power of control, rather than to the right itself. It would therefore seem to follow that the criterion of "importance" as a definitional characteristic of an unalienable natural right is not related to its value. In other words, unalienable natural rights have no greater normative force than alienable natural rights. Both establish claims to freedom of action. But the power to control the exercise of some rights is more significant in some cases than in others. The question arises, When would the power to control a natural right be of such importance so as to be unalienable? The answer suggested by Parsons's account is that this would be the case only when one could receive no equivalent for the power to control the natural right. This would be true when the right is "unalienable and inherent," and therefore "of that importance that no equivalent can be received in exchange." Thus, if unalienable natural rights are unalienable because of their importance, they appear to be important because they are unalienable and, therefore, inherent. This point may be phrased in another way. If a natural right is inherent, then it must be essential to the very existence *as a human being* of him who possesses it. If this is the case, then it must be quite literally impossible for that individual to forfeit the power of controlling it. Therefore, it is unalienable because it cannot physically be alienated. And the converse would appear to hold for alienable natural rights. These rights are of such a character that the power to control them can be relinquished. They are, therefore, not essential to the existence as human beings of those who possess them. Because they are not essential, it is possible to find some equivalent for them. The calculus in this case becomes strictly utilitarian.

The notion that unalienable natural rights are somehow basic to human nature, as well as being very desirable, is reflected in the first article of the Declaration of Rights of the Constitution of 1780. "All men are born free and equal, and have certain natural, essential, and unalienable rights; among which may be reckoned the right of enjoying and defending their lives and liberties; that of acquiring, possessing, and protecting property; in fine, that of seeking and obtaining their safety and happiness." The exact wording of this article is of critical importance. The rights described here are "natural, essential, and unalienable." Rights comprehended by this description must be natural: they must inhere to man as man, a part of human nature derived from God. They must be essential to man as man: without them a man would cease to be a man. (They are, therefore, very important; indeed, so important that no equivalent can be received in exchange.) And they must be literally unalienable: no man will give them up because no man can give them up (i.e., no man can give up the power of controlling them).

What rights are of such a character? The examples listed in Article I are very instructive. Contrary to the teaching of the Declaration of Independence, Article I of the Declaration of Rights does not hold that man has an unalienable right to life, liberty, and happiness. Men do as a matter of fact give up their right to live, and their liberties, and under the Constitution men could be compelled to give up their power of controlling their lives, liberties, and property. Article X of the Declaration of Rights is a good case in point. There it is held that an individual has the right to be protected in the enjoyment of his life, liberty, and property; but there also, it is held that society can commandeer his liberty and property when it is in the public interest to do so. The fact that it is made incumbent upon society to provide reasonable compensation (i.e., an equivalent) for property appropriated implies that property, at least, is an alienable natural right. The really unalienable natural rights of men, according to Article I, consist not of life, liberty, happiness, or property; but rather they are the "right of enjoying and defending their lives and liberties," and the right of "acquiring, possessing, and protecting property." Society can take a man's property, but not his right to acquire or possess it. It may take away his freedom, but not his right to try to keep it. It may even take his life, but the individual still has the right to fight in order to defend it. These rights are "natural, essential, and unalienable" because they define the very meaning of being a human being. A man who could not do these things would not be a man. These unalienable natural rights are the rights to do the things that man was put on earth to do. Indeed, they can be comprehended in terms of a more general right, the right to seek and obtain happiness. No man can avoid seeking and obtaining his happiness and still be a man. It would be contrary to human nature.

These unalienable natural rights are so fundamental to human nature and to human existence that it is difficult to conceive of a way in which they might be abridged. It is evident that the violation of these rights could take place only at the most extreme level of political tyranny. A government that could prevent an individual from controlling his rights to try to earn a living, to enjoy his life and liberty, and to seek and obtain happiness, would be an absolute government indeed. And it therefore appears that as claims on behalf of individuals against political authority, the unalienable natural rights of man operate only in rare cases of extreme abuse. Under most circumstances, the unalienable natural rights of man afford no claim for an individual against poltical authority.

The best an individual can hope for, then, is that he will indeed receive an equivalent when he relinquishes his alienable natural rights. Prior to examining the concept of equivalency in operation, however, one other unalienable natural right must be considered. This is the unalienable natural right of conscience. No right was more widely heralded in revolutionary Massachusetts, but the precise meaning and significance of the unalienable natural right of conscience was more complex than the rhetoric by which it was often expressed would lead on to believe.

The unalienable natural right of conscience may be described as the prototypical unalienable right, in that it perfectly fulfills the definitional requirement of all unalienable natural rights: there can be no substitute for the private right of judgment in matters of conscience. "The unalienable right of private judgment in religious concerns, or right to judge for ourselves in things pertaining to God, as accountable creatures, is another of these immovable foundations of the righteous," said Elisha Fish in 1775. Three years later "The Essex Result" spoke of the unalienable right of conscience in these terms: "Those rights which are unalienable . . . are called the rights of conscience. We have duties, for the discharge of which we are accountable to our Creator and benefactor, which no human power can cancel. What those duties are, is determinable by right reason, which may be, and is called, a well informed conscience. What this dictates as our duty, is so; and that power which assumes a controul over it, is an usurper; for no consent can be pleaded to justify the controul, as any consent in this case is void." The town of New Salem, in 1780, was more succinct: "Religion

must at all Times be a matter between GOD and individuals."
The unalienable status of the right of conscience reflects the relationship between natural law and natural rights. The liberty of
the state of nature was seen as necessitating the choice between
good and evil. The need for civil society arises out of the fact
that not all men come to know what good is, or choose to do
good. Therefore, there is a need for temporal authority to regulate life on earth. The establishment of society and government
does not, however, abrogate the responsibility for choice that is
imposed on individuals by the law of nature. This responsibility
cannot be abrogated because it is the essence of man's status as
an agent accountable to God for his actions and beliefs. In the
words of Samuel Stillman, "Some of the natural rights of mankind are unalienable. and subject to no control but that of the
Deity. Such are the SACRED RIGHTS OF CONSCIENCE. Which in
a state of nature, and of civil society are exactly the same. They
can neither be parted with nor controled, by any human authority whatever."[12]

There are two senses in which a right may be unalienable:
when it is impossible for an individual to give it up and/or when
it is impossible to receive an equivalent for it because there exists in nature no possible equivalent. The right of conscience is
concluded by both of these criteria. No man can give up the
right to make moral decisions because it is impossible to do so.
To accept the advice of another in matters of conscience, or ev-
en to acknowledge the command of one with power to compel
obedience, *is* a moral choice. And even where action can be compelled, judgment, the internal act of conscience, can never be
compelled. "The care of souls cannot belong to the civil magistrate, because his power consists only in outward force; but true
and saving religion consists in the inward persuasion of the
mind, without which nothing can be acceptable to God. And
such is the nature of the understanding, that it cannot be com-

12. Fish, *A Discourse*, p. 6; Parsons, "The Essex Result," in Handlin and
Handlin, *Popular Sources*, p. 330; "The Return of the Town of New Salem
on the Constitution of 1780," ibid, p. 482; Stillman, *A Sermon*, p. 11. For
other references to the right of conscience, see: Samuel Baldwin, *A Sermon Preached at Plymouth, December 22, 1775* (Boston, 1776), p. 14;
Murray, *Nehemiah*, p. 8; Vox Populi [pseud.], *Independent Chronicle*,
July 16, 1778; Mentor [pseud.], *Boston Gazette*, January 20, 1778; Handlin and Handlin, *Popular Sources*, p. 436, 555, 764.

pelled to any thing by outward force."[13] And beyond this, even were it possible to command the judgment as well as the action of individuals, by hypnotism, brainwashing, drugging, or any other means, it would be impossible to provide an equivalent for the alienation of the right of choice. This is evidently true because the purpose of the right of conscience is to enable individuals to be judged in the eyes of God, and this judgment presupposes and requires that individuals have the freedom to make decisions in matters of conscience. This purpose cannot be fulfilled by any surrogate, therefore it is not capable of being compensated for; in other words, no equivalent can possibly be supplied for it. Thus, in both senses, the right of conscience is an unalienable right.

Both the logic of the concept of unalienable rights and the testimony of the literature seem to confirm the unalienable status of the right of conscience in unequivocal terms. The question of the right of conscience was, as has been seen in chapter 1, a sharp political issue in revolutionary Massachusetts. That the right of conscience was unalienable was not a matter of contention. What was at issue was the question of whether or not it was adequately secured by the provisions of Article II and Article III of the Declaration of Rights. It is apparent that a correct understanding of the theoretical issues underlying the debate over Article III is necessary in order to determine the real significance of the unalienable natural right of conscience.

The opponents of Article III contended that the state had no proper role in religious matters. Just how far they were willing to carry the separation of church and state is not clear, however. For example, no one objected to the qualifications of the right of conscience in Article II, where it was provided that the exercise of the right of conscience was limited by a concern for the public peace and the rights of others. Indeed, many who objected to Article III expressed the view that Article II adequately comprehended all that needed to be said on the subject of the right of conscience. The return of the town of Needham illustrates this point: "With respect to the Third Article in the Bill of Rights, we disapprove it in the whole; being fully persuaded the Principle on which it was founded is wrong and that it can-

13. John Locke, *A Letter on Toleration*, quoted in Stillman, *A Sermon*, p. 23.

not by any alteration be made Consistant with the Rights of
Conscience —It appears to us that all that is Necessary in the
Form of Civil Government respecting Religion is fully and
happily exprest in the Second Article."[14] The fact that Article
II was unopposed establishes that the needs of society do set
a standard against which the exercise of the right of conscience
must be tested. And such standards were obviously not perceived
to be inconsistent with the unalienable status of the right of
conscience. The question which arises from this observation is,
Where is the line to be drawn between the demands of society
and the right of conscience? If the answer to this question were
known, it might be easier to comprehend how any limitation on
the right of conscience can be compatible with the notion of
unalienability. As Article III, in its provision for public support
of the ministry, was perceived by its opponents as having transgressed this theoretical line, it will be useful to consider in more
depth the rationale behind the opposition to the public support
of the ministry.

Although the opponents of this practice denied that "piety,
religion, and morality" were necessary prerequisites of civil government, they could hardly deny that they were useful qualities
for the members of a civil society to possess. Nor could they
deny absolutely the right of a civil society to take actions
deemed necessary to its survival, or actions beneficial to its well
being. In the face of these realities, the dissenters attempted to
turn the criterion of public utility to their own advantage. This
they accomplished through the technique of *argumentum ad
absurdum*. "Perhaps it will be said," held Philanthropos, "that
the civil magistrate has a right to oblige the people to support
the ministers of the gospel, *because the gospel ministry is beneficial to society*." If so, he said, "it will follow, by the same law,
that he may adopt any of the maxims of the religion of Christ
into the civil constitution, which he may judge will be beneficial
to civil society. . . . if magistrates may adopt any the least part
of the religion of Christ into their systems of civil government,
that supposes magistrates to be *judges* what parts shall be taken,
and what left; power, then which nothing can be more dangerous, to be lodged in the hands of weak and fallible men."[15] The

14. "The Return of the Town of Needham on the Constitution of 1780,"
in Handlin and Handlin, *Popular Sources*, p. 791. For other town returns
expressing similar views, see pp. 482, 597, 633, 674, 682-683, 855.
15. Philanthropos [pseud.] , *Continental Journal*, April 6, 1780.

point of this argument is that the power to achieve the public good may be abused. Therefore it is in the public interest to set some limitation on that power. This argument failed in the end, of course, because in the case at hand it was not the civil magistrates who were acting, it was the majority of the people; and the people were not enacting the New Testament, only requiring that it be taught. Nevertheless, the argument did succeed in raising the question, How far should the civil authority of society extend?

A second argument employed by those opposing the public support of religion was an attempt to answer this question. It is necessary, they held, to distinguish between the legitimate sphere of civil authority, and that of religious authority. "As members of civil society, we are accountable for our actions to the community to which we belong," held Mentor. But, he continued, "as members of the kingdom of Christ, we are accountable only to Him who is the sole fountain of authority and rule in this new and glorious kingdom. The civil magistrate hath, undoubtedly, a right to make laws relative to the civil good, establish them by penalties and sanctions. The head of the church hath the same right in his kingdom." This argument was fundamental for those who wrote in opposition to public support of religion. According to Philanthropos, "the *power* of the legislature depends upon the right of the people. If the latter have not the *right*, the former cannot have the *power*." The critical question was, Do the people have a *right* to provide for the public support of religion? This argument, narrowly confined to the issue of public support, skirts the question of public utility entirely. The contention is that public utility is a legitimate concern only within the legitimate sphere of public activity, and that matters of conscience fall outside the sphere.[16]

Now it is evident that even the opponents of Article III did not contend that *all* matters of conscience fall outside the power of civil society, as is evident in Article II. That article, however, may be characterized as an attempt to control the exercise of the right of conscience, as opposed to conscience itself. The exercise of the right of conscience then is at least alienable to some extent. In what sense may it be said to be unalienable? In examining the charges against Article III it can be seen that it

16. Mentor [pseud.], *Boston Gazette*, January 20, 1778; Philanthropos [pseud.], *Independent Chronicle*, March 16, 1780.

was perceived to transgress the line which bounded the legitimate authority of civil society, whereas Article II did not. The language of protest makes it clear that the protesters thought that the public support of the ministry under Article III violated the right of conscience itself. The return of the town of Buxton makes this clear:

> The Declaration of Rights (the 3d. Article excepted) we Conceive to be Just and Equittable, Which 3d. Article Apears to Stand thus, That although it is to be Acknowledged that every one has an Indisputable and Uncontrolable Right to dispose of his property to the Support of his own SECT or to a public Teacher of his own Denomination if he Can give his attention, but if he Cannot, then it is to be left with the Legislative Authority to dispose of his Monies as they shall think proper, Notwithstanding any Liberty before Allowed in the 2d. article, Which we Conceive to be an Infringement upon Conscience, As Matters of Religion Apears Intirely to be between GOD and Individuals, and that the Legislative Authority Ought not to Interfere in Matters of Religion, Except it be in Cases of Disturbances of the peace in time of Worship.[17]

It appears from this that the power of the government to regulate actions was in some cases regarded as a violation of the right of conscience, while in some cases it was not. But the types of government powers that were opposed were different from those that were acknowledged, and in comprehending the distinction between the two the meaning of the unalienable right of conscience comes into clearer perspective.

It was nowhere suggested in the literature that the government could have no right to regulate the practice of religion in any way whatsoever. In particular, it was not held that the government could not proscribe religious practices that are antisocial, obstructive of public order, or regarded as morally outrageous by a Christian community. It was, in short, not held that the government could not set *limits* on the external practice of religion, and in fact it was often suggested that persons who professed certain religious beliefs should not be accorded full rights of citizenship. For example, the town of Wareham insisted

17. "The Return of the Town of Buxton on the Constitution of 1780," in Handlin and Handlin, *Popular Sources*, p. 731.

"that Roman Catholicks may not Enjoy equal priviledges with Protestant Christians yet Nevertheless to enjoy a Toleration in Particular places as the Legislature shall Direct." It was held, however, that the government ought not take positive actions in regard to religious practices. That is to say, that the government has no right to compel religious observance of any kind or the unwilling support of any individual in respect to religious establishments. The protesters against Article III often expressed the view that government had no power in respect to religion, but it was conjoined frequently with a specific statement of what kind of power the government did not have. A few examples from town returns of 1780 will illustrate this.

It appears doubtfull in said articles whether the Rights of Conscience are sufficiently secured or not to those who are really desirous to, and do attend publick Worship and who are not limited to any perticular outward Teacher. . . . we humbly conceive it interely out of the power of the legislature to establish a way of Worship that shall be agreable to the Conceptions and Convictions of the minds of the individuals, as it is a matter that solely relates to and stands between God and the Soul before whose Tribunal all must account each one for himself. [The town of Dartmouth]

We hold the Right of Conscience to be an unaliable right which never ought to be given up to any man or body of men therefore to invest the Legislator with power in Religious matters we Look upon it absurd and Contrary to Christian liberty, provided always that no man under the pretence of Conscience prejudice his neighbour in his life or estate or do any thing destructive to or inconsistent with human society in which Case the Law is for the transgressor and justice to be administered upon all without respect of Persons. [The town of Natick]

All men have a Natural and unalienable Right to Worship God almighty according to their own Conscience and Understanding, And no Man Ought or of Right can be compelled to attend any religious Worship or erect or Support any place of Worship or maintain any ministry contrary to or against his own free will and consent: nor can any man who acknowledges the being of a God be justly depreived or abridged of any peculiar mode of religious Worship and

that no Authority can or Ought to be vested in, or Assumed by any power whatever that shall in any Case inter-
fere with or in any Manner Control the Right of Conscience
in the free exercise of Religious Worship. [The town of
Westford] [18]

It is apparent in these passages that those who opposed Article III on the grounds that it violated the right of conscience,
did so because they believed the government to have no right to
take positive actions in religious affairs. Now it has already been
established that such positive action could not, in the strict
sense, serve to violate the internal conscience of individuals; so
the question arises, Why would such action be held illegitimate?
The answer to this is fundamental to an understanding of the relationship of natural rights and the institution of civil society
based on a social contract. Positive government action in religious affairs was not believed to be illegitimate because it would
invade the minds of men. Rather, it was held to be illegitimate
because it was a power that individuals could not give away.
Individuals in a state of nature could only choose to forfeit their
alienable natural rights. The power to exercise one's religion in
a way that disturbed the public peace was alienable. The right
to believe, and the power to practice one's beliefs peaceably
were not. Since the right to worship God according to one's
conscience is unalienable, it cannot lie within the legitimate
sphere of government activity to control it. This is so because
the legitimate sphere of political authority is determined in the
social compact on the basis of a calculation involving a trading
of rights and benefits.

Finally, it must be noted that at all times the opposition to
the public support of the ministry was a minority point of view.
The majority believed the provisions of Article III to be compatible with the right of conscience. In so far as the right of
conscience, or the power to control that right, is alienable, it is
subordinate to a majority determination of public utility. In the
sense that it is unalienable, it is unlikely that political action can
violate the right of conscience because, like the other unalienable rights expressed in Article I, the right to believe what one
will is so fundamental to human nature that it is nearly impossible to eradicate it. The supporters of Article III accused those

18. Handlin and Handlin, *Popular Sources*, pp. 711, 510, 683, 672. See
also: *Boston Gazette*, September 6, 1779.

who opposed it of confusing the public right to compel actions with the power to compel beliefs. These would merge if the people were to compel action in order to compel belief, and all agreed that such a move would violate the right of conscience. But merely to require an individual to pay money toward the support of a teacher upon whom he does not wish to attend does not violate the unalienable right of conscience. Theophilus Parsons, author of "The Essex Result," was later to defend Article III in these terms: "The great errour lies in not distinguishing between liberty of conscience in religious opinions and worship, and the right of appropriating money by the state." He said "The former is an unalienable right; the latter is surrendered to the state as the price of protection." Parsons recognized that "if the state claimed the absurd power of directing or controlling the faith of its citizens, there might be some ground for the objection." But, he said, "no such power is claimed. The authority derived from the constitution extends no further than to submit to the understandings of the people the evidence of truths deemed of public utility, leaving the weight of the evidence, and the tendence of those truths, to the conscience of every man."[19] As suggested by Parsons, individuals surrender certain rights upon entering society in return for specified advantages. This notion of trading rights for benefits was central to the social compact theory, and it is fundamental to the relationship between individual rights and public authority. Therefore it must be examined in greater depth.

Men enter into society because the natural rights that they possess in the state of nature are insecure. In joining society certain of their rights are forfeited to the community, at least in the sense that the power to control their exercise is given over to the community. The distinction between alienable and unalienable rights is fundamental to social organization: the individuals who form the society cannot give up their unalienable natural rights; they only surrender their alienable rights to the extent necessary for the good of society (and then only when they are adequately compensated for the forfeiture). This concept is described in "The Essex Result."

When men form themselves into society, and erect a body politic or State, they are to be considered as one moral

19. Theophilus Parsons, *Defence of the Third Article of the Massachusetts Declaration of Rights* (Worcester, Mass.: 1820), pp. 6–7, reprinted from Barnes v. Falmouth, 6 *Massachusetts Reports*, 404.

whole, which is in possession of the supreme power of the
State. This supreme power is composed of the powers of
each individual collected together, and voluntarily parted
with by him. No individual, in this case parts with his unalienable rights, the supreme power therefore cannot controul them. Each individual also surrenders the power of
controuling his natural alienable rights, ONLY WHEN THE
GOOD OF THE WHOLE REQUIRES IT. The supreme power
therefore can do nothing but what is for the good of the
whole; and when it goes beyond this line, it is a power
usurped. If the individual receives an equivalent for the
right of controul he has parted with, the surrender of that
right is valid; if he receives no equivalent, the surrender
is void, and the supreme power as it respects him is an
usurper.[20]

This concept of society originating on the basis of a fair trade
needs a name, and here it will be called the compensation theory
of social organization. The compensation theory was widely evident in the literature of revolutionary Massachusetts. In 1776
Samuel Baldwin held that "what are called natural rights, are in
part surrendered, whenever mankind voluntarily enter into society and form into bodies politick." Two years later the town of
Lexington agreed that "in emerging from a State of Nature into
a State of Well regulated Society, Mankind give up some of their
natural Rights, in order that others, of greater Importance, to
their Well-being, safety and Happiness, both Societies and Individuals, might be the better enjoyed, secured and defended."
The compensation theory was tied explicitly to the idea of a
bill of rights in 1779, by the town of Stoughton:

> You are directed to use and employ your most assiduous
> Endeavours as Soon as the Convention Meets that a Bill
> of Rights be in the first place compiled, wherin the inher-
> ent and unaleinable Rights of Conscience and all those
> aleinable rights ar not necessary to be given up in to the
> hands of government together with the equivalent individ-
> uals ought undoubtedly to Recive from Government for
> their relinquishing a part of their natural and alienable
> rights for the nesessary Support of the Same. . . .

20. Parsons, "The Essex Result," in Handlin and Handlin, *Popular Sources*,
p. 330.

That the Design of man in entering into society and Submitting him self to Controul of the Supreme Power of the State is to obtain greater benefitts and advantages than he could possiblely enjoy by being out of it that is he expects, lays claim and is justly entitled to the Protection and Security of his person and property together with the enjoyment of all those natural Rights whether alienable or unalienable that he has not explicitly given up to the Controul of the Supreme power in the Social Contract.

It is apparent that this terminology lends itself to the conclusion that, since some alienable rights and all unalienable rights are reserved from the grant of authority given to society by the social contract, the authority of society is limited to just the extent of the reservation. As Stoughton noted, this is the presumptive function of a bill of rights. However, determining just what that extent was seen to be is the crucial step in ascertaining the conception of political society held by the people of Massachusetts.[21]

It is evident that the unalienable rights of man do not set great limits on the power of civil society. It has been seen that the rights that are categorized as unalienable in Article I of the Declaration of Rights are only operative at the extremes of political authority. The unalienable right of conscience, more sensitive to government invasion than other natural rights, does not preclude political coercion in favor of religion, even to the extent of commandeering property for religious purposes. And the most that can be deduced from the debates over Article III of the Declaration of Rights is that there was a strong minority sentiment opposing positive government action of this sort in religious matters.

If individuals are to gain security from the power of the social compact and the compensation theory on which it is based, that security must be derived from the equivalent they receive from the exchange of their alienable rights. The question then arises, What would be a fair equivalent for the forfeiture of the alienable rights which men enjoy in the state of nature? These rights include freedom of action, and property, in the narrow sense of

21. Baldwin, *A Sermon*, p. 14; "The Return of the Town of Lexington on the Constitution of 1778," in Handlin and Handlin, *Popular Sources*, p. 317; "Instructions of the Town of Stoughton to its Delegate to the Constitutional Convention," ibid, pp. 422–423.

material possessions. The answer is dependent upon the security of these rights in the state of nature. If the state of nature is generally a tolerable condition, and the benefits to be gained from entering civil society are therefore of marginal importance, it may be argued that the power individuals relinquish to the state by the social compact is minimal, and that the reserved rights of individuals are extensive and set strong limits on the power of the state. On the other hand, if the state of nature is a condition in which rights are generally insecure, it may be the case that the individual need only receive as a just equivalent a minimum of security in the enjoyment of his liberty and property. It would follow that the degree of society's control over his liberty and property, as well as any other of his alienable natural rights, would be nearly total. In order to understand the extent to which the concept of natural rights places limitations on political authority, it is necessary to examine the state of nature in greater depth.

As it was for Locke, the state of nature was for the people of Massachusetts a two-stage operation. Unlike Locke, however, the transition in the state of nature did not revolve around the introduction of money; instead, it came about as a result of that most important event of all, the Fall from Grace. According to Gad Hitchcock, the original liberty of man in the state of nature was paralleled by a natural rectitude and attachment to God. Under these circumstances, the contentions and oppressions that are seen to beset man would never occur. This does not necessarily mean that there would have been no political organization among men in such a state. "Government of some sort, adapted to the human nature and circumstances, would indeed, probably, have been instituted among them, as. . . . it is among the Angels themselves; but there would have been no such laws as are made for the lawless and disobedient, for the ungodly and for sinners." This government would be simple and benign, having no other objective than to secure the bodily wants of the people. Since there would be no sin, there would be no need to control sinners, and disputes would always be peaceably settled.

> As there would however, be no evil inclination, or design in any individual, or suspicion of it in others, to invade the property, retain the rights, or check the liberty of any; and as these disputes would take place in consequence only of those errors of the memory, misapprehension and mistake

to which the human mind, from its natural imbecility, tho' innocent, must be liable; they would always be issued in the most amicable manner, and to the entire satisfaction of the parties; and every one left to the free exercise of the gifts of nature, and the unmolested enjoyment of the bounties of providence.

This enchanting picture represented the ideal—man in a state of nature, before the Fall. "Such was the primitive state of man— happy in the divine image and favor, and in the purity and freedom of his own faculties."[22]
But this prospect did not last long.

But alas! how changed! what a reverse of things did he undergo at the fall! when he violated the law of his maker, given for the tryal of his fidelity and obedience, and commenced rebel against God, what forfeiture did he make of the divine presence, and favour! what a sinful nature! What irregular propensities! What strong untoward and eccentric appetites and passions were introduced into his constitution! and how by one man's disobedience were many made sinners, and brought under the condemnation of the righteous law of God!

Certainly a different picture is presented here! Man is no longer by nature good, and mankind is no longer by nature contented and harmonious. Men have "fallen into a disordered, and perverted state," and the prospects for human happiness have diminished. Have they been lost forever? Fortunately, the answer is no.

The rational faculties of the human mind, though sadly darkened, and indisposed to moral and religious performances, were not destroyed; the passions, though depraved, were not eradicated: In every idea of the soul, but its primitive purity and rectitude, there remained the essential properties of humanity; particularly the love of liberty; which is an original passion, not meerly innocent, but requisite both before and since the fall, to all virtuous exertions, and happy enjoyments, though now extremely liable to abuse by ourselves, and restraint from our fellowmen.

22. Hitchcock, *A Sermon . . . December 22d, 1774*, pp. 9, 10.

Thus the love of liberty, one of the original passions, and the rational faculty, darkened yet operative, were to guide men into social organization in order to compensate for the disorder and perversion caused by the Fall.[23]

The effects of the Fall on life in the state of nature were evident in the sermon of Samuel West in 1776. The state of nature, he said, though perfectly free, is not a state of licentiousness. "The law of nature gives men no right to do anything that is immoral, or contrary to the will of God, and injurious to their fellow-creatures; for a state of nature is properly a state of law and government, even a government founded upon the changeable nature of the Deity, and a law resulting from the eternal fitness of things." This informal government is only effective for beings who are in a state of grace, however.

> The law of nature is a perfect standard and measure of action for beings that persevere in a state of moral rectitude; but the case is far different with us, who are in a fallen and degenerate estate. We have a law in our members which is continually warring against the law of the mind, by which we often become enslaved to the basest lusts, and are brought into bondage to the vilest passions. The strong propensities of our animal nature often overcome the sober dictates of reason and conscience, and betray us into actions injurious to the public and destructive of the safety and happiness of society.

Since the law of nature is not an adequate form of government, the power of a civil authority is the only alternative. Men have no choice but to form into political societies. "Men of unbridled lusts, were they not restrained by the power of the civil magistrate, would spread horror and desolation all around them. This makes it absolutely necessary that societies should form themselves into politic bodies, that they may enact laws for the public safety, and appoint particular penalitie for the violation of their laws." West was thus driven to the same conclusion as Hitchcock had been: civil society is the only solution to the problems of life in the state of nature. And for West explicitly, as for Hitchcock by strong implication, civil society is "absolutely necessary." The Fall occurred very early indeed, and even

23. Ibid., pp. 10, 11.

if life before it had offered the promise of an alternative, man now must always live with the effects of it.[24]

Even those who did not stress the distinction between life before and after the Fall describe the state of nature in dismal terms. One of the fullest descriptions was that of Simeon Howard, in 1780. "Suppose, then," he said, "a number of men living together, and maintaining that intercourse which is necessary for the supply of their wants, but without any laws or government established among them by mutual consent, or in what is called a state of nature; —in this state every one has an equal right to liberty, and to do what he thinks proper." Disputes might arise in this state of nature, but they would be settled by the parties, because there would be no common judge to whom to appeal for a resolution of the issue. Such disputes would rarely be settled amicably, because "prejudice and self-love would render them partial judges." Thus, "the dispute must at last be ended by the strongest arm, and thus the liberty of the weak would be destroyed by the power of the strong." This pattern of events, often repeated, would lead to "an endless reciprocation of injuries," in which parties would be formed as individuals banded together to protect and advance their interests at the expense of the rights of others. The formation of parties would bring about "rapine, devastation, and murder, and the peaceful state of nature soon exchanged for a number of little, contending tyrannies, or for one successful one that should swallow up the rest." Thus the alternatives arising out of the state of nature are either a continual state of war or an eventual tyranny of the strong. This is hardly a promising prospect! What is the solution? For Howard, as for West and Hitchcock, there is only one: civil society. There is no way that men can ever "secure themselves against all manner of violence and injuries from bad men but by uniting together in society, agreeing upon some universal rules to be observed by all." The state of nature is no alternative, because the laws that control men in that state are not strong enough. "Man is not to be trusted with his unbounded love of liberty, unless it is under some other restraint than what arises from his own reason or the law of God, —these, in many instances, would make but a feeble resistance to his lust or avarice; and he would pursue his liberty to the

24. West, *A Sermon*, in Thornton, *The Pulpit*, pp. 271, 273, 274.

destruction of his fellow-creature, if he was not restrained by human laws and punishment."[25]

Civil society was not required only by the vicissitudes of the state of nature. It was also demanded by human nature, for man is a social animal, driven by his nature to commune with his fellow creatures. "As in a state of nature much happiness cannot be enjoyed by individuals, so it has been conformable to the inclinations of almost all men, to enter into political society." These were the words of "The Essex Result," in 1778, and three years earlier Samuel Williams had made the point even more emphatically: "As our Maker designed us for such a state, he has given us natures adapted to, and tending towards it. The disadvantages of a solitary state are so many and obvious, that they must have been early, and unavoidably felt. To avoid these, and with a view to enjoy the many advantages no otherwise to be had, mankind naturally fell into the practice of resolving themselves into a social state: Combining together in some form of society for the purposes of mutual benefit, protection, and defence." Reason, God, and nature thus all combined in teaching men the necessity of society. In the words of Benjamin Hitchborn, "The advantages of social life, are the result of such evident necessity, so extensively diffusive and universally felt, that all Mankind will readily acknowledge their existence without the aid of metaphysics or history."[26]

The evident conclusion is that the state of nature is not a viable alternative to civil society in any sense. The inference to be drawn from this conclusion is also clear: civil society need not offer much in the way of an equivalent in order to justify the bargain struck in the social contract. In a Hobbesian world, man is driven by his wants, his instincts, and his needs into the arms of society. In light of these considerations, it must be concluded that the forfeiture of rights on which the social contract is based is nearly total, and that the power of civil society over the individual is likewise nearly total. In order to confirm this conclusion however, it is necessary to proceed to the next stage in the analysis of the social contract theory, the examination of political power in civil society.

25. Howard, *A Sermon*, in Thornton, *The Pulpit*, pp. 362-363.
26. Parsons, "The Essex Result," in Handlin and Handlin, *Popular Sources*, p. 327; Samuel Williams, *A Discourse on the Love of Our Country* (Salem, Mass., 1775), pp. 7-8; Benjamin Hitchborn, *An Oration Delivered March 5th, 1777* (Boston, 1777), p. 5.

Civil Society

Upon the occasion of the social compact, the individuals in the state of nature enter into the state of civil society, which is the second stage of the social compact theory. Civil society is distinguished from the state of nature by virtue of the fact that every individual in the society has bound himself to the authority of the whole, and is therefore no longer possessed of the same liberty that he enjoyed antecedent to the compact. It is distinguished from the governmental or constitutional stage of the compact theory by the fact that no formal political institutions have yet been established. Indeed, the principle event to take place in civil society is the establishment of a constitution and form of government. The institution of government is essential to the good ordering of civil society, and is therefore of paramount importance. Because of this, it is invariably the case that civil societies initiate governments almost as soon as they become civil societies. There is, in fact, nothing to preclude the simultaneous occurrence of these two events, even though the formation of society is logically prior to the formation of government. Whatever the case may be in regard to the sequence of events in a particular case, civil society is theoretically antecedent to government, and the authority of civil society is antecedent to the authority of government. Therefore the determination of where authority resides in the state of civil society is crucially important, for upon it hinges the answers to the related questions of, Who establishes government? and Who may dissolve it?

Upon entering civil society each individual surrenders to the community his alienable rights, in order that all might be regulated for the common good. As has been seen, this forfeiture of control over the natural rights of individuals is virtually total. In civil society, the repository of authority over the rights of individuals is the body of people who constitute the community. Nothing can be done without the consent of the people. In particular, no form of government can be established for the community on a legitimate basis without the consent of the people. This proposition is derivable as a strict matter of logic from the political freedom and the political equality of the state of nature. In his sermon before the House and Council in 1779, Samuel Stillman discussed the relationship between the state of nature and civil society. After establishing the principles of freedom and equality in the state of nature, he went on to say: "If we admit the truth of these principles, we come by an easy transition to the foundation of civil society, viz The consent of the people. For if all men are equal by nature, it must depend entirely upon themselves, whether they will continue in their natural condition, or exchange it for a state of civil government. Consequently the sovereignty resides originally in the people." These sentiments were echoed by the men of Berkshire County, who held that "as government is only the administration of the affairs of a number of men combined for their own security and happiness, such a society have right freely to determine by whom and in what manner their own affairs shall be administered."[27]

This endorsement of popular sovereignty permeates the various town returns also. In 1777, Attleborough held "that as the End of Government is the Happiness of the People; so the Sole Power and right of forming a Plan thereof is essentially in the People." The town of Lexington, although perceiving the practical difficulties inherent in popular government, embellished on the same theory: "It appears to us that as all Government Originates from the People and the Great End of Government is their Peace, Safety and Happiness; so it is with the People at large, or where that is impractible, by their Representatives freely and equally elected and impowered for that purpose, to form and agree upon a Constitution of Government, which being considered and approved by the Body of the People, must be enacted, ratified and established." It must be remembered that in exercising their power of consent with respect to the establishment of government the people act, and must be considered, collectively rather than individually. But the collectivity must itself have an operational decision rule, and for the people of Massachusetts, this was rule by the majority. Because the sovereignty of the people is coextensive with civil society, the authority of the majority must be so also. That the majority must, at all times and in all cases, be taken as representing the people as a whole, was a proposition derivable from both the logic of the social compact theory and from consideration of utility.[28]

27. Stillman, *A Sermon*, p. 9 (see also pp. 18, 25); "Statement of Berkshire Country Representatives, November 17, 1778," in Handlin and Handlin, *Popular Sources*, p. 375.
28. "The Return of the Town of Attleborough on the House of Represen-

Both of these concerns are evident in a 1774 sermon of Nathaniel Niles on the subject of liberty. As liberty is a valuable possession for an individual, it is in a state of nature equally valuable for each individual. It follows from this that in a community, the liberty of a number of citizens must be of greater worth than the liberty of a single citizen, "for if one Man's enjoyment of it was a good, the enjoyment of two must be a greater good, and so on through the whole community." It follows from this, said Niles, that "CIVIL LIBERTY IS A GREAT GOOD," and he proceeded to consider how it might best be secured. "Civil Liberty consists, not in any inclinations of the members of a community: but in the being and due administration of such a system of laws, as effectually tends to the greatest felicity of a state." A good constitution is necessary in order for liberty to be achieved, one in which "the laws extend to all the members of the society alike." But such a constitution is not a sufficient condition. "A good foundation for liberty is laid in such a constitution, but its whole worth lies in due administration. Perfect liberty takes place where such a constitution is fully administred: But where the administration is imperfect, liberty is likewise imperfect. In a perfectly free state, both the constitution, and the administration of it, are full of propriety, equality, and equilibrium." What tends to bring about good administration? "One general inference from the whole will be, that liberty is much rather to be expected in a state where a majority, first, institutes, and then varies the constitution according as they apprehend circumstances require, than in any other." Why is this the case? Niles lists two reasons. In the first place, "a majority has a more general and distinct knowledge of the circumstances and exigencies of a state than a minority; and of consequence, is more able to judge of what is best to be done." In the second place, because each individual will be apt to act on the basis of private interest, the majority of individuals are more apt to reflect the interests of the community as a whole: "Add to this, that private interest is the great idol of the human mind; and, therefore, when a majority unite

tatives Resolution of September 17, 1776," in Handlin and Handlin, *Popular Sources*, p. 143; "The Return of the Town of Lexington on the House of Representatives Resolution of September 17, 1776," ibid, p. 149. See also: *Boston Gazette*, July 12, 1779; Cooper, *A Sermon*, p. 11; Murray, *Nehemiah*, pp. 38–39; Webster, *A Sermon*, p. 31; Handlin and Handlin, *Popular Sources*, pp. 65, 91, 136, 173, 213, 226, 233, 302, 333, 374, 385.

in any measures, it is to be supposed, they are such measures as are best calculated to secure the particular interests of the members of that majority; and, consequently, the general interests of the body are more effectually provided for, in this way, than by the security of the private interests of any minority whatever." It follows from this that, "though liberty is not necessarily, nor invariably connected with the voice of a majority; yet, it is much more likely to be found in connection with such a voice, than with that of a minority. Indeed, there is in general, no reason to expect liberty where a majority is counteracted, and, on the contrary, we may hope for some good degree of it, where a majority governs."[29]

The most radical dissentients in the state, the disaffected Berkshire Constitutionalists, were among the strongest endorsers of the majority principle. They were particularly vociferous in asserting the rights of the majority in the establishment of a constitution. Their repeated protests to the General Court, and their appeals to other counties in the state for support of their position form some of the most interesting chapters in the revolutionary history of Massachusetts and in the constitutional history of the United States.

Majority rule was not, for the Berkshireans, a mere political device. Indeed, it was counted among the unalienable rights of man.

> These [rights] which are unalienable, are those which belong to Conscience respecting the worship of God and the practice of the Christian Religion, and that of being determined or governed by the Majority in the Institution or formation of Government. . . . It is of the unalienable Rights, particularly that of being determined or governed by the Majority in the Institution or formation of Government of which something further is necessary to be considered at this Time. That the Majority should be governed by the minority in the first Institution of Government is not only contrary to the common apprehensions of Mankind in general, but it contradicts the common Law of Justice and benevolence.
>
> Mankind being in a state of nature equal, the larger Number (Caeteris paribus) is of more worth than the lesser, and

29. Nathaniel Niles, *Two Discourses on Liberty* (Newburyport, Mass., 1774), pp. 5, 6, 8, 9, 18, 19-20, 20.

the common happiness is to be preferred to that of Individuals. When Men form the social Compact, for the Majority to consent to be governed by the Minority is down right popery in politicks, as submission to him who claims Infallibility, and of being the only Judge of Right and rong, is popery in Religion.

Ironically, in making this strong plea for majority rule the Constitutionalists were attempting to argue their independence from the authority of the government of the province of Massachusetts-Bay. In arguing their case they were led to contend that while they meant to be bound by the majority ("we always mean to be governed by the majority"), that nevertheless they were not, precisely because no compact could be shown to have taken place to which they were a party. "We think it undeniably follows from the preceeding Reasonings that the Compact in this state is not yet formed: when did the Majority of the people at large assent to such Constitution, and what is it? If the Majority of the people of this state have adopted any such fundamental Constitution it is unknown to us."[30] This position, consistently held by the Constitutionalists from 1775, was expressed in 1778. In that year they were addressed by one of their own countymen, who challenged their position on precisely the majoritarian grounds which they had attempted to claim for themselves. This pamphlet was written by William Whiting, and entitled *An Address to the Inhabitants of the county of Berkshire.*

According to Whiting, the principal error into which the Constitutionalists had fallen was their failure to distinguish between the several stages of the social compact theory. By equating the social compact with the compact of government (or the formation of the constitution) they were led to the conclusion that, since no constitution had been formed, the province had fallen into a state of nature. If so, then Berkshire County was not bound by the legislature of the Province of Massachusetts-Bay, because the legislature acted without the sanction of the majority of the people. The assumption underlying this reasoning was that, where there is no constitution there can be no government, and it was this assumption which Whiting called into question. The objection of Berkshire County, he said, can

30. "Statement of Berkshire County Representatives, November 12, 1778," in Handlin and Handlin, *Popular Sources*, pp. 374–375, 377.

be "comprehended in these few words, viz. 'We have no constitution of government. And how can we have government without a constitution, or a foundation for it to stand upon?' " In order to demonstrate the inadequacy of this view, Whiting found it necessary to trace political authority from the state of nature into civil society, and his reasoning is sufficiently important to be quoted here at length.

In a state of nature, each individual has a right, not only to dispose of, order, and direct, his property, his person, and all his own actions, within the bounds of the law of nature, as he thinks fit, but he also has a right in himself, not only to defend, but to judge and to punish the person who shall make any assault or encroachment, either upon his person or property, without asking leave, or depending on the will of any other man, or any set of men whatever.

Now when any number of men enter into a state of society with each other, they resign into the hands of the society, the right they had, in a state of nature of disposing, directing and ordering their own persons and properties, so far as the good of the whole may require it. And as to the right of judging and punishing injuries done to any of the individuals, that is to be wholly given up to the society. Hence, it is obvious, there can be no medium between being in a state of nature, and in a state of civil society.

Again, in all societies of men, united together for mutual aid, support and defence, there exists one supreme, absolute, and rightful judge over the whole; one, who has a right, at all times, to order, direct, and dispose of the persons, actions and properties of the individuals of the community, so far as the good of the community shall require it; and this judge is not other than the majority of the whole. . . . let it be carefully observed, that when men emerge from a state of nature, and unite in society, in order to form a political government; the first step necessary is, for each individual to give up his alienable natural rights and privileges, to be ordered, directed, and disposed of, as the major part of the community shall think fit; so far as shall be necessary for the good of the whole, of which the majority must be the judges. And this must necessarily take place previous to the community's forming any particular constitution, mode, or form of government whatever: For to be in a state of society, so far as to be under obligation to obey the rules and orders prescribed by the majority part of the society, is one thing; and for that society to be under any particular constitution or form of government, is another. The latter is necessarily subsequent to the former, and must depend entirely on the pleasure of the supreme judge; that is, the major part of the community, who have an undoubted right to enter upon, or postpone that matter, when, and so long as they see fit; and no individual can, on that account be justified in withdrawing their allegiance, or refusing to submit to the rules and orders of the society.[31]

31. William Whiting, *An Address to the Inhabitants of the County of Berkshire* (Hartford, Conn., 1778), pp. 9, 9–11. This pamphlet is partially reprinted in Robert Taylor, ed., *Massachusetts, Colony to Commonwealth* (Chapel Hill, N.C.: The University of North Carolina Press, 1961), pp. 101–105. Gordon Wood contends that "Whiting's argument depended upon equating the constitution with the form of government, an identification most Americans were rapidly abandoning, since the government must clearly be only the creature of the constitution" (*Creation*, p. 286). Wood further contends that the "Berkshire Constitutionalists perceived the difference and now subtly shifted their emphasis away from a purely political contract. . . . What was now needed was a 'social compact,' uniting men one to another and justifying majority rule." Now while it is true that the Berkshire statement of November 1778 does reflect a shift in the position which that county had taken in previous statements, Wood misperceives the direction of the shift. While at all times endorsing the majority principle, and while at all times having in view only a single contract to justify it, the Constitutionalists were forced by the logic of Whiting's arguments to move from the unequivocal statement of May 1776 that "since the Dissolution of the power of Great Britain over these Colonies they have fallen into a state of Nature" to the more moderate view of November 1778, that "we do not consider this state in all Respects as in a state of Nature tho' destitute of such fundmental Constitution." This shift in the argument of Berkshire County, however subtle it may be, can only evidence an effort to conform to Whiting's reasoning, rather than to defeat it. The effort does not succeed, however, precisely because the Constitutionalists were not willing to recognize Whiting's emphatic conclusion: that there can be no middle ground between a state of nature and civil society. Finally, there is nothing in the Whiting pamphlet to warrant the observation that his argument "depended upon equating the constitution with the form of government." Indeed, the relationship between the second and third stages of the compact view was not central to Whiting's argument at all. It may be more accurately said that the argument of the Constitutionalists depended upon equating the constitution with the

While denying the legitimacy of majority rule in the province of Massachusetts-Bay, the Berkshire protesters were not reluctant to enlist majoritarian arguments in their own defense. They could see no reason why the majority principles should not operate within the boundaries of their own county, and indeed, the fact that a considerable majority of Berkshireans supported the intransigencies of their political leadership was advanced as an argument in support of their claims of autonomy from province rule. "We shall retain the aforesaid Character," they held, "if grounded upon the Non-admission Law, as abundantly appears to Us this Day by the Yeas and Nays, brought in from the Respective Towns We represent, taken in Town Meeting, especially called for that purpose, there being four fifths of the Inhabitants of said County against supporting the Courts of Law, untill a Constitution be formed and Accepted by the people." The evident absurdity of this position was soon brought to the attention of the Constitutionalists by the Worcester Committee of Correspondence.

> We cannot agree with you, Gentlemen, with respect to the non-admission of the Courts of Quarter Sessions and Common Pleas, untill the formation and acceptance of a new Constitution. . . . The people sanctified the measure by their consent, it therefor is constitutional so long as such consent shall continue, as the Consent of the Majority of the State: For it is a principal laid down by some of the best political writers, that whatever, in government, is publicly allowed at any perticular period, has been regularly and openly introduced and established by the approbation of the majority of those who have the power of establishing it is constitutional at that period. Now that so small a minority as four fifths of one County in this State which cannot possibly be supposed to be more than one fourteenth of the whole, should not only oppose such a great majority of a State, but act directly contrary to the sense and reccommendation of the whole Continent, in our opinion is acting like persons that do not understand the true principles of Liberty and are durating from the end of this

social compact, and this was precisely the point which Whiting undertook to refute. Compare the Berkshire statements in Handlin and Handlin, *Popular Sources*, pp. 61–64, 70–72, 88–94, 366–368, 374–379.

Country had in view in commencing the Contest with Great Britain.[32]

What was really at issue here was the question of the definition of the political community, and on this point as well Whiting attacked the Constitutionalists.

> But perhaps you will say, that you do not act, in this affair, as individuals, but, as a community: For, when the minds of the inhabitants of the county were lately taken upon the expediency or inexpediency of setting up courts, there appeared to be a very great majority against it. Here let me repeat a former question: Are the inhabitants of the county of Berkshire members of the political society of the Massachusetts-Bay? Or, are they not? Your conduct, in sending members to the general court, answers this question in the affirmative. A Majority of the inhabitants of the county therefore, can be of no more real avail in this matter, than a majority of any particular town, or, than evan a majority of any particular family in any particular town in the county. For, it is only a major part of the community that have a right to determine matters of this kind.

What was the community? Whiting's answer was emphatic: "The plain truth of the case is in fact no other than this . . . the inhabitants of the state of Massachusetts-Bay, are . . . at least in a state of civil society," and it was evident therefore that a majority of the whole must, and only a majority of the whole could, bind the rest.[33]

If the authority of the majority is not significantly limited by the antecedent rights of individuals, it may yet operate under limitations derived from the ends for which civil society is established, for it is an obvious inference that the supreme authority in a civil society cannot legitimately act contrary to the ends for which that society is established. What are the ends of civil society? The answer of the literature is unequivocal on this point: the only end of civil society is the common good. And the sine qua non of the common good is public safety—salus

---

32. "Berkshire County Remonstrance, August 26, 1778," Handlin and Handlin, *Popular Sources*, p. 367; "Response of the Worcester Committee of Correspondence, October 8, 1778," ibid, p. 370.
33. Whiting, *An Address*, pp. 14, 16.

populi suprema lex est. Contrary to what some have supposed, the common good is the good of the whole and not the good of the sum of the parts. In 1777 the Massachusetts General Court proclaimed "that, the Happiness of mankind depends very much on the Form and Constitution of Government they live under, and that the only Object and Design of Government should be the Good of the People, are Truths well understood at this day, and taught by Reason and Experience, very clearly, at all times." Samuel West held in the same year that "as the public safety is the first and grand law of society, so no community can have a right to invest the magistrate with any power or authority that will enable him to act against the welfare of the state and the good of the whole." Phillips Payson found the rationale for the common good in both reason and revelation. "The voice of reason and the voice of God," he said in 1778, "both teach us that the great object or end of government is the public good." Even those who did not subscribe to the metaphor of the social compact believed in the common good, as was evidenced by Samuel Adams in 1776: "Political Right and Public Happiness are different words for the same idea. They who wonder into metaphysical Labyrinths, or have recourse to original Contracts, to determine the Rights of Man, either impose upon themselves or mean to delude others. Public Utility is the only certain critierion." Peter Powers summed it up best. "The public good," he said, "should ever be the highest aim, next to God and his own soul, of every one constituted to any office in the state." [34]

Even those who spoke of the obligations of society to secure the happiness of individuals recognized the importance of the

34. "Resolve of May 5, 1777," Handlin and Handlin, *Popular Sources*, p. 174; West, *A Sermon*, in Thornton, *The Pulpit*, p. 284; Phillips Payson, *A Sermon Preached Before the Honorable Council and the Honorable House of Representatives . . . May 27, 1778* (Boston, 1778), ibid, p. 330; Samuel Adams, *Oration Delivered at the State House in Philadelphia, August 1, 1776*, Massachusetts Historical Society, DA 27; Powers, *Jesus Christ*, p. 13. For other references to the common good, see: John Adams, "The Earl of Clarendon to William Pym, III," in *The Works of John Adams*, ed. Charles F. Adams, 10 vols. (Boston: Charles C. Little and James Brown, 1851) 3: 479; Hitchcock, *A Sermon . . . May 25th, 1774*, pp. 7, 12, 20, 21, 28–31; Howard, *A Sermon*, in Thornton, *The Pulpit*, p. 365; Murray, *Nehemiah*, p. 42; Niles, *Two Discourses*, pp. 8–9; Webster, *A Sermon*, pp. 12, 18; Williams, *A Discourse*, pp. 9, 15; Handlin and Handlin, *Popular Sources*, pp. 65, 137, 143, 149, 158, 171, 245, 317, 329, 423, 435.

good of the whole. Samuel Stillman, for example, holds that "the great end for which men enter into a state of civil society, is their own advantage"; but he also says that, both the interest and duty (of constituents) oblige them to reverence the powers that be. It is their duty in consequence of their own appointment. And their interest because the good of the community depends much upon it." This tension is evident in the 1774 election sermon of Gad Hitchcock. "Rulers," said Hitchcock, "are under the most sacred ties to consult the good in society. . . . The great end of a ruler's exaltation is the happiness of the people over whom he presides; and his promoting it, the sole grounds of their submission to him." Since the authority of rulers has its origin from the people, those rulers "have not only a right, but are bound in duty" to preserve "the property and liberty of the whole society." Rulers, he concluded, "are the trustees of society, as their authority, under God, is derived from the people, delegated to them with design it should be exercised for, and to no other purpose than, the common benefit." But in spite of this firm endorsement of the common good, Hitchcock also holds that the ends of society consist in "the precuring of a greater good to each individual, on the whole, than could be had without it." Is this a contradiction?[35]

It is evident that these passages are inconsistent only if the public and private good are inconsistent. The resolution of the paradox took the form of two propositions: first, that there was usually no inconsistency between public and private interest, precisely because it was in the interest of each individual to advance the common good; and second, that where the public and private good came into conflict, the interest of the individual must be subordinated to the interest of society. The first proposition was maintained by an anonymous author writing in the *Independent Chronicle* in 1777. Since, he said, "the author of our nature has determined us, irresistably to desire our own happiness, and has so constituted us, that private good depends on the publick; and the happiness of every individual, on the happiness of society: It follows that the practise of all the social virtues is the law of our nature, and the law of our nature is the law of God; who by determining the end, and proportioning the means, has plainly pointed out to us the necessity of pursuing

35. Stillman, *A Sermon*, pp. 11, 16; Hitchcock, *A Sermon . . . May 25th, 1774*, pp. 12, 21, 28, 30.

the latter to obtain the former." Both propositions were articulated by Nathaniel Niles in 1774. He said, "Let us then, for once, imagine a state whose members are all of a free spirit; and then attend to the glory and pleasures of liberty." What would such free spirits do? "The individuals are all of one mind. They unite in the same grand pursuit, the highest good of the whole. Only suppose all the members of such a state to be acquainted with the best means of promoting their general end; and we shall see them all moving in perfect concert." But such perfect concert could only be directed toward the common good. "The good of the body will be their first aim. And in subserviency to this, they will impartially regard the particular interests of individuals. You and I shall perfectly unite in our regard for your interest and for mine." The subordination of the individual's interests for the public good was stated emphatically by Samuel West in 1776. "Thus we see that both reason and revelation perfectly agree in pointing out the nature, end, and design of government, viz., that it is to promote the welfare and happiness of the community . . . for every good man will be ready to forego his private interest for the sake of being beneficial to the public."[36]

The end of political society is the good of the people, and all other considerations are subordinate to this goal. This raises a further problem in determining when and under what circumstances the alienable rights of man can be forfeited. If the interests of the individual can only be realized if the interests of the people as a whole are first achieved, then it would appear to follow that it is in the interest of the individual to have his immediate interest sacrificed in order for the interests of the whole to be attained, since this is a necessary condition of his securing his interests in the long run. At least, this will be so when in fact the sacrifice of his interest is necessary in order for the public interest to be achieved. If this is the case, however, then it must always be true that the individual receives an adequate equivalent when he gives up his alienable natural rights, in such a situation. But then, the crucial determination in deciding the extent to which the alienable rights of individuals set limits on the exercise of political authority in civil society is to be made in answering the question, Who decides?

36. *Independent Chronicle*, December 4, 1777; Niles, *Two Discourses*, pp. 26–27; West, *A Sermon*, in Thornton, *The Pulpit*, p. 296; cf. p. 281.

Who decides, that is, when the good of the whole will be advanced by demanding the forfeiture of an individual's alienable natural rights, in whole or in part? And the answer to this question was unequivocal also. "For he (an individual) parts with the power of controuling his natural rights, only when the good of the whole requires it; and of this there can be but one absolute judge in the State. If the minority can assume the right of judging, there may then be two judges; for however large the minority may be, there must be another body still larger, who have the same claim, if not a better, to the right of absolute determination."[37]

The majority of the people of Massachusetts was seen as the binding political authority in the community which the people of the state comprised. Obviously, this absolute majority rule allows for cases where a majority might take actions that individuals and minority groups perceive as being contrary to their interest. What could such an individual or such a minority do? According to Samuel West, the minority, while free to protest and express peaceable dissent, must recognize its obligation ultimately to submit to the authority of the public.

> It is also necessary that the minor part should submit to the major; e.g., when legislators have enacted a set of laws which are highly approved by a large majority of the community as tending to promote the public good, in this case, if a small number of persons are so unhappy as to view the matter in a very different point of light from the public, though they have an undoubted right to show the reasons of their dissent from the judgment of the public, and may lawfully use all proper arguments to convince the public of what they judge to be an error, yet, if they fail in their attempt, and the majority shall continue to approve of the laws that are enacted, it is the duty of those few that dissent peaceably and for conscience' sake to submit to the public judgment, unless something is required of them which they judge would be sinful for them to comply with; for in that case they ought to obey the dictates of their own consciences rather than any human authority whatever.

West's position is interesting in at least two respects. First, it asserts unequivocally that the minority has no right to take mat-

37. "The Essex Result," in Handlin and Handlin, *Popular Sources*, p. 331.

ters into its own hands over policy issues. The right of revolution is a majority right, as is made explicit by West further on:
"And, besides, it is the major part of a community that have the
sole right of establishing a constitution and authorizing magistrates; and consequently it is only the major part of the community that can claim the right of altering the constitution,
and displacing magistrates." Second, even where the voice of
conscience forbids an individual to comply with a public
decision, there is no suggestion that the individual is authorized
to extend his protest beyond the point of peaceable protest and
noncompliance. The ultimate implications of the relationship
between this right of conscience and political obligation under a
morally decadent regime is not explored by West. However, his
position here is consistent with the view that government
cannot legitimately compel actions contrary to conscience.[38]

In light of these considerations, it appears that there is no
effective limit to the power of a majority of the people in civil
society. This is a harsh conclusion to reach, not only because it
is so unpalatable for contemporary libertarians to contemplate
such a nonlibertarian heritage, but also, and more fundamental-
ly, because such a conclusion runs smack in the face of traditional teachings concerning the revolutionary notions of limited
government, natural rights, and government by consent. Is there
no element of historical veracity in the traditional accounts?
Was the language of natural law merely a historical chimera?
Were the revolutionaries in fact majority rule political absolutists? The answer to these questions is a qualified no, but in order to understand the sense in which, and the extent to which,
the people of Massachusetts were not majority-rule absolutists,
it is necessary to return to a consideration of life in the state of
nature.

It has already been established that the law of nature and the
law of God were each binding in the state of nature. Even where
there is no temporal authority to regulate human behavior, individuals are responsible to their own consciences and before the
judgment of the Lord. As we have seen, according to Samuel

38. West, *A Sermon*, in Thornton, *The Pulpit*, pp. 277, 278. For other
statements affirming that the right of revolution is a majority right, see:
Hitchcock, *A Sermon . . . May 25, 1774*, p. 25; Samuel Langdon, *A Sermon Preached Before the Honorable Congress of the Colony of Massachusetts-Bay . . . May 31, 1775*, in Thornton, *The Pulpit*, p. 250.

West the "state of nature, though it be a state of perfect freedom, yet is very far from a state of licentiousness. The law of
nature gives men no right to do anything that is immoral, or
contrary to the will of God, and injurious to their fellow-creatures; for a state of nature is properly a state of law and government, even a government founded upon the unchangeable nature
of the Deity, and a law resulting from the eternal fitness of
things."[39] It is abundantly evident from the debate over Article
III that it was agreed on all hands that God's kingdom was not
of this earth. Yet the fact that God sits in judgment and the fact
that his law is a moral standard for men on earth, are both relevant facts for the problem of political authority, even though
God does not himself choose to enforce the moral code on
earth. For the moral law is still an absolute standard by which
God judges men, and God's administration of that law sets an
example to which legitimate human authority should repair.

It is incumbent upon society to determine what the moral
standards are, however, and God has provided men with reason
as their instrument for knowing his will. In moving from the
state of nature to civil society the people assume the right of
judging, which in the state of nature was solely God's prerogative. It is in this sense that the saying, the voice of the people
is the voice of God, is strictly true. "The people, under God, are
the fountain of all authority among men," said Peter Powers in
1779. In exercising that authority, the people were responsible
to God. Although by establishing political institutions the people give up the immediate right of judgment in temporal affairs,
they forfeit this right to rulers of their own choice. "Every ruler
is, or ought to be, appointed by the people, and accountable to
them," Powers held, but magistrates, like the people whose servants they are, are also accountable to God. According to Samuel
West, "though magistrates are to consider themselves as the
servants of the people, seeing from them it is that they derive
their power and authority, yet they may also be considered as
the ministers of God ordained by him for the good of mankind;
for, under him, as the Supreme Magistrate of the universe, they
are to act." Just as the people collectively are the surrogates of
God on earth, so the magistrates whom they appoint to rule in
their stead are the surrogates of God in respect to individual
members of the society. Indeed, the "covenant between prince

39. West, *A Sermon*, in Thornton, *The Pulpit*, p. 271; cf. above p. 92.

and people, most naturally represents the covenant between God and his creatures." Now if the people in the first place, and their appointed magistrates in the next, are acting as surrogates for the rule of God, then it follows that the political institutions set up by the people and the administration of them by magistrates should correspond as closely as possible with God's rule in the state of nature. Because of this, the attitude of the Massachusetts people toward God himself, as well as toward the method of his rule, becomes a relevant consideration for determining how institutions should be shaped and how they should be administered in the kingdom of earth.[40]

In regard to the divine judgment, one thing is certain. It treats all men alike. All men are equal before the eyes of God. The rule of God is impartial and it is just. The rules of equity are observed in the court of heaven. "We cannot but approve the divine administration as just and equal," said Samuel Baldwin in 1775. According to Gad Hitchcock this same justice and equity was what God expected of his surrogates on earth. "It is the character of one who is exalted from among his brethren, to rule over men, drawn by God himself, the Almighty guardian of the Rights of mankind—that he 'must be just, ruling in the fear of God,' The safety of society greatly depends on the good disposition of rulers, and the regard they have to equity in their measures of government. If they rule in the fear of God, they will make his laws their pattern in framing and executing their own." According to Hitchcock, "Although government is not explicitly instituted by God, it is from him," and those who come to hold political power are accountable to him for their behavior. "And as they are responsible to him who is no respecter of persons; they are not to expect their public conduct is to be exempted from his most strict and impartial scrutiny." Because rulers wish to be approved by God and accepted by those they rule, they will be "careful to . . . be just and impartial in every part of administration."[41]

The most extensive treatment of the relationship between divine and temporal authority is to be found in the 1774 sermon of Nathan Fiske, entitled *The Importance of Righteous-*

40. Powers, *Jesus Christ*, pp. 12, 13; West, *A Sermon*, in Thornton, *The Pulpit*, p. 275; Fish, *A Discourse*, p. 13.
41. Baldwin, *A Sermon*, p. 12; Hitchcock, *A Sermon . . . May 25th, 1774*, pp. 16, 29, 30, 31. See also Jacob Cushing, *Divine Judgment Upon Tyrants* (Boston, 1778).

ness. Fiske contends that "the execution of judgment, and the practice of righteousness, are what God expects and demands from a people." This proposition, he says, can be argued from both the nature of man and the nature of God. "Mankind in general shew the work of the law written in their hearts; particularly the law of justice and equity." This justice and equity, written in the hearts of men, is also the principle characteristic of divine rule. "Our natural notions of God will not allow us to think of him as any other than an all perfect, and consequently, as an infinitely holy and righteous being: As one, who will do no wrong to any of his creatures; but, in all his transactions with them, will observe the strictest equity." Scripture serves to buttress this conclusion regarding the nature of God and his requirements for temporal authority. "And the laws both of the old and new testament require strict justice between man and man." Because of this command of the divine will it "is incumbent on legislators to contrive and enact the most equitable laws. . . . And when such laws are ordained, justice requires that they should be observed." In order that equitable laws will be observed, executive officers must, "hold the balances of justice with an equal and impartial hand. In their decisions between man and man, they will pronounce uprightly, without respect of persons."[42]

Equity, impartiality, justice, and righteousness are, according to Fiske, the characteristics of morally upright temporal administration, and they are what God demands of earthly administration. In civil society they set limits on the power of the people and of their appointed rulers. But what specifically did these terms mean? Strictly, justice and righteousness—two terms which were used synonymously—denoted the concept of giving to each his due. "The rules of righteousness oblige people to render to all their dues; 'tribute to whom tribute is due; custom, to custom; etc.' " Equity, a concept deriving out of the com-

42. Nathan Fiske, *The Importance of Righteousness* (Boston, 1774), pp. 7, 8, 9, 10, 11, 12. For other references to the relationship between equity and justice, see: "The Address of the Convention at Concord," *Boston Gazette,* October 25, 1779; An Old Roman [pseud.], *Boston Gazette,* April 13, 1778; Cooper, *A Sermon,* pp. 14, 16, 31; Powers, *Jesus Christ,* pp. 23, 30, 33, 35-36; Warren, *An Oration,* pp. 8, 12; Webster, *A Sermon,* pp. 12, 32; Whitney, *American Independence Vindicated,* pp. 33-34; Handlin and Handlin, *Popular Sources,* pp. 83, 87, 249, 328, 330, 731-732; Thornton, *The Pulpit,* pp. 240, 243, 274, 279.

mon law, denoted equality before the law and, in a procedural
sense, the reservoir of power which judges had at their disposal
to tailor general legal rules and principles to specific cases. Impartiality, as Fiske notes, meant that the law was not a respecter of persons, but rather that it would view all equally. Thus it
was a correlate, if not the very definition, of equity. It is perhaps surprising, in view of the wide currency these terms enjoyed, that so little effort was expended in defining them. It
does not violate the evidence that exists, however, to conclude
that they constituted a package of closely related ideas, each of
which could be expressed in procedural terms. The word "equity" for example, was often defined as the golden rule, a procedural notion, and was synonymous with the procedural concept
of impartiality. Thus, Abraham Ketaltas, in a sermon on the
subject of extortion, held that "it [extortion] is a flagrant con-
travention of that excellent and universally approved golden
rule of equity, Whatsoever ye would that men should do unto
you, do you even so unto them." Justice, the corollary of righteousness, was itself understood in procedural terms. For the
people of Massachusetts, procedure was more tangible and ultimately more important than substance. If government could
be made impartial and if each citizen could stand equally before known and standing laws (which were themselves impartially determined), as individuals in a state of nature stand equally
before God, then righteousness and justice, the giving to each
his due, would naturally follow. According to Fiske, it is because "so much of the peace and welfare of a people . . . depends
so much on the unbyassed sentence of judges, that this is the
reason . . . why the word judgment, which is properly the sentence or decision of a judge, is so often, in scripture, put for the
practice of justice and equity in general."[43]

43. Fiske, *The Importance*, pp. 13, 12-13. See also Abraham Ketaltas, *Reflections on Extortion* (Newburyport, Mass., 1778). Wood contends that
in distinguishing between written and unwritten law, Americans were recognizing the difference between the fundamental principles and rights of
the common law, and the arbitrary determinations of Parliament (*Creation*,
pp. 264-268). However, this is not the way the people of Massachusetts
perceived the situation. For them, the shift was not from the arbitrary
procedure of parliamentary rule to the nonarbitrary substance of fundamental principles and rights. They were moving from one type of arbitrary
procedure (legislative supremacy), to another arbitrary procedure (popular
sovereignty)—fundamental law beyond the power of government, but not
beyond the power of the people.

A good system of laws was seen as being fundamental to procedural justice, laws which would treat all citizens alike. And the first step in establishing such a system of laws lay in erecting a constitutional system. Nathaniel Niles's definition of civil liberty, which has been analyzed above in relation to the procedure of majority rule, also stresses the relationship between a constitution and an equal system of laws.

> Civil Liberty consists, not in any inclinations of the members of a community; but in the being and due administration of such a system of laws, as effectually tends to the greatest felicity of a state. Herein consists civil liberty, and to live under such a constitution, so administered, is to be the member of a free state. . . . Where there is no system of laws, not liberty, but anarchy, takes place. Some degree of liberty may, indeed, exist where neither the constitution nor the administration of it is perfect. But in order to perfect freedom, the law must extend to every member of the community alike, both in its requisitions and prohibitions.[44]

For Niles, the essence of a constitutional system was a system of impartial laws. In order to insure that such a system would prevail, it was thought necessary to establish and enshrine the fundamental law in a written constitution, the provisions of which would set a standard for the more ephemeral statutory law of legislatures. Such a constitution would protect the individual members of society against the power of the government by setting limits to its power and by establishing procedures by which its power must be exercised. These limitations and these procedures were reasonable and binding precisely because they were sanctioned by the majority of the people upon the inception of government. The fact that they would be self-imposed by the people is also significant in terms of the analogy between divine authority and popular sovereignty. No one, after all, imposes limits upon God, except God himself; and the only limits upon the authority of the people in civil society are those that the people choose to impose upon themselves.

What should such a constitutional system look like? Here, questions of value shade over into questions of structure, as we move to the third stage of the social contract theory. For if it

44. Niles, *Two Discourses*, p. 8.

was agreed by all that a constitution should be erected in order to secure justice and equity for each individual, as well as to achieve the common happiness, the question of what should go into such a constitution was one that occasioned less agreement. Lying beneath the disputes over the form of government that was to be created in the Constitution of 1780, however, was a unifying faith in the procedures of constitutional democracy.

IV

The Theory of Government

Republican Society

The making of constitutions was, for John Adams, a science. In his *Thoughts on Government* he put it this way: "As the divine science of social happiness, and the blessings of society depend entirely on the constitutions of government, which are generally institutions that last for many generations, there can be no employment more agreeable to a benevolent mind than a research after the best." But the challenge of designing a new government would not be a simple one. It is much easier to break away from an old government than it is to set up a new one, because it is easier to see what is not working than it is to know what will work. Adams was emphatic in his belief that the erection of new governments was "the most difficult and dangerous part of the business Americans have to do." In order to approach the construction of a government scientifically, Adams contended, it is necessary to consider first the sort of people over whom that government is to rule. "The foundation of every government is some principle or passion in the minds of the people," he said. "The noblest principles and most generous affections in our nature, then, have the fairest chance to support the noblest and most generous models of government." The noblest affection in human nature is virtue. "All sober inquirers after truth, ancient and modern, pagan and Christian, have declared that the happiness of man, as well as his dignity, consists in virtue. . . . If there is a form of government, then, whose principle and foundation is virtue, will not every sober man acknowledge it better calculated to promote the general happiness than any other form?" And happily, such a form of government does exist. "There is no good government," stated Adams flatly, "but what is republican."[1]

1. John Adams, *Thoughts on Government* (Boston, 1776), in *The Works of John Adams*, ed. Charles F. Adams, 10 vols. (Boston: Charles C. Little

But if a republican government is ideally the best, it does not follow that it is necessarily suited for all people. "That government must upon the whole be esteemed best for a people," said Samuel Williams, "which is best suited to their temper and genius; to the nature of their soil, and climate; to their situation, extent, connections, dangers, and wants." By these criteria, what sort of government should Massachusetts have? "On such, and all accounts, a free and equal government is best suited to our infant and rising state."[2] But why? What specific characteristics of the people of Massachusetts made them well suited for such a government? What made them a republican society?

The literature of revolutionary Massachusetts reveals five key ingredients for a republican society: piety, moral virtue, knowledge, public virtue, and shared values. In Article III of the Declaration of Rights the framers affirmed their belief that "the happiness of a people, and the good order and preservation of civil government, essentially depend upon piety, religion, and morality," and while there were those who disputed the implication that any sort of government required these elements of good character, there was little doubt that republican government had a better chance to succeed in a pious and morally upright society. This emphasis on piety and morality was a constant of the Revolution. Many were the days of fasting and prayer that the people of Massachusetts underwent in the name of these virtues. In January 1776, soon after they resumed the colonial charter, the General Court issued a proclamation for the purpose of encouraging "Piety and Virtue" and in order to suppress "Vice and Immorality." The Court praised the form of government, yet at the same time, recognized the need to support it by encouraging good behavior.

> But, as a Government so popular can be Supported only by universal knowledge and Virtue, in the Body of the People, it is the Duty of all Ranks to promote the Means of Education, for the rising Generation, as well as true Religion, Purity of Manners, and Integrity of Life, among all orders and degrees. ... That Piety and Virtue, which, alone

and James Brown, 1851) 4: 193; "The Adams-Warren Letters," *Collections of the Massachusetts Historical Society* 72 (1925): 222; Adams, *Thoughts*, in *Works*, 4: 194, 193, 194.

2. Samuel Williams, *A Discourse on the Love of Our Country* (Salem, 1775), pp. 17, 10.

can secure the Freedom of any People, may be encouraged, and Vice and Immorality suppressed, the great and general Court have thought fit to issue this Proclamation, commanding and enjoining it upon the good People of this Colony, that they lead Sober, Religious and peaceable Lives, avoiding all Blasphemies, contempt of the holy Scriptures, and of the Lord's day and all other Crimes and Misdemeanors, all Debauchery, Prophaneness, Corruption, Venality, all riotous and tumultuous Proceedings, and all Immoralities whatsoever.

This concern for religion and morality was echoed in the *Boston Gazette* of April 20, 1778, by a writer publishing under the pseudonym of Mentor. "There is nothing upon which the well being of a community so much depends as a due regard to religion and morality," contended Mentor. "If a sense of religion is once removed from the minds of men, they will soon find a thousand means to evade the laws of their country." In a society pervaded by corruption, despotism is inevitable, "For when the manners of a people become universally corrupt, they are incapable of liberty."[3]

The General Court and Mentor were not alone in their concern for piety and morality, nor were they concerned without reason. As was noted in chapter 1, the period from 1775 to 1780 was one of political disorientation in Massachusetts. Many citizens, particularly those of the colonial gentry, were justifiably concerned about the moral condition of the state. Said Mentor:

> I have taken the liberty of offering these few observations to the public, because I have seen, with great anxiety, the rapid progress which vice has made in a few months past. Principles and manners have been lately introduced into this town, which, in my humble opinion, are utterly inconsistent with true honor, and productive of every evil which we would wish to prevent. Principles and manners hitherto never adopted and practiced here, and which

3. "Proclamation of the General Court, January 23, 1776," in Oscar and Mary Handlin, eds., *The Popular Sources of Political Authority* (Cambridge: Harvard University Press, Belknap Press, 1966), pp. 65–66. Where a complete citation to a newspaper source is given in the text, the citation will not be repeated in a footnote. See also Moses Everett, *Early Piety Recommended* (Boston, 1779).

every sober citizen earnestly hopes that gentlemen of professed honor and good breeding will not persist in obtruding upon us.

This point was made most caustically by an "officer in the American army," whose views were reproduced in the *Independent Chronicle*, from the *Pennsylvania Gazette*, in 1779.

> While we are pleasing and amusing ourselves with Spartan Constitutions on paper, a very contrary spirit reigns triumphant in all ranks, we may look out for some fatal catastrophy to befal the people. Our political constitutions and manners do not agree; one or the other must fall—give way —otherwise America is a phenomenon in civil society. Spartan constitutions and Roman manners, peculiar to her declining state, never will accord.[4]

If there was some doubt about whether or not Massachusetts was a society of sufficient virtue to justify republican government, there was no doubt that virtue should be promoted in the new constitution. The framers recognized their responsibility to provide for training that would tend to encourage the type of manners and mores they deemed essential for the lasting success of their political experiment. The public support of the ministry, provided for in Article III of the Declaration of Rights, was one such measure, and has already been discussed at length. A second important provision relating to the problem of promoting virtue was the provision for public education in Chapter V of the Frame of Government.

It was widely accepted that education was a keystone of republican government. One of the best illustrations of this fact was an article written for the *Massachusetts Spy* of May 4, 1780, by a writer under the appropriate pseudonym of A True Republican. "We are now," he said, "drawing to a close of a bloody war, by which was here secured our sovereignty and independence; and accordingly are about to establish a form of government of the republican kind. Learning and virtue are the pillars of this species of government, while ignorance is the principle of a despotick." Nowhere, said A True Republican, is the need for knowledge greater than among the political leadership of

4. Mentor [pseud.] *Boston Gazette*, April 20, 1778; *Independent Chronicle*, June 3, 1779.

the community, who "ought . . . to be men of learning and virtue." But knowledgeable leaders are not enough. Knowledge
must be diffused throughout the community. "It is not only
necessary that officers in a republic should be men of learning
and virtue; but as they are all elected from and by the people
at large, either mediately or immediately, the people themselves
ought also to be possessed of the same qualities." In order to
achieve this diffusion of knowledge among the people, a good
system of grammar schools is necessary. "The minds of children
are like a fertile garden, that courts the labour of the industri-
ous husbandman, but without it, weeds of every poisonous
kind will grow with a most deadly luxuriance." If the grammar
schools are neglected the future of the state is in danger. "In
a little time the present generation must be gone, and then, if
this neglect of schools continues, where will be found the men
of learning and virtue to fill up the almost innumerable offices,
in a republic government." Learning and virtue without public
support for education will remain the province of the rich, and
it will be only the rich who will hold political power. "But as
men of learning and virtue will but rarely to be found among
the mass of the citizens, all offices of course must fall into the
hands of men of fortune, figure and education."

And this is one of the ironies of republican government. For
although it is useful that political leaders should be good men,
and although educated men are most likely to be good, republican theory does not hold that only the rich and well-born
should have power on account of their superior education. Indeed, some were willing to risk having uneducated men in power, rather than run the risk of turning over the state to those
who might be well-educated, but whose interests would not be
consistent with the interests of the rest of the community. Such
was the view of Democritus, writing in the *Massachusetts Spy*
of July 5, 1775.

> Men of liberal education . . . are not to be trusted with the
> reigns of government. . . . If it should be objected that to
> exclude men of learning from any share in the government,
> is to exclude all that are fit to govern, I readily own it, and
> therefore mean only to exclude such as have learned to
> think and act as if the laity was their property, as much as
> cattle are the property of their lawful owners. However
> strange it may seem, this is a part of a colledge education if

we may judge the tree by its fruit. Therefore I advise that you choose men of learning, I mean men that have learnt to distinguish villains from honest men. . . . Choose men that have learnt to get their living by honest industry, and that will be content with as small an income as the generality of those have who pay them for their services. If you would be well represented, choose a man in midling circumstances as to wordly estate.

It is apparent that Democritus objects not to education per se, but rather to the type of person who might come to a position of influence because of it. Sentiments such as these were not lost upon the men of liberal education. John Adams, writing to Joseph Hawley in 1776 commented that "knowledge is among the most essential foundations of liberty. But is there not a jealousy or an envy taking place among the multitude, of men of learning, and a wish to exclude them from the public councils and from military command?" Democritus himself was the object of a scathing reply in the *Spy* from a writer styling himself Lysurgus. The calumniations of Democritus, he said, are "replete with consummate barefaced impudence. . . . One would be inclined to think, from the complexion of his advice, that he had been bred and brought up in Turkey; where a man of real learning is as much despised and rediculed, as a hottentot would be among the learned and polite part of mankind. And it is highly probable that he is peculiarly ignorant, from the ungrammatical and unclassical construction of his peice." Beneath all this rhetoric was an agreement in principle. The argument of Democritus rested on an empirical generalization to the effect that men of education cannot be trusted. He ascribed this to the fact of their education, but it must be remembered that he was still speaking within a frame of reference which presupposed that only the elites of wealth would be well educated. The establishment of a system of general education of the sort recommended by A True Republican, which would succeed in bringing about an equality of education, could reconcile the differences between Democritus and Lysurgus. And it was for just this purpose that Chapter V was included in the Constitution of 1780.[5]

5. John Adams to Joseph Hawley, in *Works*, 9:434; Lysurgus [pseud.], *Massachusetts Spy*, July 12, 1775. See George H. Martin, "The Early School Legislation of Massachusetts," *New England Magazine* 8 (1893):

Republican government must rest on virtue, but there are two sorts of virtue—private and public. Private virtue is the virtue of the soul; it is the moral virtue of a good man. Public virtue, on the other hand, is the virtue of a good citizen. For Phillips Payson public virtue was identical with patriotism: "I shall also mention the love of our country, or public virtue, as another essential support of good government and the public liberties. No model of government whatever can equal the importance of this principle, nor afford proper safety and security without it." How is public virtue to be secured? Payson mentions two factors that will contribute to its attainment: knowledge and religion. "The general diffusion of knowledge is . . . the likeliest method to beget and increase that public virtue, which, under God, will prove, like the promises of the gospel, an impregnable bulwark to the state." This emphasis on the extension of knowledge is consistent with the view that public good and private good are compatible, and that a man sufficiently well informed will recognize his own interest in that of the public. Religion also promotes public virtue because of the relationship between public and private virtue.

> I must not forget to mention religion, both in rulers and people as of the highest importance to the public. This is the most sacred principle that can dwell in the human breast. . . . The importance of religion to civil society and government is great indeed, as it keeps alive the best sense of moral obligation, a matter of such extensive utility, especially in respect to an oath, which is one of the principal instruments of government. The fear and reverence of God, and the terrors of eternity, are the most powerful restraints upon the minds of men.[6]

Public virtue, or patriotism, was the subject of an extensive essay by Samuel Williams in 1775, entitled *A Discourse on the Love of Our Country*. In this essay, Williams stressed the relationship between the prerequisite of public virtue and that of shared values. "By the Love of our country then, we are to un-

526-538; Martin, "Massachusetts Schools Before the Revolution," *New England Magazine* 9 (1893): 356-368.
6. Phillips Payson, *A Sermon Preached Before the Honorable Council, and the Honorable House of Representatives . . . May 27, 1778* (Boston, 1778), in John W. Thornton, ed., *The Pulpit of the American Revolution* (Boston: Gould and Lincoln, 1860), pp. 337, 339.

derstand a regard and affection to the common good; to the interest and welfare of that community, or body politic, of which we are a part." This public virtue is necessary for a free government.

> In a despotic government, the only principle by which the Tyrant who is to move the whole machine, means to regulate and manage the people, is Fear; by a servile dread of his power. But a free government, which of all others is far the most preferrable, cannot be supported without Virtue. This virtue is the Love of our country. And after all the devices that sound policy or the most refined corruption have, or can suggest; this is the most efficacious principle to hold the different parts of an empire together, and to make men good members of the society to which they belong.

This last clause is crucial for Williams because, "Love to our country supposes that there is a proper community, or public society formed." He says, "We must therefore first of all suppose, a real and proper community, or state of civil society, to have taken place." A real or proper community is one in which individuals are bound together by a common stock of shared values. "The great community of which we are a part, is such a body politic, or well regulated society. And to this society we are joined, by many and strong connections. We live in her dominions, we believe in her religion; we think her laws and government are best suited to our state, disposition, temper, and climate; and we partake in all her calamities and prosperity. Joined to our country by such numerous, extensive, and lasting ties, she becomes the object of our attention, veneration, reverence, and regard." Williams was articulating the basic sense of the people of Massachusetts. Massachusetts was a body politic. It was a community that rested on a secure foundation of shared values, religious belief, moral rectitude, a general diffusion of knowledge, and a commitment to an even broader dissemination of learning. It was a community tied together by tradition, circumstances, and the bonds of necessity forced upon it by the separation from England. And in all of these respects, it was a society possessed of the essential prerequisites of republican government.[7]

7. Williams, *A Discourse* (Salem, 1775), pp. 10, 13, 7, 9-10.

But to possess the necessary prerequisites of a republican government is not sufficient. Within a republican society, as within any other type of society, the darker side of human nature operates. Ambition will play its course, and independence can shade into selfishness. The science of government must account for these aspects of society as well, and in this sense a theory of good government is integrally related to a knowledge of what bad government might do. In approaching this problem, the first problem that the science of government must consider is self-love. Self-love is a primary force in human nature and the primary datum of any theory of political organization. It is a constant from which all else must be designed to flow. This view was articulated clearly by a writer in the *Independent Chronicle* of December 4, 1777, writing under the pseudonym A Gentleman in the Country. God, he said, has stipulated that happiness is the end of human action, and he has provided man with reason "to be our guide in the pursuit of it." But the goal and the capability are not sufficient. What is needed is motive.

> To stimulate us in the pursuit of it [happiness] has he not unkindly implanted in us, a principle of *self love*, which is the original spring of human actions, Under the direction of instinct first; and of reason afterwards? We are no sooner sensible of our wants and our *personal* inability to supply them, than self-love directs us necessarily to *sociability*. Instinct leads us into it, by a sense of pleasure, and reason, that, recalling the past, forsees the future, confirms us in it, by a sense of happiness. The necessaries, the conveniences of life, and every agreeable sensation are the objects of both. But happiness is a continued enjoyment of these, and that is an object, proportioned to reason alone, neither is obtained out of society: Sociability, therefore, is the foundation of human happiness. Society cannot be mentioned without *benevolence justice,* and the other moral virtues. These virtues, therefore, are the foundations of society. Self-love operates in all their stages. We love ourselves, we love our families, we love the particular societies to which we belong, and our benevolence extends at last, to the whole race of mankind; like so many vortices, the center of them all is self-love, and that which is the most distant from it, is the weakest.

But if self-love is the major incentive to the love of others, it is

also the greatest obstacle to achieving it, for as noted by A Gentleman, "that which is the most distant from it is the weakest."
Because the object of self-love, one's self, is more immediate
than other loves, including the love of one's country, there will
always exist a conflict of interest on the part of those persons
whose business it is to manage public affairs. In the words of
Phillips Payson, "The public interest being a remoter object
than that of self, hence persons in power are so generally disposed to turn it to their own advantage."[8]

The temptations of political power are enormous. Public
trusts provide many opportunities for selfish men to aggrandize
themselves at the public expense. Even men of honest disposition
may be led to act partially toward friends and supporters. But
in a republican government, rulers should pursue the interest of
the public. "This, certainly is the great object which magistrates,
as such, are under obligation to keep in their eye—as men, they
have, like other men, private interest, and private views, and
may as lawfully pursue them; but in their public capacity, they
can, of right, have no other end, than the public advantage."
When rulers elevate their own interest above that of the public,
the worst kind of calamity can be sure to follow. According to
Nathan Fiske:

> If avaracious men are in authority, they will be disposed to
> sacrifice the public, to their own private interest. . . . If
> ambition be their leading principle, every thing else, even
> liberty itself, and the most sacred rights, must give way
> thereto. If their tempers are naturally severe, they will "in-
> cline to write their laws in blood; which will keep a society
> unquiet, and be apt to approach the verge of tyranny."
> And where men of arbitrary principles are at the helm,
> they will "dispose of liberty, property and life, in spite of
> the most venerable rights descended from distant ages; in
> spite of the voice of reason, the maxims of equity, and
> the claims of conscience. No justice restrains; no mercy
> relents."[9]

8. Payson, *A Sermon*, in Thornton, *The Pulpit*, p. 339. See also: George
Lesslie, *The Nature and Tendency of Selfishness Considered* (Newbury,
Mass., 1779).
9. Gad Hitchcock, *A Sermon Preached Before His Excellency Thomas
Gage, Esq.*, . . . *May 25th, 1774* (Boston, 1774), p. 36; Nathan Fiske, *The
Importance of Righteousness* (Boston, 1774), p. 19.

Of all the possible corruptions of public life, the most to be feared is ministerial corruption. This was the great lesson of the Revolution. "If a prince is disposed to be just," said Fiske, "yet if his councellors are not actuated by the same principle, they will obstruct the free course of justice, and occasion much wrong and injury." The most searing indictment of ministerial corruption published in Massachusetts during the Revolution was the 1775 lecture on the commemoration of the Boston Massacre, by Oliver Noble. The subtitle of this discourse claimed that it would show "The Power and Oppression of STATE MINISTERS tending to the Ruin and Destruction of GOD's People." Noble undertook this task with great zeal.

> Such is the accursed nature of lawless ambition that the greatest misfortunes of kingdoms, and states, as well as of lesser communities, and individuals, have arisen from, and are owing to an insatiate lust of power in men of abilities, and influence.
>
> Voracious like the grave, they can never have enough, i.e., of power and wealth: And are therefore prompted on by restless desires, to seek the means of accumulating these, and that by expedients, however profitable to themselves, are destructive to their country. . . . Such false, designing, and detestable patriots have in every age, nation, and country in the world, at one time or other, led their blind confiding country-men, into the very jaws of slavery, vassalage, and ruin.

These "court-locusts" are able to use their influence to turn the authority of the most benevolent king against the interest of the people. Indeed, even the legislature is not immune to the influence of such courtiers. "When a state, by the influence of minions, and court parasites, those bloodsuckers of the constitution, begins, and goes on, to establish unrighteousness by law; and legislative authority is prostituted, to the iniquitous, and low purpose of aggrandizing individuals, instead of the good of the whole, then it receives a mortal blow; of which would it will certainly perish, unless timely healed. . . . This shows us how dangerous over-grown ministers and courtiers are, both to kings and estates, which every wise prince will forever guard against, and every state sound in politics always prevent."[10]

10. Fiske, *The Importance*, p. 18; Oliver Noble, *Some Strictures Upon the*

   This emphasis on corruption on the part of rulers, and in particular on the part of ministers, is significant in two respects.
First, it suggests that the people of Massachusetts were more
concerned about the problem of tyranny than they were about
the problem of anarchy. That these were perceived as alternatives is clear. "We are not fighting," said a writer in the *Independent Chronicle* in 1777, ". . . for a formidable Court interest;
but, for our lives, liberties, and estates; nor are we fighting for
this or that Form of Government, but to be free from arbitrary
power, and the iron rod of oppression, on the one hand, and
from popular licentiousness, anarchy, and confusion, on the
other hand; dreadful alternatives!" The relationship between
corruption in rulers and the Scylla and Charybdis of anarchy
and despotism was evident in the *New England Chronicle* on
July 11, 1776. Two articles adorned the front page of this edi-
tion of the *Chronicle*. One, subscribed by the initial A, discussed
the problem of choosing leaders for a new government. A argued that "something more than great abilities is necessary for
rulers; —however great their abilities may be yet if they are void
of virtue, sooner or later the public will suffer. Whenever there
is a competiton between their private interest and that of the
public, it is no hard matter to determine which must give way."
The other article was a selection of quotations from Richard
Price's *Observations on the Nature of Civil Liberty* in which the
following passage appears:

> It appears from hence, that licentiousness and despotism
> are more nearly allied than is commonly imagined. They
> are both alike inconsistent with liberty, and the true end
> of government; nor is there any other difference between
> them, than that one is the licentiousness of little men; or
> that, by the one, the persons and property of a people are
> subject to outrage and invasion from a King, or a lawless
> body of Grandees; and that, by the other, they are subject
> to the like outrage from a lawless mob. In avoiding one of
> these evils, mankind have often run into the other. But all
> well-constituted governments guard equally against both.
> Indeed of the two, the last is, on several accounts, the least
> to be dreaded, and has done the least mischief. It may be
> truly said, that if licentiousness has destroyed its thou-

Sacred Story Recorded in the Book of Esther (Newbury-Port, Mass., 1775),
pp. 5, 8, 11.

sands, despotism has destroyed its millions. The former, having little power, and no system to support it, necessarily finds its own remedy; and a people soon get out of the tumult and anarchy attending it. But a despotism, wearing the form of government, and being armed with its force, is an evil not to be conquered without dreadful struggles. It goes on from age to age, debasing the human faculties, levelling all distinctions, and preying on the rights and blessings of society.

The clear implication of these passages is that a people whose practical experience led them to become profoundly suspicious of political leadership in general, would take care in designing their political institutions to guard against the abuse of power by political leaders. As we shall see, the people of Massachusetts were very concerned to do just that.[11]

But these passages suggest more than a general suspicion of politicians. They stress the fear of a particular type of politician: the corrupt ministers of the executive branch of government who are able to act arbitrarily and capriciously toward the public because there are no popular controls on their power. Not only were the colonial governors appointed by the Crown, and therefore unresponsive to the will of colonial majorities, but their appointees were equally resistant to public opinion. Through their extensive power of appointment the governors were able to exercise control over colonial affairs, internally and externally. Thus, another significant aspect of the attitude of the revolutionary publicists was their repeated condemnation of executive power. A people besieged by this type of propaganda would be likely to want strong curbs on executive power in particular, and as shall be seen, this was the case in Massachusetts.

The people of Massachusetts possessed the necessary characteristics of a republican society, but they were as prone as any other group to the vices of human nature. They wished to erect a constitutional system which would take advantage of their virtues and guard against their vices. This system would be based upon three principles: popular control of government, government by law, and the dispersal of power. In examining each of these principles the logic that connects them may be perceived.

11. A Faithful Friend to his Country [pseud.], *Independent Chronicle*, August 7, 1777; Richard Price, *Observations on the Nature of Civil Liberty* (London, 1776).

Popular Control of Government

The most important question that faced the framers of the Constitution of 1780 was, How can we give to the virtuous people a sufficient amount of control over their corruptible rulers? The answer falls under the heading of popular control of government. This was a principle that was new to the science of government, just as the principle of popular sovereignty was new to political and legal theory. There was, in Massachusetts, a deep-seated conviction that the people should maintain a close watch over their representatives, but there was less consensus on how this should be done. Among the numerous practices and policies which were considered or adopted during this period, there emerged two rival interpretations of the principle of popular control of government: consent and accountability. Of these, consent was by far the most widely discussed, but in the end, the people of Massachusetts had to settle for accountability.

In the matter of consent it is first necessary to distinguish between individual and collective consent. When the people of the town of Sutton, in 1778, held that "law to bind all must be assented to by all," they were advancing a principle of individual consent. Law (any law) to bind all (to bind each individual) must be assented to by all (must be approved by each individual). The strong implication of this argument is that where law is not assented to by all, it does not bind all, and the suggestion is that it is those individuals who do not assent who are not bound. In other words, no individual is bound to obey a law to which he has not assented. This is the principle of individual consent. The principle of collective consent is different. Writing in the *Independent Chronicle* of July 3, 1777, A Freeman held that "the consent of the people is now most openly allowed to be the only foundation of civil government," by which he meant that the collective consent of the people is a necessary prerequisite for any system of government. The same view was expressed by the General Court in a proclamation in January of 1776.

> As the Happiness of the People, (alone) is the sole end of Government, so the Consent of the People is the only Foundation of it, in Reason, Morality, and the natural Fitness of Things; and therefore every Act of Government, every Exercise of Sovereignty, against, or without, the Consent of the People, is Injustice, Usurpation, and Tyranny.

Although this principle is not necessarily incompatible with the principle of individual consent, it might be, in a case where one or more individuals opposes what the people collectively wish to do. Nothing is said here about the obligation of individuals to obey specific laws. The principle of collective consent is thus less demanding than that of individual consent. Which of the two (if not both) was logically entailed by the theory of popular sovereignty? In answering this question let us first consider the principle of individual consent.[12]

The underlying rationale of the principle of individual consent is simple and clear. By consenting in advance to a law, an individual becomes, in a sense, an author of that law. By obeying it, then, he is doing no more than obeying his own judgment. In a civil society predicated upon the concept of individual consent, each individual shares in the sovereignty of the people at large. "Is not a country a constitution—an established frame of laws; of which a man may say, 'we are here united in society for our common security and happiness. These fields and these fruits are my own: The regulations under which I live are my own: I am not only a proprietor of the soil, but I am a part of the sovereignty of my country.' " This principle would be clearly operative in a political system where all of the people met and unanimously approved all of the laws by which they were to be governed. In such a system, the principle of individual consent would be completely fulfilled, and the problem of political obligation would never arise. However, such a system is impractical. According to the town of Boston, in 1776: "The Right to legislate is originally in every Member of the Community; which Right is always exercised by a State: But when the Inhabitants are become numerous, 'tis not only inconvenient, but impracticable for all to meet in One Assembly; and hence arose the Necessity and Practise of legislating by a few, freely chosen by the many. When this Choice is free, and the Representation, equal, 'tis the People's Fault if they are not happy." This view was universally shared. There were no proposals in Massachusetts for everyone to get together in order to pass laws. But if "in a large society, inhabiting an extensive country, it is impossible that the whole should assemble to make laws," then it is necessary that there be some delegation

12. "The Return of the Town of Sutton on the Proposed Constitution of 1778," in Handlin and Handlin, *Popular Sources*, p. 231; "Proclamation of the General Court, January 23, 1776," ibid, p. 65.

of authority. Having arrived at such a practical decision, however, a crucial theoretical question is raised. Can the practical
remedy of delegated authority be reconciled with the normative
doctrine of individual consent?[13]

If each individual is not to consent to each act of legislation,
he must exercise his individual consent at some prior stage of
the political process. For the purposes of this analysis, we may
distinguish three other opportunities that the social compact
theory affords for individuals to consent: (1) each individual
may consent to the specific individual to whom his power of
consent is delegated, i.e., to his representative; (2) each individual may consent to the system under which that delegation
takes place, i.e., he may consent to the constitution; (3) each individual may consent to the political society which sanctions
that particular system, i.e., he may consent to join society in
the original social compact. Of these, the first would seem to be
the closest thing to the pure principle of individual consent.

There can be no doubt that in all cases where a representative
system is established, the consent of an individual was seen by
the people of Massachusetts to be fully embodied in the consent
of his representative. Individual and representative consent are
of identical authority. This identity was frequently indicated by
conjoining the two types of consent in declarations of the right
of property. Thus, Nathan Fiske held that, "it is essential to a
free state, that no member of it shall have his property taken
from him by taxation, or any other way, unless by his own consent, given personally, or by his representative." William Stearns
endorsed this view in almost identical terms. "It is in opposition
to that plain dictate of reason and common sense," he said,
"that no man is to have his property taken from him without
his own consent, or that of his representative." The town of
Pittsfield in the center of rambunctious Berkshire County could
only agree that "no man's property of right can be taken from
him without his consent, given either in person or by his representative." These statements parallel the phrasing of Article X
of the Declaration of Rights, and leave no doubt that the consent of a legislature is as good as the consent of an individual as

13. Samuel Cooper, *A Sermon Preached Before His Excellency John Hancock Esq.,* . . . *October 25, 1780* (Boston, 1780), p. 27; "Boston's Instructions to Its Representatives, May 30, 1776," in Handlin and Handlin, *Popular Sources,* p. 95; Adams, *Thoughts,* in *Works,* 4:194.

far as it applies to the unalienable right of property. Peter Powers applied the identity of individual and representative consent to all natural rights. "All men, indeed, are by nature equal: and all have, most certainly, an equal right to freedom and liberty by the great law of nature," he contended. "No man or number of men," therefore, "has or can have a right to infringe the natural rights, liberties or privileges of others: or to dominion or government over any one, but by his free consent personally, or by his legal representative."[14]

Samuel Baldwin made the same point in regard to the issue over which the colonies originally rebelled, taxation: "The colonies, in their late, and present struggle for their liberties, have had occasion to revert to the first principles of the English Constitution; and opposition to the assumed right of Great Britain, of forming a tax upon them, have declared it to be an essential right of Englishmen, to be taxed only by themselves, or their legal representatives freely chosen." But this right of Englishmen applied to all just government, and it was the particular providence of the new American states to have lived under a just system during most of their colonial experience. "If we compare this system of government with the situation, state, and wants of the colonies," said Samuel Williams of the old colonial charter, "it would appear to have been widely adapted to promote their interest. It gave to the people here a share in their own government; and put us in the happy situation of being ruled by laws, to which we had consented, by representatives chose from among ourselves." The principles of the social compact, the theory of republican government, and even the long history of colonial independence served to confirm the simple fact stated by the Hampshire County Convention in 1779: "It is the Opinion of this Convention that all men are Born Equally Free and Independent, and that no man Can be bound by a Law that he has not Given his Consent to, Either by his Person, or Legal Representative."[15]

14. Fiske, *The Importance*, p. 32; William Stearns, *A View of the Controversy* (Watertown, Mass., 1775), p. 18; "Instructions of the Town of Pittsfield to their Representatives to the State Convention," in Handlin and Handlin, *Popular Sources*, p. 411; Peter Powers, *Jesus Christ the True King* (Newburyport, 1778), p. 10.
15. Samuel Baldwin, *A Sermon Preached at Plymouth, December 22, 1775* (Boston, 1775), p. 25; Williams, *A Discourse*, p. 18; "Opinions of Hamp-

What legitimates the equation of individual and representative consent? One possible answer is that in the act of participating in the electoral process, i.e., in the act of voting, each individual transmits his consent to his representative. On this account, the right to vote is a prerequisite of political liberty in that it is only through the act of voting that an individual can express his consent to government. This point of view was illustrated in 1780 by the town of Northampton in their return on the Constitution of 1780. The citizens of Northampton objected to the property qualifications for electors for the House of Representatives, wondering if these qualifications could be made consistent with the principle of personal equality embodied in Article I of the Declaration of Rights. Can it be said, asked Northampton,

> that the citizens of the State, who . . . do not answer the description of the said fourth article, as it now stands, have ever covenanted, consented, and agreed, or will ever covenant, consent, and agree, with the rest of the people, to be governed by Laws founded on an article of a constitution, which totally excludes them from any share or voice in appointing the legislature for the State; . . . the exclusion which we complain of directly militates and is absolutely repugnant to the genuine sense of the first article of the declaration of Rights; unless it be true that a majority of any State have a right without any forfeiture of the minority to deprive them of what the said first article declares are the natural, essential, and unalienable rights of all men. . . . Very strange it would be, if others should have a right by their superior strength, to take away a right from any individual, which he himself could not alienate by his own consent and agreement. . . . if one hundred . . . equal freemen should be at once on the earth together, of what age soever they were, and some one of the hundred, should happen to have an hundred times as much brutal strength, as all the other individuals taken singly, or, perhaps, what is an equivalent thereto, an hundred times as much natural cunning, as any individual of the rest, he would not have any rights against the will of any one of his bretheren, to assume the exercise of dominion and jurisdiction over him,

shire County Towns, March 30, 1779," in Handlin and Handlin, *Popular Sources*, p. 385.

however easy it might be for him to do it; and if no one of the hundred would have a right to do so, we suppose that no ten together would have any right to it, and if not ten, then ninety nine of the hundred would not have any right to dominion over the remaining hundredth man; for nought to nought gives but nought; the inevitable consequence then is, that if the ninety nine should endeavour to subjugate, and exercise government, over the hundredth man, without his consent, he would have a good right to resist, and in case the ninety nine should overcome and subdue him, the hundredth man would have a good right, at any time, when any lucky moment presented, to do any thing that should be necessary, to regain his natural liberty and freedom, whereof he had been thus wrongfully deprived. . . . Now Gentlemen in case the form of Government which you have sent out to the people, shall be affirmed and established, is it not intended that every rateable poll of this state, of the age of twenty one years, shall be obliged to submit, and be subject to such a legislative body, as is therein projected and described? Is it not intended that all such persons shall be the subjects of their legislation? . . . If they are to be subject to the jurisdiction and legislation of your legislature, with regard to life, liberty, and their day wages or whatever small property they may acquire, and yet have no voice in the appointment of that legislature, what is the difference of their condition from that of the hundredth man who without his consent had jurisdiction usurped over him, by the other ninety nine or any single one of the above mentioned hundred of superior animal strength or natural cunning?

This is the clearest statement of the relationship between natural rights, individual consent, political equality, suffrage, and representation to be found in the literature of revolutionary Massachusetts. Without suffrage, individual consent is denied, and without individual consent, political equality is likely to be abridged; and the clear implication is that where suffrage is granted, individual consent is embodied in it. It would follow that in each act of voting, the individual transmits his power of consent to his elected representative.[16]

16. "The Return of the Town of Northampton on the Constitution of 1780," in Handlin and Handlin, *Popular Sources*, p. 579-581.

This argument is, however, not without difficulty. For it is undeniably the fact that not all persons are granted the right to vote, while all persons are supposed to be obligated to obey the law. In a 1776 letter to James Sullivan, John Adams squarely confronted the relationship between individual consent, suffrage, and representation.

It is certain, in theory, that the only moral foundation of government is, the consent of the people. But to what extent shall we carry this principle? Shall we say that every individual of the community, old and young, male and female, as well as rich and poor, must consent, expressly, to every act of legislation? No, you will say, this is impossible. How, then, does the right arise in the majority to govern the minority, against their will? Whence arises the right of the men to govern the women, without their consent? Whence the right of the old to bind the young, without theirs? . . . But let us first suppose that the whole community, of every age, rank, sex, and condition, has a right to vote. This community is assembled. A motion is made, and carried by a majority of one voice. The minority will not agree to this. Whence arises the right of the majority to govern, and the obligation of the minority to obey? . . . From necessity, you will say, because there can be no other rule. . . . But why exclude women? . . . You will say, because their delicacy renders them unfit for practice and experience in the great business of life, and the hardy enterprises of war, as well as the arduous cares of state. Besides, their attention is so much engaged with the necessary nurture of their children, that nature has made them fittest for domestic cares. And children have not judgment or will of their own. True. But will not these reasons apply to others? Is it not equally true, that men in general, in every society, who are wholly destitute of property, are also too little acquainted with public affairs to form a right judgment and too dependent upon other men to have a will of their own? . . . Your idea that those laws which affect the lives and personal liberty of all, or which inflict corporal punishment, affect those who are not qualified to vote, as well as those who are, is just. But so they do women, as well as men; children, as well as adults. What reason should there be for excluding a man of twenty years eleven months and twenty-seven days old, from a vote, when you admit one who is twenty-one? The reason is, you must fix upon some period in life, when the understanding and will of men in general, is fit to be trusted by the public. Will not the same reason justify the state in fixing upon some certain quantity of property, as a qualification? . . . Society can be governed only by general rules. Government cannot accommodate itself to every particular case as it happens, nor to the circumstances of particular persons. It must establish general comprehensive regulations for cases and persons. The only question is, which general rule will accommodate most cases and most persons.[17]

Adams could not have done a better job of preparing a reply to the return of Northampton had he been able to read it in advance. For Adams, individual consent is not the only, and perhaps not even the most important value in designing a representative system. It is theoretically subordinate to competency, and as a practical matter, it is bound by human frailty. Not all men in a free state are possessed of free will. In each of the cases cited by Adams, that of women, children, and men of no property, the concept of individual consent provides no explanation of, nor justification for, majority rule. Yet no one denied that women, children, and paupers were obligated to obey the laws of the majority. While individual consent is a sufficient justification for the obligation of those who do in fact consent, it can hardly be a necessary condition for the obligation of those who do not consent. What explains their obligation? What justifies majority rule? What has happened to the principle of individual consent? The only apparent answer to these questions is that if individual consent is not provided for, for all, in the system of representation, then it must enter at a prior point for some.

Another possibility is that individual consent could be embodied in the act of framing a constitution. It might thus be argued that while not all individuals are able to consent to the actions of representatives on a continuing basis, at least by consenting to the adoption of the representative system in general, with its restricted suffrage, each individual indirectly consents to everything that the representative assembly does. It is inter-

17. John Adams to James Sullivan, in Adams, *Works*, 9:375-378.

esting to note in regard to this that, in the case of Massachusetts, a distinction was clearly made between the act of framing the Constitution and the act of voting for officers elected under it, in that the suffrage for each was different. While all freemen of age twenty-one were enfranchised to vote on the ratification of the Constitution, the Constitution itself limited the suffrage to only those freemen who had a minimum estate. Thus it is possible that there were those among the electorate that approved the Constitution who voted to disenfranchise themselves. It is certainly arguable that anyone who did vote to disenfranchise himself thereby consented to be governed by a legislature in which he had no voice, and it would appear from this that the people of Massachusetts did recognize something like anterior consent as a sufficient justification for obligation to obey the state. But it does not follow that the problem of accounting for political obligation to the state on the basis of the anterior consent of individuals is solved by this example. After all, the suffrage for ratification did not include women or children. Thus the original question remains unanswered: How does their obligation to the state arise?

It appears that the only possible explanation is that the anterior consent must have occurred at the point of the original social compact. At that point all individuals are acknowledged to have participated. This seems to have been the argument of Theophilus Parsons in "The Essex Result." Parsons begins by defining political liberty in terms of consent: "Political liberty is by some defined, a liberty of doing whatever is not prohibited by law. The definition is erroneous. A tyrant may govern by laws. . . . Let it be thus defined; political liberty is the right every man in the state has, to do whatever is not prohibited by laws, TO WHICH HE HAS GIVEN HIS CONSENT. This definition is in unison with the feelings of a free people." Some standards are necessary, however, in order to determine that an individual has in fact consented to the law he is asked to obey. Without a standard of judgment the principle is obviously meaningless. "If a fundamental principle on which each individual enters into society is that he shall be bound by no laws but those to which he has consented," holds Parsons, "he cannot be considered as consenting to any law enacted by a minority." This follows from the fact that in the original compact the individual agrees to forfeit his power of consent only when the good of the whole requires it. But there can be only one judge of the common good. "If the minority can assume the right of judging, there may then be two judges; for however large the minority may be, there must be another body still larger, who have the same claim, if not a better to the right of absolute determination." It follows from this that if "the supreme power should be so modelled and exerted, that a law may be enacted by a minority, the inforcing of that law upon an individual who is opposed to it, is an act of tyranny."[18]

Parsons's argument may be reconstructed as follows: individual consent is a prerequisite of political liberty, and the only condition under which an individual enters society in the first place is a guarantee that his political liberty will be secured. Yet the individual also agrees upon making the compact that he will give up this right of consent, the definitional requirement of political liberty, when, and only when, the good of the whole requires it. Since the majority is the sole judge of this, he may only be bound by a law that he opposes when the majority requires it of him. Thus, majority rule, a logical derivative of the popular sovereignty of the social compact, embodies the right of consent or is tantamount to the same thing in political life. And this right of the majority is directly derived from the consent embodied in the original social compact.

But if popular sovereignty and majority rule are ultimately traceable to individual consent, it is at a point far removed from day-to-day experiences of political life. From the point of the initial social compact on, individual consent is subordinate to majority rule as the legitimizer of political actions. In cases where it is demonstrable that an individual has consented to obey a law, a representative assembly, or a political system, individual consent is a sufficient condition of political obligation and is an effective principle of popular control. It is only a necessary condition of political authority, however, at the very beginning, i.e., in the social compact. After that, popular sovereignty and majority rule are sufficient conditions of political authority. The predominance of these two principles is evident in the erection of the constitution and in the selection of public officials. It is hardly tenable to argue that an individual who votes on the ratification of a constitution approves of it or con-

18. "The Essex Result," in Handlin and Handlin, *Popular Sources*, p. 331. This passage from "The Essex Result" was considered in chapter 3 in relationship to the justification of majority rule in civil society. Compare Locke, *Second Treatise*, chapter 13, sections 95-99.

sents to its adoption, if he votes against it. By the act of voting, one does not consent to be ruled by a representative against whom one has voted. In both of these cases, the only pretense of consent derives from the fact that the constitution is established, and the representative is selected, by the majority. Only the majority, as Parsons noted, can speak for all individuals. This is because the sole thing to which all individuals have agreed is to be bound by the decisions of the majority. The conclusion is clear. As an operational principle of republican government, individual consent must and does give way to majority rule.

If individual consent is not a viable principle on the basis of which to construct a theory of republican government, is the entire concept of consent a huge irrelevancy? The answer is no. In the Declaration of Independence, it is held that governments derive "their just powers from the consent of the governed," and it is in this collective sense that the concept of consent operates as a foundation of republican government. While it is not possible to identify a case where the overt consent of an individual is necessary in order to account for his obligation to a law, it is clearly the case that the people as a whole can choose to demand such prior consultation whenever they wish, through the majority. The government, after all, derives its authority from a collective decision of the people, i.e., from their consent. It is, of course, true that the people do not ordinarily require that their approval be secured for every action the government might take, for this would subvert the very purpose of their having delegated authority to the government. And so the enactment of this or that law is not the object of the original consent of the people. Rather, the people consent to be governed by a particular decision-making system and agree to abide by the decisions which that system produces. This is the purpose of the governmental agreement.

It may be thought unusual that the right of consent, which would seem to inhere in individuals only, can in fact be ascribed only to a collectivity, the people as a whole. Indeed, the distinction between consenting to a decision-making system, as opposed to a particular decision, suggests that the consent of the individual might operate after all, if each individual is understood to have consented only to the system, and not to the laws it produces. But this is simply not the case, for the very good reason that when the decision-making system is erected by the framing of the constitution, the will of the individual has already been supplanted by the will of the majority. This took place at the moment of the social compact. Thus, even though certain individuals may participate in the process of determining the majority will, it does not follow that either the authority of that majority, or the authority of the system produced by it, is derived from the consent of those participating individuals. Both the authority of the majority and the legitimacy of the government are derived from the collective sovereignty of the people. Each individual is bound by the authority of the majority, and that of the government, whether or not he consents to the actions taken by either. Since popular sovereignty is itself derived from the individual consents of the residents of the state of nature, the ultimate normative sanction of majority rule may be regarded as the consent of individuals. In terms of the practical and immediate political consequences of the theory, however, individual consent is subordinate to collective consent, which translates into majority rule.

The subordination of individual consent to popular sovereignty and majority rule was evident in the debate over representation, which was center stage during the entire revolutionary era. To judge from the frequency of its appearance in the literature of the period, there was no more widely endorsed principle than that of equal representation. The great problem, however, lay in deciding to what the concept of equality was to apply. In order to understand why the people of Massachusetts placed high value on equality of representation, it is essential to recall the rationale of the representative system; a representative assembly was needed because it was not possible to have all citizens meet in order to make public decisions. Writing in the *New-England Chronicle* of June 26, 1776, a writer using the name of Watchman put it in these terms:

> Our avowed constitution is, that all power rests in the people at large, but that for the benefit of society, the same must be delegated to a select number of individuals, freely and fairly chosen by the majority of the whole, to whom they are answerable for the due discharge of the trusts committed to them, and by whom they must be supported in such discharge to prevent the anarchy that would otherwise ensue. The foundation principle on which this constitution rests, is, that great bulwark of liberty, an EQUAL REPRESENTATION.

Since the deputation of authority to a representative assembly is only a substitute for the original sovereignty of the people and is sanctioned by the approval of their majority, it seemed apparent to the people of Massachusetts that it should as closely as possible approximate their original sovereignty. And this could only be accomplished if the representation were equal, or in other words, if the representative body was an exact representation of the people in fact as well as in name.

This was clearly the position of John Adams, expressed in one of the most famous passages of his *Thoughts on Government.*

> As good government is an empire of laws, how shall your laws be made? In a large society, inhabiting an extensive country, it is impossible that the whole should assemble to make laws. The first necessary step, then, is to depute power from the many to a few of the most wise and good. But by what rules shall you choose your representatives? Agree upon the number and qualifications of persons who shall have the benefit of choosing, or annex this privilege to the inhabitants of a certain extent of ground. . . . The principle difficulty lies, and the greatest care should be employed in constituting this representative assembly. It should be in miniature an exact portrait of the people at large. It should think, feel, reason and act like them. That it may be the interest of this assembly to do strict justice at all times, it should be an equal representation, or, in other words, equal interests among the people should have equal interests in it.

According to Adams, the primary objective in securing equal representation is to achieve a balancing of interests in the assembly. This can be achieved by one of two methods: either base the representation on the principle of geography, and hope for a good random sample, or else design the suffrage in such a way so as to include a good cross section of interests. We know from what Adams has been quoted as saying on the matter of suffrage that he viewed the inclusion of all interests in the electorate as impracticable. Presumably, then, some principle of geographic representation, or a combination of the two principles, would have been his preference. In a 1776 letter to Joseph Hawley, Adams suggests that both numbers and wealth are relevant to the ratio of representation: "equality of representation in the legislature is a first principle of liberty, and the moment the least departure from such equality takes place, that moment an inroad is made upon liberty. Yet, this essential principle is disregarded in many places in several of these republics. Every county is to have an equal voice, although some counties are six times more numerous and twelve times more wealthy." It is not apparent that Adams had in mind anything like a system of interest representation of the type later advocated by Calhoun. In such a system each identifiable interest in the population would be allowed to select its own representatives. What Adams seems to have had in mind is merely to provide a mechanism whereby a sufficiently equal representation would be achieved. Sufficient for what? Adams does not say why it is that a balancing of interests is desirable. It may be assumed, however, that he was primarily concerned to prevent the domination of the government by any one interest or set of interests. If this was the case his concern was less for an inclusive electorate than it was for a safe administration of government.[19]

The concern for the avoidance of a dominant interest was reflected in the return of the town of Beverly on the Constitution of 1778. They held that representation, "which is the very basis and support of freedom in a large society, is the most exceptionable article in this Constitution."

> This most important point, the forming of a Body to represent the People, as it must be a miniature of the whole, so it ought to be, in justice and good policy too, an exact one: and the difficulty of making it so, however great, must be surmounted, For if the Representation be unequal, the Government will not long continue equal, and the time would soon arrive, when the majority of this Body, really representing but a small part of the State, might advance their own and their constituents' private interest, to the great injury and oppressive of the rest of the people. The power thus placed in their hands, combined with the almost irresistable allurements of interest will offer such a violent temptation to them to do wrong, as members of political Bodies have scarcely ever resisted with success. But, on the other hand, if that Body be a fair and exact

19. Adams, *Thoughts*, in *Works*, 4:194–195; John Adams to Joseph Hawley, ibid, 9:435.

Epitome of the People, or in other words, if the Representation be equal, it will be invariably for their interest to do strict justice; whatever is for the interest of the people at large will be for theirs too, so that the general good will be their object.[20]

Two facets of the return of Beverly are particularly interesting. First, the resemblance of this passage to Adams's *Thoughts* is striking, particularly in its adoption of his definition of equal representation as a balancing of interests. The emphasis of Beverly on the potential for abuse of power by a dominant interest is consistent with Adams's concern to achieve a balance. Secondly, and this comes as little surprise, the citizens of Beverly go beyond Adams's position to discuss their fear of a dominant interest in terms of the potential frustration of majority rule. If an equal representation is not achieved, a minority of the state may be able to pursue its own interests at the expense of the rest of the community. The grand end of civil society, the good of the whole, will not be achieved under such circumstances.

In recommending a mode of representation, the citizens of Beverly stressed equality of numbers based on equal geographic representation. "Were we to point out a mode of representation which we think right and best, we should place all on an equal footing. . . . Each county may be divided into districts and every district throughout the State contain an equal number of Freeman."[21] It is clear from this recommendation that the people of Beverly did not perceive any inconsistency between the problem of balancing interests, and that of achieving equal numerical representation. If the latter was achieved, the former would automatically follow, and majority rule would be secured. This position, however, was not endorsed by the propertied elements in the state. They perceived that a strictly numerical basis for representation might lead to a situation where the majority of persons with relatively little property would tyrannize over the property rights of those persons who held a lot of it. In attempting to justify special representation for property under the new constitution, those who had this point of view were led to develop an alternative account of equal representation which began with well-established premises, but led to

20. "The Return of the Town of Beverly on the Proposed Constitution of 1778," in Handlin and Handlin, *Popular Sources*, p. 293.
21. Ibid., p. 294.

conclusions which were at variance with the basic premises of the social compact theory. In examining their arguments, it will be possible to demonstrate that in attempting to reconcile their special concern for property with the fundamental principles of popular sovereignty and majority rule, they unintentionally reinforced those principles at the expense of their own argument.

The most complete, the most famous, and the most influential case for the property holders was presented in "The Essex Result." Indeed, the "Result" has received so much homage in the secondary literature that it has been described as ushering in a new era in the problem of political representation. According to Pole, the success of the arguments presented in the "Result" altered the terms of the debate over representation for the entire half century following its writing. Whatever may have been the impact of the "Result," its argument was faulty and theoretically at variance with the fundamental principles of the social compact theory that served as the general basis for the Constitution of 1780; it can be shown to be so on its own terms.[22]

We have already seen how, in the argument of the "Result," consent is subordinated to majority rule. This fact, however, suggests a problem. Can individual consent, especially in regard to property, be reconciled with the right of the majority to set public policy? In other words, How can the inalienable right of property be institutionally protected? In order to accomplish this somewhat intimidating task, Parsons returns to the state of nature and the original trade, on which society was based. In a state of nature each individual had control over two things: his body and his property. In respect to these two things each individual was, as it were, sovereign. Parsons has already argued, that "in a state of nature much happiness cannot be enjoyed by individuals," and so "it has been conformable to the inclinations of almost all men, to enter into a political society." But such incommodiousness did not serve to deny to each individual his *right* to control his person and property, it only limited his *power* to do so. Thus when he entered society, each individual handed over the power of controlling his person and property but only when the good of the whole required it, which determination must be made by the majority. Since the only things over which an individual has control in the state of nature are

22. Jack R. Pole, *Political Representation in England and the Origins of the American Republic* (Berkeley and Los Angeles: University of California Press, 1966), p. 172.

his person and his property, it followed on Parsons's account that "the only objects of legislation, therefore, are the person and property of the individuals which compose the state. If the law affects only the persons of the members, the consent of a majority of any members is sufficient. If the law affects the property only, the consent of those who hold a majority of the property is enough. If it affects, (as it will very frequently, if not always), both the person and property, the consent of a majority of the members, and of those members also, who hold a majority of the property is necessary. If the consent of the latter is not obtained, their interest is taken from them against their consent." What justifies this special power of consent on the part of property holders? Strangely, Parsons's answer is the principle of political equality, in a slightly bastardized form. "If each member, without regard to his property, has equal influence in legislation with any other, it follows, that some members enjoy greater benefits and powers in legislation than others, when these benefits and powers are compared with the rights parted with to purchase them. For the property-holder parts with the controul over his person, as well as he who hath no property, and the former also parts with the controul over his property, of which the latter is destitute." For Parsons, political equality means not that all individuals are on a par in respect to authority, but rather that the influence which an individual has in legislation ought to be equal to the rights the individual forfeited upon entering into society.[23]

The question immediately arises, Why are persons and property the only objects of legislation? And, if the rule of proportion is to be followed, why is it not the case that those with a lot of property should have a great deal more influence than those with very little? This point was raised by the town of Middleborough: "but if this Rule Can be Right most Certainly then if one with an Estate of £60: is properly Quallified to give one vote towards a Representative another man worth £600: ought in justice to give ten votes towards the Same Representative." Parsons provides no answers for such speculation, but instead goes on rather blithely to consider just how these principles can be institutionalized in a system of representation. In so doing,

23. "The Essex Result," in Handlin and Handlin, *Popular Sources*, p. 336. Compare Locke, *Second Treatise*, sections 25–51, 94, 120–124, 134, 138–142.

however, he suggests that the principle of proportional influence might have a broader application.

> The rights of representation should be so equally and impartially distributed, that the representatives should have the same views, and interests with the people at large. They should think, feel, and act like them, and in fine, should be an exact miniature of their constituents. They should be (if we may use the expression) the whole body politic, with all it's property, rights, and privileges, reduced to a smaller scale, every part being diminished in just proportion. To pursue the metaphor. If in adjusting the representation of freemen, any ten are reduced into one, all the other tens should be alike reduced; or if any hundred should be reduced to one, all the other hundreds should have just the same reduction. The representation ought also to be so adjusted, that it should be the interest of the representatives at all times, to do justice, therefore equal interest among the people, should have equal interest among the body of representatives. The majority of the representatives should also represent a majority of the people, and the legislative body should be so constructed, that every law affecting property, should have the consent of those who hold a majority of the property. The law would then be determined to be for the good of the whole by the proper judge, the majority, and the necessary consent thereto would be obtained: and all the members of the State would enjoy political liberty, and an equal degree of it.

This passage is interesting in several respects. Like John Adams and the town of Beverly, Parsons stresses both a balancing of interests and equal numerical representation. These principles are not only seen to be compatible with each other, but they are both held to be compatible with the principles of consent and majority rule. And here again, the principle of consent is materially expressed by the procedure of majority rule.[24]

Parsons's institutional answer for achieving this concept of

24. "The Return of the Town of Middleborough on the Constitution of 1780," in Handlin and Handlin, *Popular Sources*, p. 695; "The Essex Result," ibid, p. 341. Compare Aristotle, *Politics*, Bk. 6, chapter 3, 1-6, 1318a.

equal representation is a bicameral legislature composed of one body to represent persons and another to represent property. In making this proposal, however, he diverges significantly from the positions of John Adams and the town of Beverly. Their endorsement of the balancing of interests is general, with emphasis on no particular type of interest. And both Adams and the people of Beverly envision a system of equal representation of persons as a sufficient device for bringing about such a balancing of interests. Parsons, however, chooses to isolate property both as a separate theoretical concept and as a separate institutional element. By isolating property as an interest that requires special provision, Parsons implicitly acknowledges that property interests are not compatible with popular sovereignty and majority rule at all. If they were, special interest representation would not be necessary. And Parsons is not able to escape the logic of popular sovereignty and majority rule even in trying to argue against it, for he is forced to adopt the terminology of majority rule even as he attempts to undercut it. Indeed, he even acknowledges that "where both cannot be represented without great intricacy, the representation of property should yield the preference to that of persons."[25]

Although Parsons does not touch upon them, there were at least two other arguments which were commonly advanced in favor of special property representation. One was the argument to the effect that, since the public treasury was filled primarily on the basis of the property tax, therefore those who paid for the public business should have the greater say in deciding what the public business was to be. The other was the argument that valuation was the surest guide in determining the population distribution. Of these, only the former suggests a significant variation on the theme of popular sovereignty. The argument that representation should be apportioned according to property because of inequality in taxation, however, is quite a different argument from that of "The Essex Result." This argument does not hold that property representation is justified on the basis of any inequality of the state of nature. Rather, the inequality that develops after civil society is formed is turned into an argument against the political equality that existed antecedent to

25. "The Essex Result," in Handlin and Handlin, *Popular Sources*, p. 357. The distinction between persons and property met with some criticism; see the returns of Wrentham (p. 804), and Petersham (p. 860), ibid.

the original compact. This view was advanced by Essex County in 1776 in their petition to the General Court: "If we regard Property as the Rule of Representation, it will be found that there are certain thirty Towns and Districts in the Colony, which altogether pay to the publick Expence, a sum not equal to what is paid by one other single Town in this County; yet the former may have a Weight in the Legislative Body, fifteen Times as large as the latter; nay it will be found by Examination, that a Majority of the Voices in the Assembly may be obtained from the Members of Towns, which pay not more than one fourth Part of the publick Tax." This argument is only persuasive because it calls upon a value which in the marketplace might be acknowledged by many, viz. that a person is entitled to value in proportion to his wealth. But if this type of principle were to be adopted in the political arena, it would follow that the original terms of the social compact were liable to abridgment by conditions irrelevant to it. Specifically, it would follow that citizens stand before the law according to their contribution to it, rather than according to their original equality before it. And this would be contrary to the conditions of the original compact. Thus the argument runs counter to the premises of the social compact theory.[26]

There is, then, no sense in which property can be regarded as a direct derivate of the social compact theory, and arguments toward that end must be seen as having deviated significantly from the basic principles underlying the Constitution of 1780—popular sovereignty and majority rule. Property may be recognized and institutionalized in a constitution as a distinct interest, but only as a matter of policy adopted by the majority, and not as a right entailed by the compact theory itself.

One other interest sought such special consideration in the system of representation, the small towns, but their claims were of a character slightly different from those of the property holders. The case of the small towns was stated by the town of Lincoln, in 1780.

> Because we think the Mode of Representation pointed out in this article is not founded upon the Principles of Equality as provided for in the preceeding article—we apprehend that all Circumstances ought to be taken into Considera-

26. "Essex County Convention, Ipswich, April 5, 26, 1776," ibid, p. 75.

tion to Determine a Representation founded in Equality:
and that the number of Rateable Polls nor any other Cir-
cumstance singly Considered Determine such a Representation —This State is Constituted of a great number of
Distinct and very unequal Corporations which Corporations are the Immediate Constituent part of the State and
the Individuals are only the Remote parts in many respects
—in all acts of the Legislature which Respect particular
Corporations each Corporations hath a Distinct and seper-
ate Interest Clashing with the interest of all the rest and
so long as Humane Nature remains the same it now is Each
Representative will be under an undue bias in favour of the
Corporation he Represents —Therefore Large Corporations
haveing a Large Number of Representatives will have a
large and undue Influence in Determining any Question in
their own favour. Should the number of Rateable Polls in
any particular Corporation Increase till they over ballance
all the other they Could Compleatly Tyraniz over all the
Rest; and every Degree of Inequality given power for the
same Degree of Tyranny.

The motivation behind the claim of the small towns was clearly
the same as that of the property holders: they were afraid that
the legislature would be stacked against them because they were
in the numerical minority. And their claim was based on a per-
ception of themselves as discrete interests entitled to discrete
representation. But the basis of their claim was different from
the propertied men, in that they actually advanced the town as
the basic representational unit of the state. They were not making a claim as a class of individuals entitled to special treatment
in the system of representation: they claimed to be the units on
which the system of representation should be based. In short,
they wanted a federal system for Massachusetts.[27]

This contention had much more justification in tradition
than it did in theory. Towns were not the consenting parties to
the social compact, and no one ever asserted the natural rights of
towns, or held that laws to bind all towns must be assented to
by all towns. Yet under the colonial charters it is undeniable
that each incorporated town was the basic representational unit,
no matter what its population happened to be. The fact that

27. "The Return of the Town of Lincoln on the Constitution of 1780,"
ibid, p. 663.

town representation ran completely counter to any notion of numerical equality was not lost upon the residents of the larger towns. As early as 1776 Essex County had pointed this fact out to the General Court. "There are some Towns and Districts in the Colony in which there are between thirty and fourty Freeholders and other Inhabitants qualified to elect, only; there are others besides Boston, in which there are more than five hundred, —The first of these may sent one Representative; —The latter can send only two." The historical origins of this were not lost on the Essex convention, but it held that rules of representation, if they are to remain equal, must adapt to changing circumstances.

> In the early Period of our Settlement, when thirty or forty Families were first permitted to send each a Representative to the general Assembly, there can be no Doubt, but the proportionate Equality was duly adjusted; nor is there much more Doubt, but that, as just an equality took Place in the Representation of the several Corporations of the british Empire, when the Rule was first established there —That striking, that unjust Disproportion, which fills us with Disgust and Detestation, has arisen in Britain, chiefly from the great Increase of Numbers and Wealth in some places of that Empire and a Decrease in others, and continued from a blind attachment to the Forms of Antiquity in some, and a wicked Disposition in others, who found an effectual way to turn this Inequality to their own Advantage, though to the Destruction of the State.[28]

It is not clear precisely what issues divided the interests of the large and small towns. It is clear that there was perceived on both sides a difference in these interests sufficient to constitute a threat. The men of Essex County were not at all reluctant to enlist majoritarian arguments when they were in the majority, and the small towns were clearly opposed to majority rule where it ran counter to their own interest.

The final resolution of this issue was a compromise, and was labeled as such by the convention. All new towns were required to have 150 rateable polls before being granted a representative, but all towns already incorporated were allowed to send a representative, no matter how small they were. Towns would be

28. "Essex County Convention, Ipswich, April 25, 26, 1776," ibid, p. 74.

granted additional representatives as their populations increased. "This method of calculation," held the Convention, "will give a more exact Representation, when applied to all the Towns in the State, than any that we could fix upon."[29] The fact that the scheme of representation represented a compromise, and was acknowledged to be a compromise, is quite significant. It provides a basis for the contention that the inclusion of the principle of town representation was a deviation from the predominant principles of popular sovereignty and majority rule, in the name of political expediency. And it provides some justification for the proposition that it is possible to discern in the debates over the Constitution certain principles that were regarded as being the most fundamental, in spite of the fact that not everything which was said and done comports with them.

The practice of instructing representatives was a direct correlate of the principle of town autonomy. Jack R. Pole argues that the practice of instructions involved contradictory assumptions. His contention is that, given that the principal rationale for having a representative assembly in the first place is that it serves in lieu of a meeting of the entire body-politic, it is essential that the assembly be an exact microcosm of the population as a whole. Why? Because the decisions produced by the assembly should be the same decisions that would have been produced had everyone assembled in the first place. The assembly must, in other words, "think, feel, reason and act" like the people as a whole. But in order to do this, its individual members must have the latitude to think, reason, and act, in a natural way, without the constraints of binding instructions. Otherwise the process of deliberation would be stifled, and would not be an exact substitute for a meeting of the whole.[30]

Pole's point is well taken, and he is correct in supposing that the practice of instructions, codified under Article XIX of the Declaration of Rights of the Constitution of 1780, was logically inconsistent with the rationale for having a representative system. The point is equally telling against another plausible theory of representation. If the representative assembly is viewed as a select group of decision makers whose authority derives from their collective wisdom rather than their collective representative character, it would be absurd to admit a practice

29. "Address of the Convention, March, 1780," ibid, p. 438.
30. Pole, *Political Representation*, p. 541.

that constrained the use of the reason that justifies their use of political power in the first place. The practice of instructions is, however, compatible with the town-unit theory of representation. Assuming that each town, being possessed of a distinct interest, is a constituent part of the state, it becomes logical to suppose that it is appropriate for the town to instruct its representative. It is understood that he is functioning in the capacity of a delegate or message carrier rather than in the capacity of a trustee, or as a piece in a jigsaw puzzle, the whole of which is designed to replicate society. Indeed, the practice of instructing delegates is common to federal bodies.[31]

There was no theoretical discussion of the practice of instructing delegates in the literature, just as there was no critical discussion of the role of a representative in a republican government. Comments made in passing in the various town returns show that two principles were generally recognized. One, it was unquestionably the case that a town had the right to issue binding instructions on its representative whenever it wished. Two, it was widely recognized that a certain amount of discretion was necessary if a representative was to secure the interests of his constituents. No systematic development of the relationship between these two principles was attempted. One thing is certain, however. The practice of instructing representatives was one that accrued to towns and not to individuals, and it was not perceived as a derivative of the concept of individual consent. If it is related to consent at all, it derives from some notion of collective consent, with each town representing the collectivity.

It has taken a long time to dispose of the concept of consent as an instrument of popular control of government. We have seen that the only sense in which consent operates as an effective means of popular control of government is in a collective sense. At the outset of this discussion it was posited that there is, in addition to consent, one other principle of popular control—that of accountability. Accountability means that public

31. The point here is that if the towns are the units of representation, then there is one representative for each unit. Thus the relationship resembles the fiduciary relationship between client and attorney where the client clearly has the right to instruct, even when he chooses not to exercise it. If persons are regarded as the unit of representation, of course, there are many clients and only one lawyer, and it becomes problematical that any one of the clients should be able to tell the agent what to do. Therefore, in the absence of unanimity among the units of representation, the concept of instructions loses its plausibility.

officials are answerable to the people for their official actions. Like collective consent, accountability is a derivative of the principle of popular sovereignty, as was made express in Article V of the Declaration of Rights. "All power residing originally in the people, and being derived from them, the several magistrates and officers of government, vested with authority, whether legislative, executive, or judicial, are their substitutes and agents, and are at all times accountable to them." The distinction between the individual and the collectivity, germane to the concept of consent, does not apply to that of accountability. While there is a prima facie plausibility to the notion that an individual can and should exercise a power of prior consent, there can be no plausibility to the contention that public officials can be accountable to each member of society on an individual basis. By voting in elections, each individual member of the electorate participates in a collective judgment. In making this collective judgment, the will of the majority must prevail. Thus, the principle of accountability means that public officials are accountable to the majority. In the words of the town of Stoughton: "that the Majority of the people wherein the Supreme power is vested has a Controul over all the delegated Powers of the State; or other words, that all persons entrusted with any of the Delegated powers of the State are Servants of the people and as Such are elective by them and accountable to them and removeable for breach of Trust incapacity or misbehavior."[32]

The great advantage of the principle of accountability is that it can be made operative. All that it entails is that there be regular elections, open to all qualified citizens. It is not necessary to determine whether or not representatives are acting with the consent of the people. If they are not, they will be voted out of office. The principle of accountability is thus related to that of consent, for it carries with it the presumption that if the representatives are not doing what the people would have consented to, had they been given the chance, the representatives will be removed from office in favor of those who will. Therefore, accountability can be interpreted as a means of achieving consent (collective consent). But the theoretical strength of the principle of accountability lies in the fact that it is a purely pro-

32. "Instructions of the Town of Stoughton to its Delegate to the Constitutional Convention of 1779," in Handlin and Handlin, *Popular Sources*, p. 425.

cedural concept. It is not necessary to determine what the people want before acting, which would be an impossible task. All that is required is that the people are free to bring about changes if they are not satisfied.

Accountability was without a doubt the primary mechanism for popular control in the view of the people of Massachusetts. The stress of Articles IV, V, VII, VIII, and IX on accountability is evident, and the provisions of the Constitution for short terms of office (e.g., Chapter I, Section III, Article I), and for exclusions from offices (Chapter VI, Article II) were part of the means of achieving this end. But accountability, like collective consent, is an operational rule that is most responsive to the will of the majority. It is not a mechanism primarily designed to secure the rights of individuals against majority will. And correlatively, it is a mechanism that is very sensitive to majority indifference. Indeed, accountability is something of a vacuous safeguard in a society where the majority of the people do not care what the government does. Thus, while the principle of collective consent may be operative in the establishment of government, and in the choice of people to run it; and while the principle of accountability may be operative in that public officials are liable to expulsion from office at the will of the majority; still, individuals are not sufficiently protected against the possibility of abuse of authority, and this for two reasons. One, individuals may yet be subject to the tyranny of the majority. Two, individuals may be subject to the tyranny of government, in the face of majority indifference. Therefore, the principle of popular control of government, represented by the subordinate rules of collective consent and accountability, is insufficient for the attainment of a free government. Additional security is necessary for the rights of the individuals, and this security was to be achieved through the second principle of republican government, government by law.

Government by Law

We have seen in chapter 3 that the single restraint on the principle of majority rule is that the majority is bound to treat individuals according to the principles of equity and impartiality. This limitation is derivable both from the original political equality of the social compact, and from the analogy between the rule of the people in civil society and the rule of God in the state of nature. Neither the concept of natural rights nor the concept of individual consent provides any theoretical barriers to majority rule. Ultimately, of course, there are no barriers of any sort to majority rule because any normative limitations on majority rule must be imposed in practice by the majority itself. The problem of democratic government is that democracy allows for no absolute institutional limitations on the power of the majority. The democrat who values individual liberty must assume (or hope) that the majority will wish to act impartially and equitably. Otherwise, democracy and individual liberty (or as we have defined them here, the concepts of popular sovereignty and individual autonomy) are incompatible.The majority that acts in establishing a political system has two incentives encouraging it toward this beneficient attitude. First, the majority should recognize that impartial and equitable treatment of individuals is morally correct, and second, the majority should recognize that it is in its own interest to treat individuals impartially and equitably. (The individuals who are a part of the majority at one time or on one issue may find themselves in the minority when the next period of decision is reached.) From an analytical point of view, the only rational way to proceed is on the assumption that the majority, in setting up a political system which will act with its authority, will try to reconcile the ultimate sovereignty of the people, and the desire to have a political system that is responsive to the wishes of ephemeral majorities and which provides for the fair treatment of individuals, in the same set of institutions.[33]

Thus, the task of framing a constitution should be viewed as a majoritarian act, and the proper way to state the problem is, In setting up a political system, how can the majority reconcile the principle of majority rule with a concern for the protection of the right of individuals to fair treatment? There are two directions from which this reconciliation may be assaulted, and

33. The problem of time plagues the social compact theory. Why should a son be bound by the acts of his grandfather's generation? Why should a majority today be bound by the acts of a majority of yesterday? These problems were not explored in the literature of revolutionary Massachusetts. It would seem that any answer to them within the framework of the social compact theory would have to derive from the notion of collective sovereignty, which involves the assumption that some collective entity exists and embodies moral authority over time. Can that collectivity change its mind? Of course, whenever it wishes to do so (n.b. the Declaration of Independence).

from which it must be guarded. A majority may at some time act partially toward a minority or an individual citizen; or majority rule may itself become frustrated in favor of a biased minority that may seize political power. In a civil society organized for political action, such abuses of power can take place through the political system itself, or outside the political system. The presumption that underlies the original organization of political society is that it is the purpose of government to prevent abuses of individual rights in private life. The problem of organizing a government is to do it in a way so as to prevent such abuses through the government itself. And specifically, the dual problems are, one, how to prevent abuse of power by a majority acting through the agencies of government, and two, how to prevent abuse of power by a minority acting through the agencies of government. And in both of these cases, the question, What can be done to prevent abuse? translates into the question, What can the majority do to prevent abuse?

The general answer to this question comes under the rubric of government by law, but this concept is itself complex, involving at least two facets. First, it signifies the idea of a society that regulates its political life according to known and general rules embodied in written law. Written law includes both the fundamental law of constitutions and statutory law. Second, it signifies the concept of procedural due process of law.[34]

The idea of a written constitution was America's most original contribution to political theory. But a constitution does not spring from nature. It is an organic act of a body-politic which defines and limits the power of the rulers by whom that body-politic has chosen to be governed. A constitution places only those limitations upon the power of the people organized into political society that they choose to impose upon themselves. Rights that are stipulated to individuals in a constitution, represent instances of majoritarian self-restraint, and not ultimate limitations on the legitimacy of majority rule. The great advantage of constitutional government derives not in the ultimate

34. Custom, tradition, and habit are also arguably a part of government by law, related to, but distinct from, written law. The people of Massachusetts must have had a deep respect for tradition, particularly for the tradition of common law, but they were not satisfied to rely on unwritten law as a foundation for the new political order. There was little discussion of the problem in the literature, but no one argued that unwritten laws were sufficient safeguards for individual rights.

sanctity that it bestows upon individuals, but rather in the very real protections that it affords to individuals against other individuals, particularly against those who have political power. By defining the rules of political action, by establishing procedures by which fixed laws will be established and executed, and by reserving certain important decision-making powers to the people, constitutional government is intended to provide for the liberties of individuals the maximum security that can be achieved within a social framework. This is what constitutional government can accomplish, and this is what the people of Massachusetts tried to accomplish in adopting the Constitution of 1780.

The question of how to go about establishing a written constitution was a ripe political issue in revolutionary Massachusetts, and nowhere was this more evident than in the debate over who should partake in its making. The General Court, in 1776, sought permission to frame a new constitution, but this notion was rejected by the towns, in part because the General Court was not perceived as a proper body to perform such a task. A year later, when the Court again sought, and this time achieved, popular sanction to frame a constitution, it resorted to the ruse of convening itself into special session during the period in which it did the framing. But even this attempt to disassociate the legislative body from a role in the formation of the constitution was objected to by some. Writing in the *Independent Chronicle* of May 22, 1777, Hannibal [pseud.] had this to say.

> Besides, the method proposed for forming a constitution is altogether exceptionable. It is proposed that the General Court, or the Supreme Legislative of the State, shall form and establish a constitution. This is altogether inconsistent with the very idea of a constitution. By a constitution we mean (if we mean any thing) a system of principles established to secure the subject in the enjoyment of his rights and privileges against any encroachment of the governing part. It is therefore inconsistent that the Supreme Legislative should be the formers and establishers of a constitution: For those, who form and establish it, may of consequence at pleasure alter it. A constitution therefore formed and established by the Supreme Legislative are the source of all power; and if they can at pleasure alter the

constitution, government may at pleasure make what encroachments upon the right of the subject they please.

Hannibal is here echoing the opinions of many of the towns. The towns of Acton and Concord were the first to come out against legislatively enacted constitutions in 1776. According to Concord, "The Same Body that forms a Constitution have of Consequence a power to alter it," and "A Constitution alterable by the Supreme Legislative is no Security at all to the Subject against any Encroachment of the Governing part on any, or all of their Rights and privileges." Acton "resolved that the Supreme Legislative in their Capacity are by no means a Body Proper to form and Establish a Constitution for the following Reason (viz) Because that a Constitution Properly formed has a System of Principles Established to Secure the Subjects in Possession of their Rights and Privileges against any Incroachments of the Governing Part and it is our Oppenion that the Same Body that forms a Constitution have of Consequence a Power to alter it, and we Conceive that a Constitution alterable by the Supreme Legislative Power is no Security to the Subjects against Incroachments of that Power on our Rights and Priveliges."[35]

Lying beneath the surface of this debate concerning who should form the Constitution, was the distinction between fundamental and statutory law. The fundamental law was perceived as the set of rules on the basis of which the political game was to be played. It had its material expression in the form of the written constitution. All laws that were passed by the government pursuant to a constitutional grant of authority must conform to the fundamental law of the constitution or else be invalid. These laws were the statutory laws. This distinction between fundamental law and statutory law paralleled the distinction between the constitution and the government or administration. In the same sense that the social compact is distinct from, and superior to, the governmental agreement, so

35. "The Return of the Town of Concord on the House of Representatives Resolution of September 17, 1776," in Handlin and Handlin, *Popular Sources*, p. 153; "Return of the Town of Acton on the House of Representatives Resolution of September 17, 1776," ibid, p. 158; See also: *New England Chronicle*, August 29, 1776; *Independent Chronicle*, June 19, 1777; Handlin and Handlin, *Popular Sources*, pp. 135, 144, 160, 178, 216, 246, 318-319.

too, the constitution is distinct from, and superior to, the continuing administration of government under it. Writing in the *Continental Journal* of May 27, 1779, a writer calling himself Benevolus quotes at length from "a late elegant writer" on precisely this point.

> By constitution we mean, whenever we speak with propriety and exactness, the assemblege of laws, constitutions and customs, derived from certain . . . principles of reason, directed to certain . . . objects of public good, that compose the general system, according to which, the community hath agreed to be govern'd. By government we mean, whenever we speak in the same manner, that particular tenor of conduct which a chief magistrate, and inferior magistrates heed, in the administration of public affairs. We call it a good government, when the execution of the laws, the observation of the institutions and customs, in short the whole administration of public affairs, is wisely pursued, with strict conformity to the principles and objects of the constitution.

The relationship between fundamental and statutory law is important, and more subtle than it may first appear. While fundamental law is expressed in a constitution, it does not follow from this that statutory law presupposes fundamental law, or a constitution. And this was a point that many people in Massachusetts failed to perceive. This was the implicit assumption of the town of Boothbay, when in 1778 they argued against the admission of any anterior law under a new constitution.

> Article XXXII disapproved, because we see no more reason for adopting the Statutes of Brittain than of Rome, and are not willing that a Constitution, which opens a new era in the State, Should bring with it any old laws, except the Law of God, natural and revealed; nor give Sanction to any Statutes, except those of Congress, and such as shall be enacted by the assembly of this state after the constitution itself is ratified and in force.

Geographically, Boothbay is almost as far from Berkshire County as one could get in revolutionary Massachusetts, but the citizens of Boothbay and the dissenters in Berkshire County shared the same view of the relationship between the two types of law. "In all free Governments duly organized there is an essential

Distinction to be observed between the fundamental Constitution, and Legislation. The fundamental Constitution is the Basis and ground work of Legislation, and assertains the Rights Franchises, Immunities and Liberties of the people." This passage is taken from the memorial of the Berkshire County representatives to the General Court of November 17, 1778. In this memorial, which has already figured in the discussion of majority rule in chapter 4, the Constitutionalists reveal that they were cognizant of the difference between fundamental and statutory law, i.e., between a constitution and the administration of government under it. This led them to share in the widespread view that the legislature, as a part of the administration of government, was an inappropriate agency to form a constitution. "Legislators," said the Constitutionalists, "stand on this foundation (of fundamental law), an enact Laws agreeably to it. They cannot give Life to the Constitution: it is the approbation of the Majority of the people at large that gives Life and being to it. This is the foundation of Legislation that is agreeable to true Liberty, it is above the whole Legislature of a free state, it being the foundation upon which the Legislature stands." The constitution was perceived by the people of Berkshire County to be superior to the legislature, because it has received "Life and being" from the "Majority." But since the majority had not acted to make a compact (i.e., form a constitution), they concluded that there was no proper foundation for legislation in Massachusetts. "In this the very essence of true liberty consists, viz. in every free state the Constitution is adopted by the Majority. . . . We think it undeniably follows from the preceeding Reasonings that the Compact in this state is not yet formed: when did the Majority of the people at large assent to such Constitution." The illogicality of this argument is apparent. The Constitutionalists equated the constitution with the social compact, and concluded that the government of the province could not operate over them because the compact or constitution had not yet been formed. In other words, they held that a constitution or fundamental law is an essential condition of any law, even one approved by the majority of the people. Yet how can a majority of the people approve of and establish a constitution if their authority is not antecedent to it? And if their authority is antecedent to the constitution, how can it be conditional on the existence of the constitution?[36]

36. "The Return of the Town of Boothbay on the Proposed Constitution

In the previous chapter the primacy of majority rule as a direct derivative of popular sovereignty has been discussed at some length. In the present context, the proper relationship between majority rule, fundamental law, and statutory law must be stressed. The social compact theory does not hold that a constitution is necessary for a government, or in other words, it does not maintain that fundamental law is not only superior to statutory law, where it exists, but also that it is necessary for it to exist before statutory law can be valid. All that is necessary for law is majority rule, which is sanctioned by the very existence of civil society. Fundamental law may be prior to statutory law, but majority rule is prior to both, because popular sovereignty is prior to both. Indeed, we may look upon the concept of fundamental law as a derivative of popular sovereignty, rather than as a limitation upon it.

This does not imply that the formation of fundamental law is not of extreme importance. Indeed, the development and enactment of a constitution are two of the most important, if not the two most important actions a political society can undertake. Precisely because they feared the potential power of government, the people of Massachusetts were very concerned to bind the government within the confines of a body of fundamental law. Only by accomplishing this can the people maintain control over their government. This goal was to be achieved primarily by the adoption of a bill of rights. But even a bill of rights is an instrument of majority will, specifying the procedures that will be followed by the government when it acts.

It is natural to suppose that the provisions of a bill of rights would be primarily substantive, i.e., that they would prohibit specific actions. In the Massachusetts Constitution of 1780 this was sometimes the case, for example in Articles XXI, XXIV, XXV, and XXVI of the Declaration of Rights. Substantive limitations such as these are distinctly in the minority in the Declaration of Rights, however. It is much more often the case that such substantive limitations are made contingent upon the procedural principle of representative consent (i.e., majority rule), as for example in Articles X, XV, XX, XXIII, XXVII, and XXVIII. The reasons for this are clear. Because majority rule is the primary procedural rule of republican government, substan-

---

of 1778," in Handlin and Handlin, *Popular Sources*, p. 251; "Statement of Berkshire County Representatives, November 17, 1778," ibid, pp. 375, 377.

tive limitations on the power of ephemeral majorities are generally undesirable; it is nevertheless desirable to impose them in some cases where the enduring majority wishes to place certain powers out of the hands of a passionate majority of the moment. In most cases, however, it is sufficient to require that majority preference be clearly declared in regard to actions the government might take against individuals. It is evident that simple substantive limitations on the power of the government were not thought to be a staple of republican government. Such limitations by their very nature call into question the relationship between majorities past, and majorities present, and it is in the nature of republican government that the majority principle should not be turned against itself except in rare and important cases.

Another category of articles in the Declaration of Rights sets limitations on the government, but of a procedural rather than of a substantive sort. These are the provisions for due process of law found in Articles X through XIV of the Declaration. The reasoning which lay behind the high value that was placed on due process was articulated with great clarity in an article published in the *Continental Journal* of November 27, 1778. The article is a speech made by a Georgia Tory to a grand jury that was considering whether or not to indict him for refusal to take an oath of allegiance to the new government. The state is now verging, said the accused, toward a "very fateful precipice" which "must soon compleat the Ruin of the State, and of every individual." The cause of this imminent downfall was the denial of due process of law.

> That nothing can be more alarming, than the establishing of a power to take away liberty and property out of the usual and due course of Law, by a power distinct from and in opposition to the only legal and constitutional judiciary department. You must be convinced, gentlemen, that if the constitution, by which a people are to be governed, may be altered, infringed, or taken away, or acted contrary against, at the pleasure of those who may chuse to do so, constitutional government is at an end. . . . If a man be taken up without any previous accusation upon oath, all liberty is at an end. If a man may be condemned without any public tryal, or presence of violation of a law, all law is at an end. If he may be determined against by his known

and professed enemies, whom he is not allowed to except against, all appearance of justice is at an end.

Justice, law, liberty, even the very concept of constitutional government itself—all are contingent upon due process of law.

This emphasis on due process of law was a principal heritage of the colonial experience, deriving from the tradition of common law. A large part of the history of the English Constitution was the continuing struggle for procedural due process in the face of entrenched executive prerogatives. The right to trial by a jury of one's peers; the right to face one's accusers; the right to a speedy and public trial; the right to stand immune from double jeopardy and self-incrimination; all of these rights became established tenets of due process of law, but only after centuries of development in the common law. While the finer points of English law were not widely known in Massachusetts, these broad principles of the English Constitution were commonly accepted practices in the colonial courts, and were the common currency of political life. Perhaps because they had been accepted for so long, the principles of due process of law reflected the deep respect that the people of Massachusetts had for procedure in general. Although it was recognized that the fairest of procedures would not guarantee a fair determination of every issue or case, nevertheless, by maintaining scrupulously fair procedures, the possibilities of a just outcome are maximized. Similarly, the procedures of a fair and open election will not always insure that good men will hold public office, nor will they insure that those who are elected will be attentive to the rights of individuals. But in this case too, good procedure is the surest road to a good outcome. In the words of Simeon Howard: "But as every people have a right to be free, they must have a right of choosing their own rulers, and appointing such as they think most proper; because this right is so essential to liberty, that the moment a people are deprived of it they cease to be free." Procedure is thus important for both popular control of government and government by law, and procedural due process is especially important as a guarantor of individual rights in a system predicated upon the sovereignty of the people.[37]

37. Simeon Howard, *A Sermon Preached Before the Honorable Council, and the Honorable House of Representatives . . . May 31, 1780* (Boston, 1780), in Thornton, *The Pulpit*, p. 365.

The Separation of Powers

But due process of law must be embodied in law itself, either written, as in a bill of rights, or unwritten, as in the English common law. And, like any other sort of law, the procedural safeguards that due process provides for individuals are, in the end, parchment barriers. Laws prescribe actions, but it is men who must act, and men may ignore the prescriptions of law. Indeed, the primary fear of the people of Massachusetts, as we have seen, was precisely that those men who have the power to make or enforce laws, might be the most inclined to disobey them. For the people of Massachusetts, it was not enough merely to demark the limits of authority substantively and procedurally. In addition, the political system itself must be structured in such a way so as to prevent the abuse of power by those whose duty it is to enact and execute laws. A republic is the best of government, said John Adams in *Thoughts on Government*, because it is by definition "an empire of laws, and not of men." But the best of republics is "that particular arrangement of the powers of society, or in other words, that form of government which is best contrived to secure an impartial and exact execution of the laws."[38] Only by organizing the powers of government correctly can a government of laws exist in fact, as well as in name. The initial mechanism for insuring government by law was the principle of popular control of government itself. Next to the electoral principle, however, for the people of Massachusetts, the idea of a proper system of government reduced to a single principle: the separation of powers.

In Article XXX of the Declaration of Rights, the framers of the Constitution posited a causal connection between a principle of separation of powers and the concept of government by law.

> In the government of this Commonwealth, the legislative department shall never exercise the executive and judicial powers, or either of them: The executive shall never exercise the legislative and judicial powers, or either of them; The judicial shall never exercise the legislative and executive powers, or either of them: to the end it may be a government of laws and not of men.

38. Adams, *Thoughts*, in *Works*, 4: 194.

The phrasing of this article would seem to imply a connection between the institutional agencies—the departments—and the powers those agencies are to exercise. The implication is that each department has a particular type of power, which is germane to it, and that each department should exercise that power, and no other. In other words, Article XXX suggests some concept of power defined in terms of the department that exercises it. Yet as we have seen in our preliminary analysis of this problem in chapter 2, it is not easy to differentiate the three departments according to the types of powers they are each assigned. Each department seems to possess powers that an abstract consideration might conclude more properly belonged to one of the others. This is true in particular of the executive negative on the acts of the legislature and the legislative power of impeachment. And it does not seem possible, in considering the powers of any one of the departments, to discern a typological principle that might operate to tie all of the powers together, precisely because of the aberrant cases.

The problem is this: we wish to understand the relationship between the separation of powers clause of Article XXX and government by law, yet we are not in a good position to do so because the meaning of the separation of powers clause is not clear. It appears that it is either the case that the framers were confused in their definition of separate powers, or else that they had in mind some other conception of power than the substantive one suggested by the wording of Article XXX. In trying to understand the specific meaning of this article's principle of separation of powers in relation to the distribution of powers under the Constitution, it would have been very helpful if the framers had elaborated upon their conception of different types of power. Unfortunately, not only did they leave no record of their views on this subject; they do not appear to have thought the subject worthy of discussion at all. *The Journal of the Convention* and the correspondences of the members of the Convention leave no hint that the question of the theoretical distinction between executive, legislative, and judicial power ever arose. That the framers would have paid so little attention to a problem that now seems so apparently significant is in itself an important fact, for it suggests strongly that they at least thought there to be no doubt that they had achieved in the Frame of Government whatever they had intended by Article XXX.

In the most extensive discussion of this problem to be found in the secondary literature, Ellen E. Brennen contends that it is incorrect to interpret Article XXX in terms of any abstract notion of a type or types of power. Brennen's analysis in chapter 5 of her *Plural Office-Holding in Massachusetts* provides a reasonably exhaustive examination of the documentary evidence relating to this question. Within the context of the present discussion, it will be appropriate to review for a moment her argument and her conclusions. The principal thesis of *Plural Office-Holding* is that the concept of separation of powers as it was understood in revolutionary Massachusetts meant no more than a prohibition on plural office-holding. Plural office-holding was by all accounts a much abused practice under the colonial regime. Through their extensive power of appointment, colonial governors were able to accrue large numbers of offices in the hands of a relatively small number of faithful supporters. In many cases, this practice resulted in the frustration of the elected colonial legislatures. The lesson of this colonial experience was clear to the revolutionaries; if their new governments were to remain free, plural office-holding must be prevented. Their solution, expressed in Chapter VI of the Constitution of 1780, was a provision for incompatibility and exclusion from office. Brennen contends that this qualification was all that the framers intended by Article XXX of the Declaration of Rights. Separation of powers actually meant separation of persons and separation of departments. The departments would be separate and independent because their personnel would be separate and independent. Therefore, the exercise of their respective powers would be separate and independent, whatever those powers happened to be.[39]

Brennen's reasons for holding this position may be summarized as follows: first, the antecedent experience and evident public disapproval of plural office-holding; second, the lack of debate on the concept of power; third, the apparent inconsistencies between the allocation of powers in the Constitution and a substantive interpretation of Article XXX; fourth, the general lack of public interest in Article XXX; fifth, the fact that the General Court under the new Constitution, in its first years of operation, assumed powers and regularly undertook activities that are difficult to reconcile with a substantive con-

39. Ellen E. Brennen, *Plural Office-Holding in Massachusetts, 1760-1780* (Chapel Hill: University of North Carolina Press, 1945), pp. 136-178.

cept of separation of powers. Brennen does take cognizance of
contrary evidence. The wording of Article XXX itself she explains away on the grounds of its ambiguity. While the language
suggests a concept of power independent of any institutional
exercise of it, it does not demand that interpretation; it can be
interpreted to mean only that each department is prohibited
from exercising the powers which are assigned to the others.
The few objections to the Constitution based upon the incompatibility between Article XXX and the executive veto and the
legislative power of impeachment are harder to explain away.
Brennen is so uncomfortable in the face of these recalcitrant
towns that it is interesting to quote her at length.

> There were several towns, however, Lincoln, Middle-
> borough, Sandisfield, and Wilbraham, which objected to
> giving the Governor a veto upon legislation, on the ground
> that a separation of departments required a separation of
> powers. They understood the veto to give the Governor
> the power of a legislator.
> "Wilbraham stated: 'That the Governor shall have no
> power in Legislation—which we conceive he has in his Ob-
> jecting to Bills and the Consequence thereof according to
> the Art (Part 2: Chap & Sect 1st): Reasons; Because we
> think it is Important for the Safety of the Rights of the
> People that the three Branches of Government Should be
> kept Distinct and that a Union of them would be Danger-
> ous—to this purpose you very well Express the Matter in
> your Address in these Words—that when the same man or
> Body of men Enact Interpret and execute the Laws Prop-
> erty Becomes too precarious to be Valuable. and the Peo-
> ple are finally born down with the force of Corruption
> Resulting from the Union of those Powers. . . . we also
> conceive it to be repugnant to the 30: Art: of the Declara-
> tion of Rights where it is Declared that the Executive Shall
> never Exercise the Legislative and Judicial Powers or either
> of them. . . . But the Governor in Consequence of his Elec-
> tion as Chief Executive Officer ought to be excluded a
> Voice in Legislation as much as the Supream Judicial
> Judges.' " In the above statement, the separation of de-
> partments would seem to be understood to extend to a
> separation of powers. The Constitution did not go far

enough in separating the departments of government, in the opinion of these towns.[40]

It is apparent that Brennen has no real explanation for the several towns who obviously did think that Article XXX should be interpreted substantively. The example she chooses to cite is an interesting one, however. The provision for a limited negative on the laws in the hands of the executive was argued for, and was argued against, on the same grounds: the separation of powers. Some thought as did Wilbraham, that to give any role in legislation to the executive violated the doctrine. Others felt that a negative power was necessary if the executive department was to remain independent of the legislative department. The former concern reflects a substantive concept of separation of powers; the latter reflects an institutional understanding of it.

Obviously there were, then, alive in the political debates in revolutionary Massachusetts, two differing concepts of separation of powers. Brennen is justified in asserting that the framers of the Constitution subscribed to the institutional view: for them, separation of powers meant the independence of departments, and this was to be achieved by separating the persons who occupied the offices of each. The weight of the evidence is heavily in favor of this interpretation. Brennen has little to say about why this was the case, however, and nothing to say at all about the relationship between these two concepts of separation of powers. Within the context of the present discussion, the following observations may be advanced.

Consider for a moment, Article XXX, but do it backwards. The objective is a government of laws, and not of men; the means is the separation of powers clause, which we now understand to mean a separation of persons. Why does the latter serve to affect the former? In order to answer this question, it is necessary to reconsider why such a high value was placed on government by law. Government by law is designed to prevent the abuse of power. It is not principally a mechanism to limit the scope of power, but on the contrary, it is a means of implementing a power which is virtually limitless. How can the abuse of power be prevented without limiting power itself? The answer is that if power cannot be limited, and if its abuse must be

40. Ibid, pp. 159–160.

prevented, then power must be dispersed and balanced so that
it can act as a check on its own potential abuse. Give some
power to a number of people, make them independent of each
other, set their powers on a collision course, and a balancing of
power will be achieved. Within this structure of power resides
an equilibrium upon which rest the rights of individual citizens.
This is the rationale behind the principle of separation of persons, and this is the reason why the separation of persons is
causally related to the concept of government by law. Law will
prevail because the dispersal of power will operate to contain
individual political actors within the bounds of law. It is, therefore, the dispersal of power which is of primary importance to
government by law, and not the particular way in which power
is dispersed. In this reasoning we see again the heavy emphasis
procedure and structure play in the theory of republican government. The only claim that the individual can legitimately
advance against the state is a claim to fair treatment, which
means fair procedure. But fair procedure can itself only be
achieved if institutions are structured properly.

The question of what type of power ought to be assigned to
which department, therefore, is not necessarily related to Article XXX. There certainly is some logic in differentiating between the power to enact, interpret, and enforce laws, as noted
by the Convention in its "Address"; and there can be no doubt
that the people of Massachusetts were aware of this logic. Writing in the *Massachusetts Spy* in 1776, O.P.Q. contended that
*"the placing the legislative and executive powers in the same
hands,* is unconstitutional, impolitic, oppressive and absurd."
The people of Massachusetts should take early provision to
guard against such an allocation of power, and the reasons for
such a provision "existed in the nature and necessity of government, before any express constitution took place, and consequently are fundamental to that constitution." O.P.Q. gave
three reasons in support of this contention. One, the separation
of powers accords with the principle of division of labor: "the
highest improvements in every art and science, as well as in every kind of business in life, is made by attending to but one
thing at a time." Two, the prevention of the accrual of undue
influence which "those who were in both might have in the
legislature." Third, the fact that for a "judge to determine upon
appeals from his own judgment, is so repugnant to the common
law, yea to the first principle of justice and equity, that it need

only be mentioned as incident to the investiture of the legislative and executive powers in the same person, to shew its absurdity, its impolicy, its unconstitutionality and oppressive tendency." Of these three reasons, the second and third make it apparent that O.P.Q. had in mind a separation of persons, since the problem derives from allowing the same persons to sit in both legislative and executive departments. But it is also apparent that O.P.Q. recognized that there were rational criteria for distinguishing between the functions of each department as well.[41]

The distinction between making, executing, and interpreting law, and the concomitant division of political institutions into legislative, executive, and judicial departments, while it may appear obvious today, was in fact brought about only after decades and even centuries of differentiation in English political institutions. As late as 1766 John Adams, in his third letter from "The Earl of Clarendon to William Pym," referred to the judicial system as a part of the executive power. After defining the English Constitution in terms of the traditional three forms of government (monarchy, aristocracy, and democracy), Adams contended that according to the definition, "the first grand division of constitutional powers is into those of legislation and those of execution." Adams's principal thesis was that under the English Constitution, there was a degree of popular control over each of these powers. In relation to the power of legislation, the people have an influence through the electoral process. In relation to the power of execution, the people have an influence through the jury system.[42]

> The other grand division of power is that of execution. And here the king is, by the constitution, supreme executor of the laws, and is always present, in person or by his judges, in his courts, distributing justice among the people. But the executive branch of the constitution, as far as respects the administration of justice, has in it a mixture of popular power too. The judges answer to questions of fact as well as law; being few, they might be easily corrupted; being commonly rich and great, they might learn to despise the common people, and forget the feelings of

41. O.P.Q. [pseud.], *Massachusetts Spy*, May 18, 1776, in Handlin and Handlin, *Popular Sources*, pp. 82–83.
42. John Adams, "The Earl of Clarendon to William Pym," in *Works*, 3: 480, 481.

> humanity, and then the subjects liberty and security would
> be lost. But by the British constitution . . . the jurors an-
> swer to the question of fact. In this manner, the subject
> is guarded in the execution of the laws. . . . Innocence
> therefore is so well protected in this wise constitution,
> that no man can be punished till twenty-four of his neigh-
> bors have said upon oath that he is guilty.[43]

Here can be seen the intimate relationship between government
by law and popular control. Adams clearly perceived popular
control of government as one means of securing government by
law. But beyond this, the passage is interesting in that it suggests just how recently prior to the Revolution was the tripar-
tite typology of political power. By 1776, Adams himself in
Thoughts on Government speaks of a separate and independent
judiciary, and the need to make the judiciary department independent of the executive was a matter of common agreement.
Probably the machinations of Governors Bernard and Hutchinson in the years between the Stamp Act and the Revolution
had much to do with solidifying this view, for they exercised
influence primarily through their appointments to the courts.
Whatever the case, the result was clear: a differentiation into,
and a demand for, three independent branches of government.

The debates surrounding two issues, the executive veto of
legislation and the method of appointing judges, reveal just how
complex the problem of separation of powers was seen to be,
particularly in relation to the principle of popular control. Because of their experience under the colonial administrations,
most people were averse to a powerful governor. Indeed, several
of the publicists and towns were against having any governor at
all, preferring simple legislative democracy. Although such a
system is apparently contrary to the principle of separation of
persons, it was not always perceived to be so. Consider the return of the town of Rehobeth in 1780.

> We therefore give our Reasons for Rejecting a Governor
> Senate and etc. is from our Being of opinion that our
> safety and happiness Esentially consists in being governed
> by one house of Representatives which shall be stiled the
> Great and General Court of the Commonwealth of the
> Massachusetts to be elected Annually. Whose Rules and

43. Ibid., p. 481.

Regulations shall be simeler to that of the Honourable
Continental Congress. And the House of Representatives
to Annually Ellect all the Executive officers and all other
Publick Officers Except Judges of Probates of Wills and
Register of Deeds which ought forever Hereafter be Done
in Each Respective Town and all Military officers to be
chosen Agreable to the Proposed form of Government
and the Judges of the Supreme Judicial Court to hold
their office During their good Behaviour and no Legislative officer to be an Judicial officer and no Judicial officer
to be an Executive officer etc. all which objections and
amendments we think absolutely Nesecary for Enjoying
a free well Regulated Government.

Although there was to be no independent executive, and only
one house in the legislature, which would have the power to appoint all executive and major judicial officers, the people of
Rehobeth believed that the principle of separation of powers
could still be preserved by a separation of persons. Their point
of disagreement with the framers and most of the other towns
was, then, not over the desirability of separation of persons,
but only over the means by which, and the extent to which, it
should be imposed.[44]

This question translates into another, viz. How independent
should the persons holding each type of power be? Most people
in Massachusetts thought that more independence was needed
than the plan of Rehobeth would have provided for. Even those
who feared a too strong executive recognized that a governor
would have to be strong enough to enforce the laws, and this
required a degree of independence. Indeed, the principal threat
to the independence of the governor was thought by most to
be the legislature itself. Those who argued for a "three-part legislature" or in other words for an absolute executive veto on
acts of legislation, did so on the grounds that it was necessary in
order to keep the executive branch from being dominated by
the legislative. In arguing thus, the town of Newburyport (the
birthplace of "The Essex Result") emphasized the need for an
independent executive and illuminated the relationship between
the separation of powers and the separation of persons.

44. "The Return of the Town of Rehobeth on the Constitution of 1780,"
in Handlin and Handlin, *Popular Sources*, p. 528.

They conceive it to be of great importance that the governor as supreme executive magistrate should have with the advice of the council a negative upon all the acts of the legislature that so the executive branch of the constitution may ever be kept distinct from and independent of the legislature, and the due balance between the two powers preserved, they are of aprehensive that without this check the legislative will encroach by degrees on the judicial as well as the executive till at length, both of the latter will be stripped of all their rights and powers. and united with the former, and if ever this event happens, if ever the legislative body shall become the judicial and executive also, if in other words, the same body of men may make interpret and execute the laws, there will be an end of civil liberty, for such a body will enact such laws, and such only as it chooses to execute, it will cause the laws in being to speak what language it pleases, and affix such a sense to them as it finds convenient, and there and then justify such interpretation, and their doings in consequence of it, However tyranical by a retrospective law, declare such sense to be the true one. . . . In short this union which each of these powers has ever attempted to effect, and against which the proposed negative of the supreme executive is the only effectual security, has in all ages been productive of innumerable mischief and the greatest calamnities.

In this exposition the citizens of Newburyport made it clear that the process of political power (i.e., the process of taking political action by law in relation to individual citizens), has an interior logic. Before a law can finally be applied to an individual it must undergo the three processes of enactment, interpretation, and execution. By assigning each of these powers to distinct persons, the integrity and impartiality of the process as a whole will be maximized, and the possibility of the entire process being corrupted at the expense of an individual will be minimized.[45]

Within this framework of separating powers by separating persons, there remained much room for variations. Allowing the governor any role in legislation at all is a violation of both principles, yet it was thought to be necessary if the separation

45. "The Return of the Town of Newburyport on the Constitution of 1780," ibid, p. 916.

of persons and powers was in other respects to work properly. Thus the principles must be excepted if they are to be achieved. Additionally, the concept of dispersing power can come into conflict with the principle of popular control. By dispersing power, each branch of the government becomes independent of each of the others to some degree. Yet there is also the possibility that they will achieve another sort of independence, independence from the people. This problem surfaced over the question of the tenure and mode of appointing judicial officers.

A great debate under the colonial regime revolved around the question of whether or not judges should hold their offices during good behavior or at the pleasure of the king. Judges who served at the will of the king could be expected to make decisions pleasing to him, a possibility of which the colonists were aware. But judges appointed during good behavior are often hard to get rid of, even when their behavior is less than exemplary. Therefore, many towns wanted to have the judges under the new constitution elected, and for relatively short terms of office. They preferred, in other words, to depend on the principle of popular control. Thus, there were two concepts of independence that related to the judiciary department, as can be seen by comparing the following quotations.

> You will readily conceive it to be necessary for your own Safety, that your Judges should hold their Offices during good behaviour; for Men who hold their places upon so precarious a Tenure as annual or other frequent Appointments will never so assiduously apply themselves to study as will be necessary to the filling their places with dignity. Judges should at all Times feel themselves independent and free. ["Address of the Convention"] [46]

> Then passed to the Consideration of the Judiciary Department—and proposed the following alteration (viz) that the Judges of the Supreme Judicial Court be Annually Elected at large through the State—The Judges of the Inferiour Court and of Probate of Wills and Justices of the peace be annually Elected by each County—For this Reason it keeps each Branch more Immediately Dependent upon the People—and therefore will Serve to keep the three Branches

46. "Address of the Convention, March, 1780," ibid, p. 439.

> Distinct and Independent of each other and as each Branch
> are the Substitutes of the People according to the Declara-
> tion of Rights, Article 5th—we think each Branch should
> also be Elected by the People,—but it is Said in the Ad-
> dress if the People Should Elect their Judicial and execu-
> tive Officers, it will forever keep them under the Countroul
> of Ambitious artful and interested Men who can obtain
> most votes for them—Observe, it is said Interested men, are
> ambitious and will do much hurt in the Society and will
> make Elections Dangerous—whence then the Reason of
> making Interest a Qualification for either Electors or Elec-
> ted, (if there is any wieght in the objection, it lies equally
> against all Elections, and if the Inconveniencies arising
> therfrom are Sufficient to give all elections, then let us
> give them all up, otherwise let us Retain them—But we are
> of opinion that it is an important right and ought to be Re-
> tained for the Welfare of Generations Yet unborn. ["The
> Return of the Town of Wilbraham"] [47]

It appears that the Convention was as concerned to keep the
judiciary free from the influence of the people as it was to maintain its independence from the other branches of the government. Wilbraham on the other hand believed that the best way
to maintain the independence of the judiciary from the legislative and executive was to give it a separate foundation in the
popular suffrage. Both passages reflect a desire to have power
dispersed among those who are to hold it. Wilbraham was less
concerned than the framers to set limits on the power of the
majority.

In both of the principal debates relative to the separation of
powers, that concerning the role of the governor in legislation,
and that concerning the independence of the judiciary, the principle criticisms of the plan of the Convention were from the
"left." That is, they were in the name of a more popular (i.e.,
more majoritarian) government. In the case of the executive
negative on the laws, the protesters wanted to insure the subordination of the executive to the legislature. They identified
the legislature with their right of self-government and viewed
the executive as the primary threat to it. In the case of judicial
appointments, they wished to keep the judges immediately de-

47. "The Return of the Town of Wilbraham on the Constitution of 1780,"
ibid, p. 623.

pendent upon the people. As it developed, of course, the more "conservative" elements did succeed in achieving their own concept of an independent executive and judiciary. And in each case the motive behind the provisions for independence was to insure government by law, which in turn translates into fair and impartial treatment of individuals in the face of the superior force of majority rule.

The only questions which remain to be answered, therefore, are, Did the framers intend to set an outer limit on the exercise of majority rule by including provisions for independent executive and judiciary branches? Did they try to frustrate the principle of majority rule while at the same time paying lip service to it? The answer to this set of questions is both yes and no, and in clarifying why this is the correct answer, we may bring the discussion of the theory of government of the Massachusetts Constitution to a close. The answer is no for the following reasons. First, neither the provision for a limited executive veto, nor the provision for life tenure during good behavior for judges, set any ultimate limit on majority rule. The governor was, after all, to be annually elected, and both he and the judges were liable to be removed from office by the legislature for misbehavior. Thus the provisions for independence of executive and judicial authority cannot be said to provide any absolute or ultimate barrier to the rule of the majority. Second, these provisions do not require an assumption of antidemocratic intent. We have already made it clear that what the framers were trying to achieve by a system of laws based on the separation of powers was the securement of fair and impartial treatment of individuals within a framework of majority-rule democracy. This involved establishing a political system that would hinder the majority from the immediate and untrammeled exercise of its will. It did not involve developing principles of minority rule. Third, and finally, it must be remembered that all the provisions of the Constitution had to be approved by an extraordinary majority of two-thirds of the freemen of the state, of age twenty-one or over, in a free and open vote. If the framers intended to subvert majority rule, they were brazen politicians indeed.

But the element of truth in these questions should not be ignored. There was disagreement in Massachusetts over the extent to which majority rule should be allowed to operate freely, and this disagreement took place among individuals who were equally committed to the theoretical premises of majority rule. Clearly the framers had more reservations about the wisdom of simple majoritarianism than did some of the people in the dissentient towns. And clearly they intended to use the principle of separation of powers as one means of effecting a limitation on the power of ephemeral majorities. In this sense, the framers were trying to frustrate the immediate operation of the majority principle, but this should be distinguished from an intention to invalidate the ultimate authority of it. It was this very caution where majority rule was concerned, this very desire to limit majority rule through the principles of government by law and the separation of powers, that made the framers a special type of democrat: it made them republicans.

V

Commonwealth

The Social Compact Theory Summarized

In a 1776 letter to Francis Dana, John Adams expressed a wish about the government of his home state. "I hope," said Adams, "the Massachusetts will call their government a commonwealth. Let us take the name manfully." Four years later Adams was to see his wish fulfilled, when the people of Massachusetts chose to style themselves as "the Commonwealth of Massachusetts" in the Constitution of 1780. In choosing this title for themselves, the people of Massachusetts were doing more than just selecting a name for their government. They were saying something about the character of their society. For them the word "commonwealth" signified the fact that, as a people, they were bound together by the bonds of blood and common heritage, as well as by those of common interest. The purpose of their joining together in society and government was to secure their collective well-being, their common wealth. Indeed, the concept of the common good was inextricably linked with the meaning of civil society itself, and this link was made express in the label "commonwealth." John Locke, in his *Second Treatise of Government* had defined commonwealth in these terms: "By *Common-wealth*, I must be understood all along to mean, not a Democracy, or any Form of Government, but *any Independent Community* which the *Latines* signified by the word *Civitas*, to which the word which best answers in our Language, is *Commonwealth*, and most properly expresses . . . a Society of Men." A commonwealth was for Locke a community, a civitas, and in adopting the title for themselves, the people of Massachusetts recognized their own sense of being a political society.[1]

1. John Adams to Francis Dana, Philadelphia, August 16, 1776, in *The Works of John Adams*, ed. Charles Francis Adams, 10 vols. (Boston: Charles C. Little and James Brown, 1851), 9:429–430; John Locke, *Two*

But what form of government should the Commonwealth of Massachusetts adopt? Theophilus Parsons, in "The Essex Result" answered the question this way:

Was it asked, what is the best form of government for the people of the Massachusetts-Bay? we confess it would be a question of infinite importance: and the man who could truly answer it, would merit a statue of gold to his memory, and his fame would be recorded in the annals of late posterity, with unrivalled lustre. The question, however, must be answered, and let it have the best answer we can possibly give it. Was a man to mention a despotic government, his life would be a just forfeit to the resentments of an affronted people. Was he to hint monarchy, he would deservedly be hissed off the stage, and consigned to infamy. A republican form is the only one consonant to the feelings of the generous and brave Americans. Let us now attend to those principles, upon which all republican governments, who boast any degree of political liberty, are founded, and which must enter into the spirit of a FREE republican constitution. For all republics are not FREE.

According to Parsons, Massachusetts should have a republican government, and this was a view which was shared by the people of Massachusetts. But Parsons was even more demanding. A republican government would be the best form of government, but that form would be an empty shell unless enlivened by the spirit of political liberty. For Parsons, the objective was a free republic.[2]

The Massachusetts Constitutional Convention agreed with Parsons. On Friday afternoon, September 3, 1779, it passed, as its first substantive order of business, the following two resolutions.

Resolved, unanimously, That the Government to be framed by this Convention, shall be a FREE REPUBLIC.

Resolved, That it is the Essence of a free Republic, that the People be governed by FIXED LAWS OF THEIR OWN MAKING.

Treatises of Government, ed. Peter Laslett (New York: The New American Library, 1960), p. 400.

2. "The Essex Result," in Handlin and Handlin, eds., The Popular Sources of Political Authority (Cambridge: Harvard University Press, Belknap Press, 1966), p. 330.

In these two resolutions are captured, in remarkably concise terms, the essential principles of the political theory of the Massachusetts Constitution of 1780. The government of Massachusetts was to be a free republic. If the end of civil society is the common good, and if this end is expressed in the term "commonwealth," then the only suitable government for that commonwealth is a republic, or in the Latin a "res publica" or "public thing." A republican government, because it is a public thing, has as its end the attainment of the public good. It was defined, however, in procedural terms. A republic is a government in which the people make the laws. Because Massachusetts was to be a representative democracy in which the laws were to be made by the elected representatives of the people, it fulfilled this definitional requirement. But the people of Massachusetts were also to be governed by fixed laws. Therefore their government would be a free republic.[3]

A free republic is best suited for a commonwealth, because in a free republic the common good is most apt to be achieved. In other words, when the people govern by fixed laws, which they have made themselves, the common good will probably be secured. In no other form of government is there any guarantee of this. Why is it the case that a free republic is more likely to achieve the common good than any other form of government? Since only the people as a whole are motivated to secure the common interest, it is therefore the people as a whole who should govern if the common interest is to be achieved. But the people as a whole might seek the common good at the expense of private rights. Therefore, only if the people govern by fixed laws that provide security for individuals, are the good of society and the good of each member of society both apt to be secured. When this is the case, the common good may be said to have been secured to the fullest possible extent.

These general conclusions are implicit in the resolutions of the Convention, but they are in fact derivable from the social compact theory underlying the Constitution, as that theory has been elucidated in this essay. In undertaking this study, it was posited that there existed in the literature of the American Revolution, a tension between two sets of principles, associated respectively with the concepts of individual autonomy and pop-

3. *The Journal of the Convention for Framing a Constitution of Government for the State of Massachusetts-Bay* (Boston: Dutton and Wentworth, 1832), p. 24.

ular sovereignty. It was asserted that determining the relative priorities of these two sets of principles is necessary, in order to understand correctly the political thinking of the Americans of revolutionary Massachusetts. Having examined in depth the social compact theory underlying the Massachusetts Constitution of 1780, it is now appropriate to make express our conclusions in respect to the question of the relative priorities of the two concepts at each stage of the social compact theory. In so doing it will be possible to clarify the way in which the conclusions expressed in the discussion of republican government, are as obviously derivative from the social compact theory as they are obviously implied in the two resolutions of the Convention.

The relationships between the concepts of popular sovereignty and individual autonomy, within the social compact theory, may be usefully illustrated in a simple chart. In Table 1, the stages of the social compact theory are listed on the side, and the major principles associated with the concepts of individual autonomy and popular sovereignty are arrayed across the top. The boxes contain brief descriptions of the status of each principle at each stage of the theory. As may be seen in this chart, the state of nature is governed by the concept of individual autonomy. All individuals are possessed of their natural rights, and no individual should be subject to any political action to which he has not consented. Each individual seeks to satisfy his own interests, and is acting rightly in so doing. In the state of nature, the individual is supreme. He is subject to the laws of God, but he is at liberty to decide whether or not to follow those dictates of conscience.

Unfortunately the supremacy of each individual in the state of nature is de jure and not de facto. For where interests conflict, the only resolution of the conflict lies in an appeal to force. Since the state of nature is not a state of physical equality, the interests of the weak must give way to the interests of the strong. Indeed, since not all men in a state of nature will obey the laws of nature and the laws of God, even the natural rights of many individuals will be insecure in the state of nature. It is the insecurity engendered by these conditions that provides the primary incentive for individuals to join together in the bonds of civil society, in order that the power of the whole may be employed to protect the rights and interests of each.

Upon the transition from the state of nature to civil society, the situation changes drastically. Since all individuals join society for their own protection, the primary obligation of civil society is to protect all individuals. The interests of all or most, must take precedence over those of one or a few. This collective interest, or the common good, is the end of civil society, and all individual interests must be subordinated to it. In forming a civil society all individuals are equal partners, and therefore in civil society all individuals must participate equally in the making of decisions. The collective consent of the people, therefore, becomes the proper procedural mechanism for the making of political decisions. Since the people as a whole will rarely agree unanimously in the making of any decision, a decision-making rule is needed in order to determine the popular will, and it must be as consistent as possible with the original political equality of all individuals in civil society. This decision rule is majority rule. The majority of the people in civil society must speak for the people as a whole in all cases, and in particular, it is the majority that must decide what is, and what is not, in the common interest. Self-interest is still the primary motivation behind individual behavior in civil society, but it is no longer the principal standard of political right. In civil society, self-interest yields to the common good as the standard of political right.

Perhaps the most significant difference between the state of nature and civil society is in the area of individual rights. In the state of nature, individuals are possessed of both alienable and unalienable natural rights. When individuals enter civil society, however, they give up their alienable natural rights and retain only their unalienable rights. This forfeiture is the price they must pay for the security of civil society. When constitutional government is established, of course, the individual members of society may be accorded civil rights by the people. During the state of civil society, prior to the framing of a constitution, the individual is protected by his unalienable natural rights only. These rights relate to the most basic manifestations of the human character, and protect the individual only under conditions where his very existence is threatened by the political authority of the people. In light of this fact, it is not surprising that civil societies invariably erect constitutional governments at the moment of their inception.

The transition from the state of nature to civil society involves a fundamental change in the relative priorities of popular sovereignty and individual autonomy. This transition is, there-

Table 1. The Social Compact Theory

Individual Autonomy

	Individual Consent	*Individual Rights*	*Self Interest*
The State of Nature	The only procedural prerequisite of any individual action. Applies to all individuals equally	Alienable and unalienable natural rights are valid. Exercise of rights is very insecure. No authority to enforce rights except individual strength	The principal end of individual behavior. Motive force behind individual actions, especially in choosing to join civil society
Unorganized Civil Society	Becomes subordinated to collective consent. Still a sufficient condition of political obligation, but no longer necessary	Unalienable natural rights are still valid. Power to control alienable rights forfeited to the majority of the political community	Still a motive force, but normatively subordinate to common good
Constitutional Government	Some individuals may consent to the substance of a constitution through popular ratification	Unalienable natural rights are still valid. Civil rights are specified in a constitution. Individuals are entitled to due process of law	Motivates individuals to participate in making a a constitution
Administration	Some individuals may consent to be governed by other individuals, through the act of voting in elections	Unalienable natural rights are still valid. Civil rights are enforced by a government limited by the dispersal of power, and the electoral process	Motivates and guides individuals in voting for public officials

Popular Sovereignty

	Collective Consent	Majority Rule	Common Good
The State of Nature			
Unorganized Civil Society	A necessary normative prerequisite of any political action	Decision-making mechanism for expressing the collective consent of the people. Majority speaks for the people in all cases	The end of civil society. The ultimate standard of political right
Constitutional Government	Creates and institutionalizes fundamental law in in a constitution	Majority expresses popular will in adopting a constitution. Exercise is limited by consent of the people	The objective of establishing a constitution. Rights of individuals are recognized to be a part of it
Administration	Establishes governmental institutions that are accountable to the people collectively	Decision rule in elections and in legislative bodies. Procedurally limited by the separation of powers, and due process of law	Governmental institutions work to achieve it within constitutional limitations

fore, the most crucial one within the social compact theory. The transition from the stage of civil society to the stage of civil society under constitutional government involves a change, but of an institutional rather than a normative sort. The relative priorities of the two concepts and their concomitants do not change when constitutional government is established. Rather, they are institutionalized in the constitution, as the civil society organizes itself for political action. Under the constitution, individuals are accorded civil rights in lieu of the alienable natural rights they forfeited when they joined into civil society. Civil rights are claims to freedom that individuals may advance against the authority of government. These rights are sanctioned by the sovereignty of the people, however, and do not constitute claims against that sovereignty, nor against the majority rule by which it is expressed.

In establishing a constitution, the people create political institutions through which they expect to effect their political will and achieve their collective well-being. The government thus created is charged with the responsibility of protecting individual citizens in the enjoyment of their civil rights, against the invasions of other citizens. In order to accomplish this, the government establishes laws by which it regulates the behavior of individuals. The political authority of the people and the political power they have invested in their government stand behind these laws. The government, of course, is itself composed of a number of individuals, and therefore must be subject to some restraint in order to prevent those individuals from turning political power to their own unjust ends. To prevent such an abuse from occurring, certain of the more important civil rights of individuals are enshrined in the constitution as fundamental law. In addition, the people may choose to set constitutional limits on the power of government by forbidding it to take certain actions, and by reserving some decisions from its grant of power to government. The fundamental law of the constitution is not, however, the only way in which government by law protects individuals from the tyranny of government. The government can only act on individuals through democratically enacted laws that are executed and interpreted on the basis of procedures specified in the constitution. Because of these constitutional requirements, statutory laws tend to be well known, impartial, and relatively stable. They are, in other words, fixed laws. Thus the principle of government by law permeates both the stage of constitutional government and the stage of administration.

Government by law is a major support of a free government, but it is not enough. It is only effective as long as the will to obey the law is strong. If those who hold political power choose to ignore the process of law, individuals will suffer the loss of their civil rights. The principle barrier against this possibility is the electoral process. Through it, the people exercise control over their public officials by holding those officials accountable for the exercise of their public trust. The principle of popular control of government is supportive of the civil rights of individuals, because the people can be expected to demand that the government honor those rights. It is in the common interest that civil rights remain inviolate, therefore the power of the whole will be employed to protect the rights of each.

In cases where a majority of the whole for some reason wishes to abridge the rights of an individual or a minority, the principle of popular control of government can be turned against the civil rights of individuals. In a republican government, there can be no ultimate institutional restraint against the majority, and therefore there can be no ultimate safeguard against this possibility. The most that can be done is to make it more difficult for the majority to act perniciously. This may be accomplished through the dispersal of power. By distributing the powers of government to make, execute, and interpret the laws among three departments of government, by making each sufficiently independent to resist the encroachments of the others, and by separating the personnel of these departments, the people make it more difficult for an ephemeral majority to use the powers of government unjustly. In order to do so, the majority would have to gain control of all three departments of the government, making its evil intentions apparent along the way, and this would be very difficult to do.

In this way the people do all that they possibly can do to protect the rights of individuals without impairing their own sovereignty. For the sovereignty of the people is the ultimate value in civil society. In a free republic, the civil rights of individuals should be protected, but these rights cannot be elevated above the source of their own legitimacy, which is the people. Indeed, the subserviency of the principles associated with the concept of individual autonomy to the principles associated with the concept of popular sovereignty is the most important characteristic of the social compact theory, as can be seen in Table 1. As soon as the people become a people through the social compact, they become more important than any individual. The government that they create is to serve their interests, and in securing those interests it faces no ultimate restraints. The only limitations upon the exercise of political power are procedural in nature, and these are instituted by the people in the constitution. There are no absolute restraints on the power of the people.

The emphasis of the social compact theory on procedure is perhaps its most important recommendation for political theory. In political life, proper procedure is all important. Political power must not be prevented from achieving its proper ends, and therefore must not be subjected to absolute limitations. By its very nature, in fact, it cannot be limited, since the people in whom it resides must also determine its limitations, a matter of procedure inherent in the nature of political life itself. Not only is it the case that the political power of the people is without effective limit in an ultimate sense; it is also true that, under the constitutional limitations imposed by the people upon government, the government must be responsive to the wishes of the people. The procedural mechanisms by which the people bring about this responsiveness are as important as any procedural limitations on the power of government, and indeed, more so. For in those procedures is embodied the principle of popular sovereignty, the most important political principle of all. In a republican government, the people, if they are persistent, must, will, and should, have their way.

The Text of the Constitution Reconsidered

The aspiration of the Convention to frame a "free republic" in which the people are "governed by fixed laws of their own making" was then, a logical derivative of their general theoretical perspective. The final question that this essay must address is simply, Were they successful? Did they, in other words, create a free republic by the standard of their own social compact theory? The answer to this question is clearly yes. In chapter 2 a number of questions were raised concerning the implicit tension between the individual and the people, which permeates the Constitution. The answers to many of those questions will by now have become apparent, and so it will suffice to conclude by returning to the text of the Constitution in order to reassess this tension between the individual and society in general terms. In so doing, the extent to which the Massachusetts Constitution of 1780 stands as an exemplary product of the social compact theory may be brought into clearer perspective.

The dichotomization between the individual and the people is the most distinguishing feature of this Constitution, just as it is the most distinguishing feature of the social compact theory. The people in this case are the people of the Commonwealth of Massachusetts, and the individuals are the citizens of that Commonwealth. The people have the right, under the Constitution that they have established, to elect those who will govern them, to hold those officials accountable for their actions, to provide for their safety and happiness by supporting religion, and to consult upon the common good. In sum they have the "sole and exclusive right of governing themselves, as a free, sovereign, and independent state." Each individual, under the Constitution, has the right to be protected by society, the right to have recourse to the laws, the right to be governed by certain laws, the right to an impartial interpretation of the laws and administration of justice, and numerous other procedural rights. The tension between the rights of the people and the rights of individuals, which was the cause of initial confusion, is easily resolved with the benefit of the enlarged understanding gained through the examination of the political thought of the period in chapters 3 and 4.

Perhaps the most important fact, which must be stressed, is that the rights of the people and the rights of individuals are not necessarily incompatible, and were not perceived to be so by the people of Massachusetts. While the tension between the two is apparent, it is also apparent that it was not a tension that worried the framers of the Constitution overly much. Indeed, the Constitution suggests that they viewed the rights of the people and the rights of individuals as operating in harmony, each supporting the other. In the Preamble, for example, it is held that it is the duty of the people to provide for equity and impartiality in the making and execution of laws, so "that every man may, at all times, find his security in them." But in the same paragraph, it is also held that "all shall be governed by certain laws, for the common good." In Article XXIX of the

Declaration of Rights the impartiality of law and the administration of justice is enshrined in the Constitution "for the security of the rights of the people, and of every citizen." Clearly, the advantages of government by law were thought to accrue to both the people and individual citizens.

But if the right of individuals to government by law is to the advantage of the people, the right of the people to control their government is even more beneficial to individuals. The right of the people to elect their public officers, noted in Article VIII of the Declaration of Rights, is necessary "in order to prevent those who are vested with authority from becoming oppressors," that is, from oppressing individual citizens. This procedural mechanism makes effective the principle of accountability, which was written into the Constitution in Article V of the Declaration of Rights; it is because public officials are accountable to the people collectively that they will behave justly and according to the law in their treatment of individuals. For individuals in the state of nature, the very purpose of forming civil society was to employ the power of the whole for the protection of each individual. It is therefore only logical that the collective sovereignty established in the social compact should be used to protect the civil rights of those individuals, and that is precisely what the people of Massachusetts attempted to do in framing their Constitution.

The relationship between individual autonomy and popular sovereignty was perceived by the people of Massachusetts to be a great extent symbiotic. There was no doubt in their minds, however, as to which one was of higher priority. The fact is that, with the possible exception of Article I of the Declaration of Rights, the Constitution of 1780 places no absolute substantive limitations on the power of government, and Article I is so generally phrased as to be of limited utility. All other absolute restrictions on the power of government are procedural in nature. In some cases procedural stipulations may be excepted with legislative approval. These facts, taken in conjunction with the broad scope of legislative power granted in Chapter I, Section I, Article IV of the Frame of Government, suggests strongly that the legislature, as the policy-making agent of the people of Massachusetts, was not to be prevented from achieving the common good by any absolute limitations in the Constitution. The procedural restrictions in the Declaration of Rights inhibited the ability of the government to act capriciously, but the numerous statements of popular sovereignty—as for example those in Articles IV, V, VII, and XIX of the Declaration of Rights—make explicit the pre-eminence of the popular sovereignty which is embodied in the structure of the government.

Majority rule, as the decision rule of the people, is the most important procedural principle in the Massachusetts Constitution. Before it, all other principles must give way. Oddly, the debates over the Constitution provided little in the way of an in-depth analysis or justification of majority rule. The relationship between majority rule and the concepts of fundamental and statutory law was not not extensively explored; the relationship between majority rule and the various theories of representation was never extensively analyzed; and even the prima facie validity of majority rule itself did not receive the critical attention it seems retrospectively to have deserved. This lack of critical analysis is probably due in large part to the fact that the principle of majority rule was never seriously challenged. Even those who wished to circumvent its effects chose to employ its language. The revolutionaries always perceived themselves as a majority party, fighting *for* the civil rights of individuals, against the tyranny of a nondemocratic power. The fight for self-government and majority rule, then, was also a fight for individual rights.[4]

In establishing their new government, the people of Massachusetts attempted to limit the power of government procedurally, in order to protect individuals from arbitrary actions by the government. In so doing they also provided a measure of protection for individuals against a tyrannical majority. Because Massachusetts was dominated by a large majority party, the time was not ripe for an airing of the majority tyranny-individual rights issue. The only issue on which this question arose was that of the right of conscience, and this was not a good issue for the purpose of illustrating the problem, because the parties involved disagreed on the question of whether or not an individual

---

4. Thus we see that Gordon Wood is partly correct in his interpretation of the relationship between majority rule and minority rights during the early years of the Revolution (c.f. above pp. 11–12). It was not that the people of Massachusetts perceived no incompatibility between majority rule and individual liberties; rather, it was that they believed that the only legitimate way to secure individual liberties was by the authority of the majority. If the will of the majority were to conflict with the claims of individuals, the people of Massachusetts had no doubt about where the final authority lay.

right had in fact been violated. It was not to be until 1787, when the number and strength of potential minority interests were proliferated by enlarging the arena of potential governmental actions, that a reasoned discussion of the problem of majority tyranny developed in America. Then, of course, it was argued, as the people of Massachusetts seem to have realized in 1780, that ultimately there is no institutional solution to the problem of majority tyranny under a republican government.[5]

The concept of majority rule is related to that of political equality. According to the social compact theory, all individuals are politically equal in civil society since all individuals participated equally in its formation. There are, however, two facets to this political equality. On one hand, there is equality of participation in the making of decisions, or equality of consent; and on the other hand there is equality in being subject to those decisions, or equality before the law. According to the social compact theory, in regard to equality of consent, the only stage in which all individuals must participate is in the state of nature, as the civil society is formed. The decisions of the majority are thereafter binding, and that majority may choose to restrict the suffrage on any insuing vote without violating the principle of political equality. In other words, if the conditions of political equality are satisfied in the making of a decision to deny political equality in the making of some future decision, then such a future decision would be valid in spite of the fact that it was made under conditions of inequality. Is the civil society, in its original unorganized state, under any moral obligations to develop political institutions that are based on the principle of political equality? The most that can be said in answer to this is that some people in Massachusetts seemed to have thought so, as was made evident in the debate over equality of representation.

Suffrage was restricted in the Constitution through the imposition of property qualifications. These property qualifications present an interesting anomaly. While they were approved by a large majority, they could not be defended on the basis of a logical deduction from the conditions of the original compact. The argument of "The Essex Result" in this regard reveals the illogicality of this position. They could, however, be defended

5. This is the implicit conclusion of the tenth *Federalist*.

on prudential grounds, as John Adams attempted to do in his letter to James Sullivan, and it is in this sense that their popular acceptance must be understood. Reasons of prudence were explicitly advanced by the Convention in defense of the property qualifications. Those who objected to the property qualifications and who were in favor of a suffrage based on numerical proportion, used the principle of political equality in arguing their case. What was essentially at issue, then, was the question, To what extent does the original political equality of civil society logically entail political equality in the making of decisions at subsequent stages? To what extent may utilitarian concerns override the prima facie claim of political equality? The relative lack of any discussion of this issue in the literature, and the corresponding failure of the revolutionary publicists to answer these questions, reflect the ambiguity in their understanding of the concept of political equality. The only available evidence which is capable of providing insight into their views on this question is the stark fact that the property qualifications, while they certainly were inegalitarian, were obviously thought to be legitimately so by a large majority of the people of Massachusetts. This evidence is insufficient, however, to allow any firm conclusion on the question of precisely where the people of Massachusetts would have drawn the line between utility and equality.

The other facet of political equality relates to equality before the laws. This concept did not require that the law make no discriminations among persons. It is, after all, the function of law to make reasonable discriminations. In order to satisfy the criterion of equality before the law, it is sufficient that all persons who are relevantly similar stand equal before the law. In other words, the law should not make arbitrary and unreasonable discriminations among individuals. The procedural requirements embodied in Articles X-XV, XXIV-XXVI, and XXIX of the Declaration of Rights, which establish the principle of due process of law, were intended to secure this equality before the law. Unlike the principle of equality of consent, the principle of equality before the law was subject to no limitations or exceptions on the ground of utility. Presumably a majority could at some time choose to alter or abridge these procedural rights by altering the constitution; but the salient fact is that the majority of the people of Massachusetts chose to set these procedural rights beyond the power of a utilitarian political judgment, which might place expediency above justice. It is problematical whether any conclusion can be wrung from the high regard in which equality before the law was held. It does suggest that political equality, as equality before the law, may have meant more to the people of Massachusetts than political equality as equal consent to the law, but this is only an inference and perhaps not the only possible one.

However great their lack of conceptual sophistication, the people of Massachusetts were rich in practical political experience, and it was upon this reservoir of experience that they drew in establishing their political institutions in the Constitution of 1780. Within the parameters established by the principle of the separation of powers, the elective branches of government were to embody the policy-making power of the people. The political abuses of the colonial governors continued to reveal in practice what republican political theory advocated in the abstract, viz. that of the two elective branches, the legislature should be ascendent over the executive. The pernicious use to which the colonial governors had put their power of appointing judges led the people of Massachusetts to value a politically independent judiciary. The tenure during good behavior that the judges were to enjoy under the Constitution did not, however, imply any superiority of the judiciary to the elective branches. As the passive branch of the government, the judiciary was never perceived as an initiator of policy, and therefore was not thought by the majority of the people to require direct popular control.

The executive power was to be constrained by annual elections and by the legislative power of impeachment. In other words, it was to be subject to popular control, rather than to extensive constitutional restrictions. The people of Massachusetts were distrustful of the executive, but there is no reason to believe that they did not recognize the need for a firm execution of the laws. The fact that the Constitution contains no extensive delineation of the executive powers suggests that the executive was expected to be guided by the legislature and reminds us that the scope of political power is itself difficult to define. The extensive power of the legislature, however, could only imply an equally extensive executive power, for whatever the legislature was empowered to enact, the executive was empowered to enforce.

Conclusion

The political theory of the Massachusetts Constitution of 1780 subordinates the individual to society. The implications of this conclusion are very significant. The myth persists that the revolutionary Americans were rugged individualists, who tolerated government only to the extent necessary to provide for civil order. Our children are taught that the famous self-evident truths passage of the Declaration of Independence, with its emphasis on individual rights, captures the "basic faith" of revolutionary America. Above all, the revolutionaries are supposed to have been believers in limited government, and their intention in framing their new constitution was to bring about a "weakening (of) the power of government." All of these things may have been true in other states, and in other constitutions. But in the most important state, and in the most influential of all the new constitutions, the myths of individual supremacy and weak government simply did not hold.[6]

Massachusetts was a commonwealth, and had been one since the days of the Puritan ascendency. Under the Constitution of 1780 it was no longer a Bible commonwealth, it was a secular commonwealth in which the common good supplanted salvation as the end of civil society. The attainment of salvation had been, for the Puritans, a collective enterprise toward an individual end, and the attainment of the common good was viewed in collective terms by the people of Massachusetts in 1780. During the Revolution the state continued public policies designed to secure the collective well-being of the people which included public education, public support of religion, public relief of the poor, public employment of the poor, and the most extensive price controls America has ever seen. Many of these activities were municipal functions, but the salient fact is that they were conducted under the sanction of the state. The control of the state over individual behavior was incredible. The penalties for blasphemy, profanity, and other misdemeanors would be regarded as cruel and unusual today.

In undertaking these activities, the people of Massachusetts

6. Current et al., *United States History* (Glenview, Ill.: Scott, Foresman and Company, 1967), p. 55; Irving Kristol, *The American Revolution as a Successful Revolution* (Washington, D.C.: The American Enterprise Institute, 1973), p. 11.

were acting on the basis of a political theory that was well established by 1780. This political theory taught them that a republican political system, created by and responsive to the wishes of the majority of the people, must enjoy a wide latitude of action in the pursuit of the public good. Such a political system, as the institutional expression of the sovereignty of the people, must not be limited by any concept of antecedent individual rights or prerogatives, and the republican government created in the Massachusetts Constitution of 1780 was not so limited. If it is true, then, that Americans have ever believed in such an ascendency of the individual over his civil society, scholars will have to look elsewhere in order to prove it.

Appendix

The Massachusetts Constitution of 1780

A CONSTITUTION * *OR FRAME OF GOVERNMENT, Agreed upon by the Delegates of the People of the STATE OF MASSACHU-SETTS-BAY,* – In Convention,—*Begun and held at* Cambridge, *on the First of* September, *1779, and continued by Adjournments to the Second of* March, *1780.*

Preamble

The end of the institution, maintenance and administration of government, is to secure the existence of the body-politic; to protect it; and to furnish the individuals who compose it, with the power of enjoying, in safety and tranquillity, their natural rights, and the blessings of life: And whenever these great objects are not obtained, the people have a right to alter the government, and to take measures necessary for their safety, prosperity and happiness.

The body-politic is formed by a voluntary association of individuals: It is a social compact, by which the whole people covenants with each citizen, and each citizen with the whole people, that all shall be governed by certain laws for the common good. It is the duty of the people, therefore, in framing a Constitution of Government, to provide for an equitable mode of making laws, as well as for an impartial interpretation, and a faithful execution of them; that every man may, at all times, find his security in them.

We, therefore, the people of Massachusetts, acknowledging, with grateful hearts, the goodness of the Great Legislator of

*Reprinted from *The Journal of the Convention, for Framing a Constitution of Government for the State of Massachusetts-Bay* (Boston: Dutton and Wentworth, 1832), pp. 222-249. May be found in Handlin and Handlin, *Popular Sources*, pp. 441-472.

the Universe, in affording us, in the course of His providence, an opportunity, deliberately and peaceably, without fraud, violence or surprise, of entering into an original, explicit, and solemn compact with each other; and of forming a new Constitution of Civil Government, for ourselves and posterity; and devoutly imploring His direction in so interesting a design, DO agree upon, ordain and establish, the following *Declaration of Rights, and Frame of Government,* as the CONSTITUTION of the COMMON- WEALTH of MASSACHUSETTS.

PART THE FIRST

A Declaration of the Rights of the Inhabitants of the Commonwealth of Massachusetts.

Art. I.   All men are born free and equal, and have certain natural, essential, and unalienable rights; among which may be reckoned the right of enjoying and defending their lives and liberties; that of acquiring, possessing, and protecting property; in fine, that of seeking and obtaining their safety and happiness.

II.   It is the right as well as the duty of all men in society, publicly, and at stated seasons, to worship the SUPREME BEING, the great creator and preserver of the universe. And no subject shall be hurt, molested, or restrained, in his person, liberty, or estate, for worshipping GOD in the manner and season most agreeable to the dictates of his own conscience; or for his religious profession or sentiments; provided he doth not disturb the public peace, or obstruct others in their religious worship.

III.   As the happiness of a people, and the good order and preservation of civil government, essentially depend upon piety, religion and morality; and as these cannot be generally diffused through a community, but by the institution of the public worship of GOD, and of public instructions in piety, religion and morality: Therefore, to promote their happiness and to secure the good order and preservation of their government, the people of this Commonwealth have a right to invest their legislature with power to authorize and require, and the legislature shall, from time to time, authorize and require, the several towns, parishes, precincts, and other bodies-politic, or religious societies, to make suitable provision, at their own expense, for the institution of the public worship of GOD, and for the support and maintenance of public protestant teachers of piety, religion and morality, in all cases where such provision shall not be made voluntarily.

And the people of this Commonwealth have also a right to, and do, invest their legislature with authority to enjoin upon all the subjects an attendance upon the instructions of the public teachers aforesaid, at stated times and seasons, if there be any on whose instructions they can conscientiously and conveniently attend.

Provided notwithstanding, that the several towns, parishes, precincts, and other bodies-politic, or religious societies, shall, at all times, have the exclusive right of electing their public teachers, and of contracting with them for their support and maintenance.

And all monies paid by the subject to the support of public worship, and of the public teachers aforesaid, shall, if he require it, be uniformly applied to the support of the public teacher or teachers of his own religious sect or denomination, provided there be any on whose instructions he attends: otherwise it may be paid towards the support of the teacher or teachers of the parish or precinct in which the said monies are raised.

And every denomination of christians, demeaning themselves peaceably, and as good subjects of the Commonwealth, shall be equally under the protection of the law: And no subordination of any one sect or denomination to another shall ever be established by law.

IV. The people of this Commonwealth have the sole and exclusive right of governing themselves as a free, sovereign, and independent state; and do, and forever hereafter shall, exercise and enjoy every power, jurisdiction, and right, which is not, or may not hereafter, be by them expressly delegated to the United States of America, in Congress assembled.

V. All power residing originally in the people, and being derived from them, the several magistrates and officers of government, vested with authority, whether legislative, executive, or judicial, are their substitutes and agents, and are at all times accountable to them.

VI. No man, nor corporation, or association of men, have any other title to obtain advantages, or particular and exclusive privileges, distinct from those of the community, than what arises from the consideration of services rendered to the public; and this title being in nature neither hereditary, nor transmissible to children, or descendants, or relations by blood, the idea of a man born a magistrate, lawgiver, or judge, is absurd and unnatural.

VII. Government is instituted for the common good; for the protection, safety, prosperity and happiness of the people; and not for the profit, honor, or private interest of any one man, family, or class of men: Therefore the people alone have an incontestible, unalienable, and indefeasible right to institute government; and to reform, alter, or totally change the same, when their protection, safety, prosperity and happiness require it.

VIII. In order to prevent those, who are vested with authority, from becoming oppressors, the people have a right, at such periods and in such manner as they shall establish by their frame of government, to cause their public officers to return to private life; and to fill up vacant places by certain and regular elections and appointments.

IX. All elections ought to be free; and all the inhabitants of this Commonwealth, having such qualifications as they shall establish by their frame of government, have an equal right to elect officers, and to be elected, for public employments.

X. Each individual of the society has a right to be protected by it in the enjoyment of his life, liberty and property, according to standing laws. He is obliged, consequently, to contribute his share to the expense of this protection; to give his personal service, or an equivalent, when necessary: But no part of the property of any individual, can, with justice, be taken from him, or applied to public uses without his own consent, or that of the representative body of the people: In fine, the people of this Commonwealth are not controlable by any other laws, than those to which their constitutional representative body have given their consent. And whenever the public exigencies require, that the property of any individual should be appropriated to public uses, he shall receive a reasonable compensation therefor.

XI. Every subject of the Commonwealth ought to find a certain remedy, by having recourse to the laws, for all injuries or wrongs which he may receive in his person, property, or character. He ought to obtain right and justice freely, and without being obliged to purchase it; completely, and without any denial; promptly, and without delay; conformably to the laws.

XII. No subject shall be held to answer for any crime or offence, until the same is fully and plainly, substantially and formally, described to him; or be compelled to accuse, or furnish evidence against himself. And every subject shall have a right to produce all proofs, that may be favorable to him; to meet the witnesses against him face to face, and to be fully heard in his defence by himself, or his council, at his election. And no subject shall be arrested, imprisoned, despoiled, or deprived of his property, immunities, or privileges, put out of the protection of the law, exiled, or deprived of his life, liberty, or estate; but by the judgment of his peers, or the law of the land.

And the legislature shall not make any law, that shall subject any person to a capital or infamous punishment, excepting for the government of the army and navy, without trial by jury.

XIII. In criminal prosecutions, the verification of facts in the vicinity where they happen, is one of the greatest securities of the life, liberty, and property of the citizen.

XIV. Every subject has a right to be secure from all unreasonable searches, and seizures of his person, his houses, his papers, and all his possessions. All warrants, therefore, are contrary to this right, if the cause or foundation of them be not previously supported by oath or affirmation; and if the order in the warrant to a civil officer, to make search in suspected places, or to arrest one or more suspected persons, or to seize their property, be not accompanied with a special designation of the persons or objects of search, arrest, or seizure: and no warrant ought to be issued but in cases, and with the formalities, prescribed bv the laws.

XV. In all controversies concerning property, and in all suits between two or more persons, except in cases in which it has heretofore been otherways used and practised, the parties have a right to a trial by jury; and this method of procedure shall be held sacred, unless, in causes arising on the high-seas, and such as relate to mariners wages, the legislature shall hereafter find it necessary to alter it.

XVI. The liberty of the press is essential to the security of freedom in a state: it ought not, therefore, to be restrained in this Commonwealth.

XVII. The people have a right to keep and to bear arms for the common defence. And as in time of peace armies are dangerous to liberty, they ought not to be maintained without the consent of the legislature; and the military power shall always be held in an exact subordination to the civil authority, and be governed by it.

XVIII. A frequent recurrence to the fundamental principles

of the constitution, and a constant adherence to those of piety, justice, moderation, temperance, industry, and frugality, are absolutely necessary to preserve the advantages of liberty, and to maintain a free government: The people ought, consequently, to have a particular attention to all those principles, in the choice of their officers and representatives: And they have a right to require of their law-givers and magistrates, an exact and constant observance of them, in the formation and execution of the laws necessary for the good administration of the Commonwealth.

XIX. The people have a right, in an orderly and peaceable manner, to assemble to consult upon the common good; give instructions to their representatives; and to request of the legislative body, by the way of addresses, petitions, or remonstrances, redress of the wrongs done them, and of the grievances they suffer.

XX. The power of suspending the laws, or the execution of the laws, ought never to be exercised but by the legislature, or by authority derived from it, to be exercised in such particular cases only as the legislature shall expressly provide for.

XXI. The freedom of deliberation, speech and debate, in either house of the legislature, is so essential to the rights of the people, that it cannot be the foundation of any accusation or prosecution, action or complaint, in any other court or place whatsoever.

XXII. The legislature ought frequently to assemble for the redress of grievances, for correcting, strengthening, and confirming the laws, and for making new laws, as the common good may require.

XXIII. No subsidy, charge, tax, impost, or duties, ought to be established, fixed, laid, or levied, under any pretext whatsoever, without the consent of the people, or their representatives in the legislature.

XXIV. Laws made to punish for actions done before the existence of such laws, and which have not been declared crimes by preceding laws, are unjust, oppressive, and inconsistent with the fundamental principles of a free government.

XXV. No subject ought, in any case, or in any time, to be declared guilty of treason or felony by the legislature.

XXVI. No magistrate or court of law shall demand excessive bail or sureties, impose excessive fines, or inflict cruel or unusual punishments.

XXVII. In time of peace no soldier ought to be quartered in any house without the consent of the owner; and in time of war such quarters ought not to be made but by the civil magistrate, in a manner ordained by the legislature.

XXVIII. No person can in any case be subjected to law-martial, or to any penalties or pains, by virtue of that law, except those employed in the army or navy, and except the militia in actual service, but by authority of the legislature.

XXIX. It is essential to the preservation of the rights of every individual, his life, liberty, property and character, that there be an impartial interpretation of the laws, and administration of justice. It is the right of every citizen to be tried by judges as free, impartial and independent as the lot.of humanity will admit. It is therefore not only the best policy, but for the security of the rights of the people, and of every citizen, that the judges of the supreme judicial court should hold their offices as long as they behave themselves well; and that they should have honorable salaries ascertained and established by standing laws.

XXX. In the government of this Commonwealth, the legislative department shall never exercise the executive and judicial powers, or either of them: The executive shall never exercise the legislative and judicial powers, or either of them: The judicial shall never exercise the legislative and executive powers, or either of them: to the end it may be a government of laws and not of men.

PART THE SECOND

The Frame of Government.

The people, inhabiting the territory formerly called the Province of Massachusetts-Bay, do hereby solemnly and mutually agree with each other, to form themselves into a free, sovereign, and independent body-politic or state, by the name of THE COMMONWEALTH OF MASSACHUSETTS.

Chapter I. The Legislative Power.

Section I. The General Court.

Art. I. The department of legislation shall be formed by two branches, *a Senate* and *House of Representatives:* each of which shall have a negative on the other.

The legislative body shall assemble every year, on the last Wednesday in May, and at such other times as they shall judge necessary; and shall dissolve and be dissolved on the day next preceding the said last Wednesday in May; and shall be styled, THE GENERAL COURT OF MASSACHUSETTS.

II. No bill or resolve of the Senate or House of Representatives shall become a law, and have force as such, until it shall have been laid before the Governor for his revisal: And if he, upon such revision, approve thereof, he shall signify his approbation by signing the same. But if he have any objection to the passing of such bill or resolve, he shall return the same, together with his objections thereto, in writing, to the Senate or House of Representatives, in which soever the same shall have originated; who shall enter the objections sent down by the Governor, at large, on their records, and proceed to reconsider the said bill or resolve: But if, after such reconsideration, two thirds of the said Senate or House of Representatives, shall, notwithstanding the said objections, agree to pass the same, it shall, together with the objections, be sent to the other branch of the legislature, where it shall also be reconsidered, and if approved by two thirds of the members present, shall have the force of a law: But in all such cases the votes of both houses shall be determined by yeas and nays; and the names of the persons voting for, or against, the said bill or resolve, shall be entered upon the public records of the Commonwealth.

And in order to prevent unnecessary delays, if any bill or resolve shall not be returned by the Governor within five days after it shall have been presented, the same shall have the force of a law.

III. The General Court shall forever have full power and authority to erect and constitute judicatories and courts of record, or other courts, to be held in the name of the Commonwealth, for the hearing, trying, and determining of all manner of crimes, offences, pleas, processes, plaints, actions, matters, causes and things, whatsoever, arising or happening within the Commonwealth, or between or concerning persons inhabiting, or residing, or brought within the same; whether the same be criminal or civil, or whether the said crimes be capital or not capital, and whether the said pleas be real, personal, or mixt; and for the awarding and making out of execution thereupon: To which courts and judicatories are hereby given and granted full power and authority, from time to time, to administer oaths or affirmations, for the better discovery of truth in any matter in controversy or depending before them.

IV. And further, full power and authority are hereby given and granted to the said General Court, from time to time, to make, ordain, and establish, all manner of wholesome and reasonable orders, laws, statutes, and ordinances, directions and instructions, either with penalties or without; so as the same be not repugnant or contrary to this Constitution, as they shall judge to be for the good and welfare of this Commonwealth, and for the government and ordering thereof, and of the subjects of the same, and for the necessary support and defence of the government thereof; and to name and settle annually, or provide by fixed laws, for the naming and settling all civil officers within the said Commonwealth, the election and constitution of whom are not hereafter in this Form of Government otherwise provided for; and to set forth the several duties, powers and limits; of the several civil and military officers of this Commonwealth, and the forms of such oaths or affirmations as shall be respectively administered unto them for the execution of their several offices and places, so as the same be not repugnant or contrary to this Constitution; and to impose and levy proportional and reasonable assessments, rates, and taxes, upon all the inhabitants of, and persons resident, and estates lying, within the said Commonwealth; and also to impose, and levy reasonable duties and excises, upon any produce, goods, wares, merchandize, and commodities whatsoever, brought into, produced, manufactured, or being within the same; to be issued and disposed of by warrant, under the hand of the Governor of this Commonwealth for the time being, with the advice and consent of the Council, for the public service, in the necessary defence and support of the government of the said Commonwealth, and the protection and preservation of the subjects thereof, according to such acts as are or shall be in force within the same.

And while the public charges of government, or any part thereof, shall be assessed on polls and estates, in the manner that has hitherto been practised, in order that such assessments may be made with equality, there shall be a valuation of estates within the Commonwealth taken anew once in every ten years at least, and as much oftener as the General Court shall order.

Chapter I

Section II. Senate.

Art. I. There shall be annually elected by the freeholders and other inhabitants of this Commonwealth, qualified as in this Constitution is provided, forty persons to be Counsellors and Senators for the year ensuing their election; to be chosen by the inhabitants of the districts, into which the Commonwealth may from time to time be divided by the General Court for that purpose: And the General Court, in assigning the numbers to be elected by the respective districts, shall govern themselves by the proportion of the public taxes paid by the said districts; and timely make known to the inhabitants of the Commonwealth, the limits of each district, and the number of Counsellors and Senators to be chosen therein; provided, that the number of such districts shall never be less than thirteen; and that no district be so large as to entitle the same to choose more than six Senators.

And the several counties in this Commonwealth shall, until the General Court shall determine it necessary to alter the said districts, be districts for the choice of Counsellors and Senators, (except that the counties of Dukes County and Nantucket shall form one district for that purpose) and shall elect the following number for Counsellors and Senators, viz:

Suffolk	Six	York	Two
Essex	Six	Dukes County	
Middlesex	Five	and Nantucket	One
Hampshire	Four	Worcester	Five
Plymouth	Three	Cumberland	One
Barnstable	One	Lincoln	One
Bristol	Three	Berkshire	Two.

II. The Senate shall be the first branch of the legislature; and the Senators shall be chosen in the following manner, viz: There shall be a meeting on the first Monday in April annually, forever, of the inhabitants of each town in the several counties of this Commonwealth; to be called by the Selectmen, and warned in due course of law, at least seven days before the first Monday in April, for the purpose of electing persons to be Senators and Counsellors: And at such meetings every male inhabitant of twenty-one years of age and upwards, having a freehold estate within the Commonwealth, of the annual income of three pounds, or any estate of the value of sixty pounds, shall have a right to give in his vote for the Senators for the district of which he is an inhabitant. And to remove all doubts concerning the meaning of the word "inhabitant" in this constitution, every person shall be considered as an inhabitant, for the purpose of electing and being elected into any office, or place within this State, in that town, district, or plantation, where he dwelleth, or hath his home.

The Selectmen of the several towns shall preside at such meetings impartially; and shall receive the votes of all the inhabitants of such towns present and qualified to vote for Senators, and shall sort and count them in open town meeting, and in presence of the Town Clerk, who shall make a fair record in presence of the Selectmen, and in open town meeting, of the name of every person voted for, and of the number of votes against his name; and a fair copy of this record shall be attested by the Selectmen and the Town-Clerk, and shall be sealed up, directed to the Secretary of the Commonwealth for the time being, with a superscription, expressing the purport of the contents thereof, and delivered by the Town-Clerk of such towns, to the Sheriff of the county in which such town lies, thirty days at least before the last Wednesday in May annually; or it shall be delivered into the Secretary's office seventeen days at least before the said last Wednesday in May; and the Sheriff of each county shall deliver all such certificates by him received, into the Secretary's office seventeen days before the said last Wednesday in May.

And the inhabitants of plantations unincorporated, qualified as this Constitution provides, who are or shall be empowered and required to assess taxes upon themselves toward the support of government, shall have the same privilege of voting for Counsellors and Senators, in the plantations where they reside, as town inhabitants have in their respective towns; and the plantation-meetings for that purpose shall be held annually on the same first Monday in April, at such place in the plantations respectively, as the Assessors thereof shall direct; which Assessors shall have like authority for notifying the electors, collecting and returning the votes, as the Selectmen and Town-Clerks have in their several towns, by this Constitution. And all other persons living in places unincorporated (qualified as aforesaid) who shall be assessed to the support of government by the Assessors of an adjacent town, shall have the privilege of giving in their votes for Counsellors and Senators, in the town where they shall be assessed, and be notified of the place of meeting by the Selectmen of the town where they shall be assessed, for that purpose, accordingly.

III.   And that there may be a due convention of Senators on the last Wednesday in May annually, the Governor, with five of the Council, for the time being, shall, as soon as may be, examine the returned copies of such records; and fourteen days before the said day he shall issue his summons to such persons as shall appear to be chosen by a majority of voters, to attend on that day, and take their seats accordingly: Provided nevertheless, that for the first year the said returned copies shall be examined by the President and five of the Council of the former Constitution of Government; and the said President shall, in like manner, issue his summons to the persons so elected, that they may take their seats as aforesaid.

IV.   The Senate shall be the final judge of the elections, returns and qualifications of their own members, as pointed out in the Constitution; and shall, on the said last Wednesday in May annually, determine and declare who are elected by each district, to be Senators, by a majority of votes: And in case there shall not appear to be the full number of Senators returned elected by a majority of votes for any district, the deficiency shall be supplied in the following manner, viz. The members of the House of Representatives, and such Senators as shall be declared elected, shall take the names of such persons as shall be found to have the highest number of votes in such district, and not elected, amounting to twice the number of Senators wanting, if there be so many voted for; and, out of these, shall elect by ballot a number of Senators sufficient to fill up the vacancies in such district: And in this manner all such vacancies shall be filled up in every district of the Commonwealth; and in like manner all vacancies in the Senate, arising by death, removal out of the State, or otherwise, shall be supplied as soon as may be after such vacancies shall happen.

V.   Provided nevertheless, that no person shall be capable of being elected as a Senator, who is not seized in his own right of a freehold within this Commonwealth, of the value of three hundred pounds at least, or possessed of personal estate to the value of six hundred pounds at least, or of both to the amount of the same sum, and who has not been an inhabitant of this Commonwealth for the space of five years immediately preceding his election, and, at the time of his election, he shall be an inhabitant in the district, for which he shall be chosen.

VI. The Senate shall have power to adjourn themselves, provided such adjournments do not exceed two days at a time.

VII. The Senate shall choose its own President, appoint its own officers, and determine its own rules of proceeding.

VIII. The Senate shall be a court with full authority to hear and determine all impeachments made by the House of Representatives, against any officer or officers of the Commonwealth, for misconduct and mal-administration in their offices. But, previous to the trial of every impeachment, the members of the Senate shall respectively be sworn, truly and impartially to try and determine the charge in question, according to evidence. Their judgment, however, shall not extend further than to removal from office and disqualification to hold or enjoy any place of honor, trust, or profit, under this Commonwealth: But the party, so convicted, shall be, nevertheless, liable to indictment, trial, judgment, and punishment, according to the laws of the land.

IX. Not less than sixteen members of the Senate shall constitute a quorum for doing business.

Chapter I.

Section III. House of Representatives.

Art. I. There shall be in the Legislature of this Commonwealth, a representation of the people, annually elected, and founded upon the principle of equality.

II. And in order to provide for a representation of the citizens of this Commonwealth, founded upon the principle of equality, every corporate town, containing one hundred and fifty rateable polls, may elect one Representative: Every corporate town, containing three hundred and seventy-five rateable polls, may elect two Representatives: Every corporate town, containing six hundred rateable polls, may elect three Representatives; and proceeding in that manner, making two hundred and twenty-five rateable polls the mean increasing number for every additional Representative.

Provided nevertheless, that each town now incorporated, not having one hundred and fifty rateable polls, may elect one Representative: but no place shall hereafter be incorporated with the privilege of electing a Representative, unless there are within the same one hundred and fifty rateable polls.

And the House of Representatives shall have power, from time to time, to impose fines upon such towns as shall neglect to choose and return members to the same, agreeably to this Constitution.

The expenses of travelling to the General Assembly, and returning home, once in every session, and no more, shall be paid by the government, out of the public treasury, to every member who shall attend as seasonably as he can, in the judgment of the House, and does not depart without leave.

III. Every member of the House of Representatives shall be chosen by written votes; and for one year at least next preceding his election shall have been an inhabitant of, and have been seized in his own right of a freehold of the value of one hundred pounds within the town he shall be chosen to represent, or any rateable estate to the value of two hundred pounds; and he shall cease to represent the said town immediately on his ceasing to be qualified as aforesaid.

IV. Every male person, being twenty-one years of age, and resident in any particular town in this Commonwealth for the space of one year next preceding, having a freehold estate within the same town, of the annual income of three pounds, or any estate of the value of sixty pounds, shall have a right to vote in the choice of a Representative or Representatives for the said town.

V. The members of the House of Representatives shall be chosen annually in the month of May, ten days at least before the last Wednesday of that month.

VI. The House of Representatives shall be the Grand Inquest of this Commonwealth; and all impeachments made by them shall be heard and tried by the Senate.

VII. All money-bills shall originate in the House of Representatives; but the Senate may propose or concur with amendments, as on other bills.

VIII. The House of Representatives shall have power to adjourn themselves; provided such adjournment shall not exceed two days at a time.

IX. Not less than sixty members of the House of Representatives shall constitute a quorum for doing business.

X. The House of Representatives shall be the judge of the returns, elections, and qualifications of its own members, as pointed out in the constitution; shall choose their own Speaker; appoint their own officers, and settle the rules and orders of proceeding in their own house: They shall have authority to punish by imprisonment, every person, not a member, who shall be guilty of disrespect to the House, by any disorderly, or contemptuous behaviour, in its presence; or who, in the town where the General Court is sitting, and during the time of its sitting, shall threaten harm to the body or estate of any of its members, for any thing said or done in the House; or who shall assault any of them therefor; or who shall assault, or arrest, any witness, or other person, ordered to attend the House, in his way in going, or returning; or who shall rescue any person arrested by the order of the House.

And no member of the House of Representatives shall be arrested, or held to bail on mean process, during his going unto, returning from, or his attending, the General Assembly.

XI. The Senate shall have the same powers in the like cases; and the Governor and Council shall have the same authority to punish in like cases. Provided, that no imprisonment on the warrant or order of the Governor, Council, Senate, or House of Representatives, for either of the above described offences, be for a term exceeding thirty days.

And the Senate and House of Representatives may try, and determine, all cases where their rights and privileges are concerned, and which, by the Constitution, they have authority to try and determine, by committees of their own members, or in such other way as they may respectively think best.

Chapter II. Executive Power.

Section I. Governor.

Art. I. There shall be a Supreme Executive Magistrate, who shall be styled, THE GOVERNOR OF THE COMMONWEALTH OF MASSACHUSETTS; and whose title shall be—HIS EXCELLENCY.

II. The Governor shall be chosen annually: And no person shall be eligible to this office, unless at the time of his election, he shall have been an inhabitant of this Commonwealth for seven years next preceding; and unless he shall, at the same time, be seized in his own right, of a freehold within the Commonwealth, of the value of one thousand pounds; and unless he shall declare himself to be of the christian religion.

III. Those persons who shall be qualified to vote for Senators and Representatives within the several towns of this Commonwealth, shall, at a meeting, to be called for that purpose, on the first Monday of April annually, give in their votes for a Governor, to the Selectmen, who shall preside at such meetings; and the Town Clerk, in the presence and with the assistance of the Selectmen, shall, in open town meeting, sort and count the votes, and form a list of the persons voted for, with the number of votes for each person against his name; and shall make a fair record of the same in the town books, and a public declaration thereof in the said meeting; and shall, in the presence of the inhabitants, seal up copies of the said list, attested by him and the Selectmen, and transmit the same to the Sheriff of the county, thirty days at least before the last Wednesday in May; and the Sheriff shall transmit the same to the Secretary's office seventeen days at least before the said last Wednesday in May; or the Selectmen may cause returns of the same to be made to the office of the Secretary of the Commonwealth seventeen days at least before the said day; and the Secretary shall lay the same before the Senate and the House of Representatives, on the last Wednesday in May, to be by them examined: And in case of an election by a majority of all the votes returned, the choice shall be by them declared and published: But if no person shall have a majority of votes, the House of Representatives shall, by ballot, elect two out of four persons who had the highest number of votes, if so many shall have been voted for; but, if otherwise, out of the number voted for; and make return to the Senate of the two persons so elected; on which, the Senate shall proceed, by ballot, to elect one, who shall be declared Governor.

IV. The Governor shall have authority, from time to time, at his discretion, to assemble and call together the Counsellors of this Commonwealth for the time being; and the Governor, with the said Counsellors, or five of them at least, shall, and may, from time to time, hold and keep a Council, for the ordering and directing the affairs of the Commonwealth, agreeably to the Constitution and the laws of the land.

V. The Governor, with advice of Council, shall have full power and authority, during the session of the General Court, to adjourn or prorogue the same to any time the two Houses shall desire; and to dissolve the same on the day next preceding the last Wednesday in May; and, in the recess of the said Court, to prorogue the same from time to time, not exceeding ninety days in any one recess; and to call it together sooner than the time to which it may be adjourned or prorogued, if the welfare of the Commonwealth shall require the same: And in case of any infectious distemper prevailing in the place where the said Court is next at any time to convene, or any other cause happening whereby danger may arise to the health or lives of the members from their attendance, he may direct the session to be held at some other time the most convenient place within the State.

And the Governor shall dissolve the said General Court on the day next preceding the last Wednesday in May.

VI. In cases of disagreement between the two Houses, with regard to the necessity, expediency or time of adjournment, or prorogation, the Governor, with advice of the Council, shall have a right to adjourn or prorogue the General Court, not exceeding ninety days, as he shall determine the public good shall require.

VII. The Governor of this Commonwealth, for the time being, shall be the commander-in-chief of the army and navy, and of all the military forces of the State, by sea and land; and shall have full power, by himself, or by any commander, or other officer or officers, from time to time, to train, instruct, exercise and govern the militia and navy; and, for the special defence and safety of the Commonwealth, to assemble in martial array, and put in warlike posture, the inhabitants thereof, and to lead and conduct them, and with them, to encounter, repel, resist, expel and pursue, by force of arms, as well as by sea as by land, within or without the limits of this Commonwealth, and also to kill, slay and destroy, if necessary, and conquer, by all fitting ways, enterprizes and means whatsoever, all and every such person and persons as shall, at any time hereafter, in a hostile manner, attempt or enterprize the destruction, invasion, detriment, or annoyance of this Commonwealth; and to use and exercise, over the army and navy, and over the militia in actual service, the law martial, in time of war or invasion, and also in time of rebellion, declared by the legislature to exist, as occasion shall necessarily require; and to take and surprise by all ways and means whatsoever, all and every such person or persons, with their ships, arms, ammunition and other goods, as shall, in a hostile manner, invade, or attempt the invading, conquering, or annoying this Commonwealth; and that the Governor be intrusted with all these and other powers, incident to the offices of Captain-General and Commander-in-Chief, and Admiral, to be exercised agreeably to the rules and regulations of the Constitution, and the laws of the land, and not otherwise.

Provided, that the said Governor shall not, at any time hereafter, by virtue of any power by this Constitution granted, or hereafter to be granted to him by the legislature, transport any of the inhabitants of this Commonwealth, or oblige them to march out of the limits of the same, without their free and voluntary consent, or the consent of the General Court; except so far as may be necessary to march or transport them by land or water, for the defence of such part of the State, to which they cannot otherwise conveniently have access.

VIII. The power of pardoning offences, except such as persons may be convicted of before the Senate by an impeachment of the House, shall be in the Governor, by and with the advice of Council: But no charter of pardon, granted by the Governor, with advice of the Council, before conviction, shall avail the party pleading the same, notwithstanding any general or particular expressions contained therein, descriptive of the offence, or offences intended to be pardoned.

IX. All judicial officers, the Attorney-General, the Solicitor-General, all Sheriffs, Coroners, and Registers of Probate, shall be nominated and appointed by the Governor, by and with the advice and consent of the Council; and every such nomination shall be made by the Governor, and made at least seven days prior to such appointment.

X. The Captains and subalterns of the militia shall be elected by the written votes of the train-band and alarm list of their respective companies, of twenty-one years of age and upwards: The field-officers of Regiments shall be elected by the written votes of the captains and subalterns of their respective regiments: The Brigadiers shall be elected in like manner, by the field officers of their respective brigades: And such officers, so elected, shall be commissioned by the Governor, who shall determine their rank.

The Legislature shall, by standing laws, direct the time and manner of convening the electors, and of collecting votes, and of certifying to the Governor the officers elected.

The Major-Generals shall be appointed by the Senate and House of Representatives, each having a negative upon the other; and be commissioned by the Governor.

And if the electors of Brigadiers, field-officers, captains or subalterns, shall neglect or refuse to make such elections, after being duly notified, according to the laws for the time being, then the Governor, with advice of Council, shall appoint suitable persons to fill such offices.

And no officer, duly commissioned to command in the militia, shall be removed from his office, but by the address of both houses to the Governor, or by fair trial in court martial, pursuant to the laws of the Commonwealth for the time being.

The commanding officers of regiments shall appoint their Adjutants and Quarter-masters; the Brigadiers their Brigade-Majors; and the Major-Generals their Aids: and the Governor shall appoint the Adjutant General.

The Governor, with advice of Council, shall appoint all officers of the continental army, whom by the confederation of the United States it is provided that this Commonwealth shall appoint,—as also all officers of forts and garrisons.

The divisions of the militia into brigades, regiments and companies, made in pursuance of the militia laws now in force, shall be considered as the proper divisions of the militia of this Commonwealth, until the same shall be altered in pursuance of some future law.

XI. No monies shall be issued out of the treasury of this Commonwealth, and disposed of (except such sums as may be appropriated for the redemption of bills of credit or Treasurer's notes, or for the payment of interest arising thereon) but by warrant under the hand of the Governor for the time being, with the advice and consent of the Council, for the necessary defence and support of the Commonwealth; and for the protection and preservation of the inhabitants thereof, agreeably to the acts and resolves of the General Court.

XII. All public boards, the Commissary-General, all superintending officers of public magazines and stores, belonging to this Commonwealth, and all commanding officers of forts and garrisons within the same, shall, once in every three months, officially and without requisition, and at other times, when required by the Governor, deliver to him an account of all goods, stores, provisions, ammunition, cannon with their appendages, and small arms with their accoutrements, and of all other public property whatever under their care respectively; distinguishing the quantity, number, quality and kind of each, as particularly as may be; together with the condition of such forts and garrisons: And the said commanding officer shall exhibit to the Governor, when required by him, true and exact plans of such forts, and of the land and sea, or harbour or harbours adjacent.

And the said boards, and all public officers, shall communicate to the Governor, as soon as may be after receiving the same, all letters, dispatches, and intelligences of a public nature, which shall be directed to them respectively.

XIII. As the public good requires that the Governor should not be under the undue influence of any of the members of the General Court, by a dependence on them for his support—that he should, in all cases, act with freedom for the benefit of the public—that he should not have his attention necessarily diverted from that object to his private concerns—and that he should maintain the dignity of the Commonwealth in the character of its chief magistrate—it is necessary that he should have an honorable stated salary, of a fixed and permanent value, amply sufficient for those purposes, and established by standing laws: And it shall be among the first acts of the General Court, after the Commencement of this Constitution, to establish such salary by law accordingly.

Permanent and honorable salaries shall also be established by law for the Justices of the Supreme Judicial Court.

And if it shall be found, that any of the salaries aforesaid, so established, are insufficient, they shall, from time to time, be enlarged, as the General Court shall judge proper.

Chapter II.

Section II. Lieutenant-Governor.

Art. I. There shall be annually elected a Lieutenant-Governor of the Commonwealth of Massachusetts, whose title shall be HIS HONOR—and who shall be qualified, in point of religion, property, and residence in the Commonwealth, in the same manner with the Governor: And the day and manner of his election, and the qualifications of the electors, shall be the same as are required in the election of a Governor. The return of the votes for this officer, and the declaration of his election, shall be in the same manner: And if no one person shall be found to have a majority of all the votes returned, the vacancy shall be filled by the Senate and House of Representatives, in the same manner as the Governor is to be elected, in case no one person shall have a majority of the votes of the people to be Governor.

II. The Governor, and in his absence the Lieutenant-Governor, shall be President of the Council, but shall have no vote in Council: And the Lieutenant-Governor shall always be a member of the Council, except when the chair of the Governor shall be vacant.

III. Whenever the chair of the Governor shall be vacant, by reason of his death, or absence from the Commonwealth, or otherwise, the Lieutenant-Governor, for the time being, shall, during such vacancy, perform all the duties incumbent upon the Governor, and shall have and exercise all the powers and authorities, which by this Constitution the Governor is vested with, when personally present.

Chapter II.

Section III. Council, and the Manner of Settling Elections by the Legislature.

Art. I. There shall be a Council for advising the Governor in the executive part of government, to consist of nine persons besides the Lieutenant-Governor, whom the Governor, for the time being, shall have full power and authority, from time to time, at his discretion, to assemble and call together. And the Governor, with the said Counsellors, or five of them at least, shall and may, from time to time, hold and keep a council, for the ordering and directing the affairs of the Commonwealth, according to the laws of the land.

II. Nine Counsellors shall be annually chosen from among the persons returned for Counsellors and Senators, on the last Wednesday in May, by the joint ballot of the Senators and Representatives assembled in one room: And in case there shall not be found, upon the first choice, the whole number of nine persons who will accept a seat in the Council, the deficiency shall be made up by the electors aforesaid from among the people at large; and the number of Senators left shall constitute the Senate for the year. The seats of the persons thus elected from the Senate, and accepting the trust, shall be vacated in the Senate.

III. The Counsellors, in the civil arrangements of the Commonwealth, shall have rank next after the Lieutenant-Governor.

IV. Not more than two Counsellors shall be chosen out of any one district of this Commonwealth.

V. The resolutions and advice of the Council shall be recorded in a register, and signed by the members present; and this record may be called for at any time by either House of the Legislature; and any member of the Council may insert his opinion contrary to the resolution of the majority.

VI. Whenever the office of the Governor and Lieutenant-Governor shall be vacant, by reason of death, absence, or otherwise, then the Council or the major part of them, shall, during such vacancy, have full power and authority, to do, and execute, all and every such acts, matters and things, as the Governor or the Lieutenant-Governor might or could, by virtue of this Constitution, do or execute, if they, or either of them, were personally present.

VII. And whereas the elections appointed to be made by this Constitution, on the last Wednesday in May annually, by the two Houses of the Legislature, may not be completed on that day, the said elections may be adjourned from day to day until the same shall be completed. And the order of elections shall be as follows; the vacancies in the Senate, if any, shall first be filled up; the Governor and Lieutenant-Governor shall then be elected, provided there should be no choice of them by the people: And afterwards the two Houses shall proceed to the election of the Council.

Chapter II.

Section IV. Secretary, Treasurer, Commissary, etc.

Art. I. The Secretary, Treasurer and Receiver-General, and the Commissary-General, Notaries-Public, and Naval-Officers, shall be chosen annually, by joint ballot of the Senators and Representatives in one room. And that the citizens of this Commonwealth may be assured, from time to time, that the monies remaining in the public Treasury, upon the settlement and liquidation of the public accounts, are their property, no man shall be eligible as Treasurer and Receiver-General more than five years successively.

II. The records of the Commonwealth shall be kept in the office of the Secretary, who may appoint his Deputies, for whose conduct he shall be accountable, and he shall attend the Governor and Council, the Senate and House of Representatives, in person, or by his deputies, as they shall respectively require.

Chapter III. Judiciary Power.

Art. I. The tenure that all commission officers shall by law have in their offices, shall be expressed in their respective commissions. All judicial officers, duly appointed, commissioned and sworn, shall hold their offices during good behaviour, excepting such concerning whom there is different provision made in this Constitution: Provided, nevertheless, the Governor, with consent of the Council, may remove them upon the address of both Houses of the Legislature.

II. Each branch of the Legislature, as well as the Governor and Council, shall have authority to require the opinions of the Justices of the Supreme Judicial Court, upon important questions of law, and upon solemn occasions.

III. In order that the people may not suffer from the long continuance in place of any Justice of the Peace, who shall fail of discharging the important duties of his office with ability or fidelity, all commissions of Justices of the Peace shall expire and become void, in the term of seven years from their respective dates; and, upon the expiration of any commission, the same may, if necessary, be renewed, or another person appointed, as shall most conduce to the well being of the Commonwealth.

IV. The Judges of Probate of Wills, and for granting letters of administration, shall hold their courts at such place or places, on fixed days, as the convenience of the people shall require. And the Legislature shall, from time to time, hereafter appoint such times and places; until which appointments, the said Courts shall be holden at the times and places which the respective Judges shall direct.

V. All causes of marriage, divorce and alimony, and all appeals from the Judges of Probate, shall be heard and determined by the Governor and Council until the Legislature shall, by law, make other provision.

Chapter IV. Delegates to Congress.

The delegates of this Commonwealth to the Congress of the United States, shall, sometime in the month of June annually, be elected by the joint ballot of the Senate and House of Representatives, assembled together in one room; to serve in Congress for one year, to commence on the first Monday in November then next ensuing. They shall have commissions under the hand of the Governor, and the great seal of the Commonwealth; but may be recalled at any time within the year, and others chosen and commissioned, in the same manner, in their stead.

Chapter V. The University at Cambridge, and Encouragement of Literature, etc.

Section I. The University.

Art. I. Whereas our wise and pious ancestors, so early as the year one thousand six hundred and thirty six, laid the foundation of Harvard-College, in which University many persons of great eminence have, by the blessing of GOD, been initiated in those arts and sciences, which qualified them for public employments, both in Church and State: And whereas the encouragement of Arts and Sciences, and all good literature, tends to the honor of GOD, the advantage of the christian religion, and the great benefit of this, and the other United States of America— It is declared, That the PRESIDENT AND FELLOWS OF HARVARD-COLLEGE, in their corporate capacity, and their successors in that capacity, their officers and servants, shall have, hold, use, exercise and enjoy, all the powers, authorities, rights, liberties, privileges, immunities and franchises, which they now have, or are entitled to have, hold, use, exercise and enjoy: And the same are hereby ratified and confirmed unto them, the said President and Fellows of Harvard-College, and to their successors, and to their officers and servants, respectively, forever.

II. And whereas there have been at sundry times, by divers persons, gifts, grants, devises of houses, lands, tenements, goods, chattels, legacies and conveyances, heretofore made, either to Harvard-College in Cambridge, in New-England, or to the President and Fellows of Harvard-College, or to the said College, by some other description, under several charters successively: IT IS DECLARED, That all the said gifts, grants, devises, legacies and conveyances, are hereby forever confirmed unto the President and Fellows of Harvard-College, and to their successors, in the capacity aforesaid, according to the true intent and meaning of the donor or donors, grantor or grantors, devisor or devisors.

III. And whereas by an act of the General Court of the Colony of Massachusetts-Bay, passed in the year one thousand six hundred and forty-two, the Governor and Deputy-Governor, for the time being, and all the magistrates of that jurisdiction, were, with the President, and a number of the clergy in the said act described, constituted the Overseers of Harvard-College: And it being necessary, in this new Constitution of Government, to ascertain who shall be deemed successors to the said Governor, Deputy-Governor and Magistrates: IT IS DECLARED, That the Governor, Lieutenant-Governor, Council and Senate of this Commonwealth, are, and shall be deemed, their successors; who, with the President of Harvard-College, for the time being, together with the ministers of the congregational churches in the towns of Cambridge, Watertown, Charlestown, Boston, Roxbury, and Dorchester, mentioned in the said act, shall be, and hereby are, vested with all the powers and authority belonging, or in any way appertaining to the Overseers of Harvard-College; PROVIDED, that nothing herein shall be construed to prevent the Legislature of this Commonwealth from making such alterations in the government of the said university, as shall be conducive to its advantage, and the interest of the republic of letters, in as full a manner as might have been done by the Legislature of the late Province of the Massachusetts-Bay.

Chapter V.

Section II. The Encouragement of Literature, etc.

Wisdom, and knowledge, as well as virtue, diffused generally among the body of the people, being necessary for the preservation of their rights and liberties; and as these depend on spreading the opportunities and advantages of education in the various parts of the country, and among the different orders of the people, it shall be the duty of legislators and magistrates, in all future periods of this Commonwealth, to cherish the interests of literature and the sciences, and all seminaries of them; especially the university at Cambridge, public schools, and grammar schools in the towns; to encourage private societies and public institutions, rewards and immunities, for the promotion of agriculture, arts, sciences, commerce, trades, manufactures, and a natural history of the country; to countenance and inculcate the principles of humanity and general benevolence, public and private charity, industry and frugality, honesty and punctuality in their dealings; sincerity, good humour, and all social affections, and generous sentiments among the people.

Chapter VI. Oaths and Subscriptions; Incompatibility of and Exclusion from Offices; Pecuniary Qualifications; Commissions; Writs; Confirmation of Laws; Habeas Corpus; The Enacting Style; Continuance of Officers; Provision for a future Revisal of the Constitution, etc.

Art. I. Any person chosen Governor, Lieutenant-Governor, Counsellor, Senator, or Representative, and accepting the trust, shall, before he proceed to execute the duties of his place or office, make and subscribe the following declaration, viz.—

"I, A. B. do declare, that I believe the christian religion, and have a firm persuasion of its truth; and that I am seized and possessed, in my own right, of the property required by the Constitution as one qualification for the office or place to which I am elected."

And the Governor, Lieutenant-Governor, and Counsellors, shall make and subscribe the said declaration, in the presence of the two Houses of Assembly; and the Senators and Representatives first elected under this Constitution, before the President and five of the Council of the former Constitution, and, forever afterwards, before the Governor and Council for the time being.

And every person chosen to either of the places or offices aforesaid, as also any person appointed or commissioned to any judicial, executive, military, or other office under the government, shall, before he enters on the discharge of the business of his place or office, take and subscribe the following declaration, and oaths or affirmations, viz.—

"I, A. B. do truly and sincerely acknowledge, profess, testify and declare, that the Commonwealth of Massachusetts is, and of right ought to be, a free, sovereign and independent State; and I do swear, that I will bear true faith and allegiance to the said Commonwealth, and that I will defend the same against traitorous conspiracies and all hostile attempts whatsoever: And that I do renounce and adjure all allegiance, subjection and obedience to the King, Queen or Government of Great Britain, (as the case may be) and every other foreign power whatsoever: And that no foreign Prince, Person, Prelate, State or Potentate, hath, or ought to have, any jurisdiction, superiority, pre-eminence, authority, dispensing or other power, in any matter, civil, ecclesiastical or spiritual, within this Commonwealth; except the authority and power which is or may be vested by their Constituents in the Congress of the United States: And I do further testify and declare, that no man or body of men hath or can have any right to absolve or discharge me from the obligation of this oath, declaration or affirmation; and that I do make this acknowledgment, profession, testimony, declaration, denial, renunciation and abjuration, heartily and truly, according to the common meaning and acceptation of the foregoing words, without any equivocation, mental evasion, or secret reservation whatsoever. So help me GOD."

"I, A. B. do solemnly swear and affirm, that I will faithfully and impartially discharge and perform all the duties incumbent on me as   ; according to the best of my abilities and understanding, agreeably to the rules and regulations of the Constitution, and the laws of this Commonwealth." "So help me GOD."

PROVIDED always, that when any person, chosen or appointed as aforesaid, shall be of the denomination of the people called Quakers, and shall decline taking the said oaths, he shall make his affirmation in the foregoing form, and subscribe the same, omitting the words *"I do swear," "and adjure," "oath or," "and abjuration,"* in the first oath; and in the second oath, the words *"swear and;"* and in each of them the words *"So help me* GOD;*"* subjoining instead thereof, *"This I do under the pains and penalties of perjury."*

And the said oaths or affirmations shall be taken and subscribed by the Governor, Lieutenant Governor, and Counsellors, before the President of the Senate, in the presence of the two Houses of Assembly; and by the Senators and Representatives first elected under this Constitution, before the President and five of the Council of the former Constitution; and forever afterwards before the Governor and Council for the time being:

And by the residue of the officers aforesaid, before such persons and in such manner as from time to time shall be prescribed by the Legislature.

II.   No Governor, Lieutenant Governor, or Judge of the Supreme Judicial Court, shall hold any other office or place, under the authority of this Commonwealth, except such as by this Constitution they are admitted to hold, saving that the Judges of the said Court may hold the offices of Justices of the Peace through the State; nor shall they hold any other place or office, or receive any pension or salary from any other State or Government or Power whatever.

No person shall be capable of holding or exercising at the same time, within this State, more than one of the following offices, viz:—Judge of Probate—Sheriff—Register of Probate—or Register of Deeds—and never more than any two offices which are to be held by appointment of the Governor, or the Governor and Council, or the Senate, or the House of Representatives, or by the election of the people of the State at large, or of the people of any county, military offices and the offices of Justices of the Peace excepted, shall be held by one person.

No person holding the office of Judge of the Supreme Judicial Court—Secretary—Attorney General—Solicitor General—Treasurer or Receiver General—Judge of Probate—Commissary General—President, Professor, or Instructor of Harvard College—Sheriff—Clerk of the House of Representatives—Register of Probate—Register of Deeds—Clerk of the Supreme Judicial Court—Clerk of the Inferior Court of Common Pleas—or Officer of the Customs, including in this description Naval Officers—shall at the same time have a seat in the Senate or House of Representatives; but their being chosen or appointed to, and accepting the same, shall operate as a resignation of their seat in the Senate or House of Representatives; and the place so vacated shall be filled up.

And the same rule shall take place in case any judge of the said Supreme Judicial Court, or Judge of Probate, shall accept a seat in Council; or any Counsellor shall accept of either of those offices or places.

And no person shall ever be admitted to hold a seat in the Legislature, or any office of trust or importance under the Government of this Commonwealth, who shall, in the due course of law, have been convicted of bribery or corruption in obtaining an election or appointment.

III. In all cases where sums of money are mentioned in this Constitution, the value thereof shall be computed in silver at six shillings and eight pence per ounce: And it shall be in the power of the Legislature from time to time to increase such qualifications, as to property, of the persons to be elected to offices, as the circumstances of the Commonwealth shall require.

IV. All commissions shall be in the name of the Commonwealth of Massachusetts, signed by the Governor, and attested by the Secretary or his Deputy, and have the great seal of the Commonwealth affixed thereto.

V. All writs, issuing out of the clerk's office in any of the Courts of law, shall be in the name of the Commonwealth of Massachusetts: They shall be under the seal of the Court from whence they issue: They shall bear test of the first Justice of the Court to which they shall be returnable, who is not a party, and be signed by the clerk of such court.

VI. All the laws which have heretofore been adopted, used and approved in the Province, Colony or State of Massachusetts Bay, and usually practiced on in the Courts of law, shall still remain and be in full force, until altered or repealed by the Legislature; such parts only excepted as are repugnant to the rights and liberties contained in this Constitution.

VII. The privilege and benefit of the writ of *habeas corpus* shall be enjoyed in the Commonwealth in the most free, easy, cheap, expeditious and ample manner; and shall not be suspended by the Legislature, except upon the most urgent and pressing occasions, and for a limited time not exceeding twelve months.

VIII. The enacting style, in making and passing all acts, statutes and laws, shall be—"Be it enacted by the Senate and House of Representatives, in General Court assembled, and by the authority of the same."

IX. To the end there may be no failure of justice or danger arise to the Commonwealth from a change of the Form of Government—all officers, civil and military, holding commissions under the government and people of Massachusetts Bay in New-England, and all other officers of the said government and people, at the time this Constitution shall take effect, shall have, hold, use, exercise and enjoy all the powers and authority to them granted or committed, until other persons shall be appointed in their stead: And all courts of law shall proceed in the execution of the business of their respective departments; and all the executive and legislative officers, bodies and powers shall continue in full force, in the enjoyment and exercise of all their trusts, employments and authority; until the General Court and the supreme and executive officers under this Constitution are designated and invested with their respective trusts, powers and authority.

X. In order the more effectually to adhere to the principles of the Constitution, and to correct those violations which by any means may be made therein, as well as to form such alterations as from experience shall be found necessary—the General Court, which shall be in the year of our Lord one thousand seven hundred and ninety-five, shall issue precepts to the Selectmen of the several towns, and to the Assessors of the unincorporated plantations, directing them to convene the qualified voters of their respective towns and plantations for the purpose of collecting their sentiments on the necessity or expediency of revising the Constitution, in order to amendments.

And if it shall appear by the returns made, that two thirds of the qualified voters throughout the State, who shall assemble and vote in consequence of the said precepts, are in favor of such revision or amendment, the General Court shall issue precepts, or direct them to be issued from the Secretary's office to the several towns, to elect Delegates to meet in Convention for the purpose aforesaid.

The said Delegates to be chosen in the same manner and proportion as their Representatives in the second branch of the Legislature are by this Constitution to be chosen.

XI. This form of government shall be enrolled on parchment, and deposited in the Secretary's office, and be a part of the laws of the land—and printed copies thereof shall be prefixed to the book containing the laws of this Commonwealth, in all future editions of the said laws.

JAMES BOWDOIN, *President.*
Attest. SAMUEL BARRETT, *Secretary.*

Bibliographic Note

Recent years have seen a resurgence of social contract theory. John Rawls, *A Theory of Justice* (Cambridge: Harvard University Press, Belknap Press, 1970) and Robert Nozick, *Anarchy, State, and Utopia* (New York: Basic Books, Inc., 1974) both claim to lie within the social contract tradition, although they understand that tradition differently. It is possible that both Rawls and Nozick understand social contract theory differently than did those who originated the tradition, and those who employed it in Massachusetts in 1780. The secondary literature on the social contract, and social contract thinkers is vast. A recent book by Andrew Levine, *The Politics of Autonomy* (Amherst: University of Massachusetts Press, 1976) brings the techniques of analytic philosophy to the study of Rousseau. This approach explores the logic of social contract thinking (in this case as exemplified by Rousseau), without the historical dimension reflected in the present study of the Massachusetts experience. The comparison is interesting. A classic statement on the social contract tradition is John W. Gough, *The Social Contract*, 2d ed. (Oxford: Clarendon Press, 1957). My study of the social contract problem departed from Willmoore Kendall, *John Locke and the Doctrine of Majority Rule* (Urbana: University of Illinois Press, 1941).

General discussions of the literature of the Revolution may be found in: Clinton Rossiter, *Seedtime of the Republic* (New York: Harcourt, Brace and Co., 1953), pp. 326-361; Bernard Bailyn, *The Ideological Origins of the American Revolution* (Cambridge: Harvard University Press, Belknap Press, 1967), pp. 1-21; and Gordon Wood, *The Creation of the American Republic, 1776-1787* (New York: W. W. Norton and Co., Inc., 1969), pp. 619-627. Virtually all pamphlets and newspapers from the revolutionary era are available on microcard in the American Antiquarian Society's series, *Early American Imprints* and *Early American Newspapers*. The town returns on the Massachusetts Constitution of 1780 and other related primary materials are to be found in Oscar and Mary Handlin, eds., *The Popular Sources of Political Authority* (Cambridge: Harvard University Press, Belknap Press, 1966). *Massachusetts, Colony to Commonwealth* (Chapel Hill: University of North Carolina Press, 1961), edited by Robert J. Taylor, contains some documentary material not included in Handlin and Handlin's *Popular Sources*. Those interested in further secondary

treatments of the political thought of the Revolution are directed to the
work of Bailyn and Wood, mentioned above, and to that of Jack R. Pole.
Pole's *Political Representation in England and the Origins of the American
Republic* (Berkeley and Los Angeles: University of California Press, 1966)
is especially worthwhile for those interested in exploring the interrelation-
ships between political ideas and political practice. Pole also provides a
very extensive bibliography (pp. 567–581).

Those who are interested in discovering the political theory of the
Revolution for themselves will have to consult primary sources. Among
the primary sources, I found the pamphlet literature to be the most fruit-
ful source of theoretical discussion. Interestingly, Gordon Wood prefers
the newspapers. He says: "Newspaper essays are sometimes more revealing
of what is happening intellectually than longer pamphlets because of their
very brevity and lack of deliberateness" (*The Creation of the American Republic*, p. 621). Here he reveals clearly the way in which his understanding
of political thought differs from mine. For Wood, ideas are things that
people are seized by at given moments in time. The task of the interpreter
is to determine what ideas have seized what people, at what moment in
time. In my view, ideas embody theoretical perspectives understood by
the people who have them to transcend the immediate context in which
they were thought. A pamphlet, which runs thirty to fifty pages, and in
which the author attempts to develop an analysis of an important political
issue, is much more likely to reveal the fundamental theoretical perspective of the author than is a two-column newspaper essay.

This distinction (between pamphlets and newspaper essays) can be related to the theoretical framework which is developed in this book. The
social compact theory views the problem of politics in stages. Beginning
with the state of nature, a condition far removed from the immediate
politics of the day, the theory traces political authority through its foundation in the social compact to its institutionalization and operation under
a constitution. The stages of the theory that are furthest removed from the
ongoing business of government are those in which the deepest understanding of politics may be found. It is not surprising, then, that one finds
the most penetrating discussions of the state of nature and the social compact in the pamphlet literature, rather than in newspaper essays. It is also
not surprising that questions of government and politics were more vocif-
erously debated in the newspapers than in the pamphlets. The footnotes
to chapters 3 and 4 of this book reveal this difference in the sources upon
which the respective discussions in each chapter draw. One may go further
and say that the debates in the newspapers over the form of government
are more reflective of the differences in interests that marked revolutionary Massachusetts, while the pamphlet literature reveals general agreement
upon the fundamental principles of politics. It is not coincidental that
most of the pamphlets were published sermons. The sermons almost always addressed a biblical text and attempted to explain its relationship to

the political issues of the day. The discussions often contained a very deep level of theoretical analysis, and indicate that the congregations of revolutionary Massachusetts were regularly regaled with lessons on the relationship between religion, political theory, and politics. Therefore, the serious student of the political theory of the Revolution must turn to the pamphlets. For such hardy souls, I provide a selected list of the best of the pamphlets produced in Massachusetts between 1774 and 1780, along with the identifying number from Evans, *American Bibliography*.

Selected Pamphlets and Broadsides
Published in Massachusetts: 1774–1780

1774

Allen, John. *The Patriotic Whisper in the Ears of the King; or the Grand Request of the People of America Made Manifest. Intended as a Chariot of Liberty for the Sons of America, and a Standing Memorial of the Rights of the American Colonies. Being a Political Liberty Oration Upon the Branches of the American Charters, Proving them to Be as Sacred as the British Constitution; Delivered on the Last Annual Thanksgiving, at Mount Pleasant in the Wilds of America.* Boston: T. and J. Fleet, 1774. [Evans, 13103]

[Allen, John.] *The Watchman's Alarm to Lord North; or The British Parliamentary Boston Port-Bill Unwrapped: Being an Oration on the Meridian of Liberty. By the British Bostonian.* Salem: Samuel and Ebenezer Hall, 1774. [Evans, 13757]

Bradbury, Thomas. *The Ass; or, the Serphent: A Comparison Between the Tribes of Issachar and Don, in Their Regard for Civil Liberty. November 5, 1712.* Newbury Port: Thomas and Tinges, 1774. [Evans, 13173]

Chandler, Thomas Bradbury. *The American Querist: or, some Questions Proposed Relative to the Present Disputes Between Great Britain, and Her American Colonies. By a North American.* Boston: Mills and Hicks, 1774. [Evans, 13222]

Cooper, Samuel. *A Discourse on the Man of Sin: Delivered in the Chapel of Harvard College, in Cambridge, New England, September 1, 1773: at the Lecture Founded by the Honorable Paul Dudley, Esq.* Boston: Greenleaf's Printing Office, 1774. [Evans, 13227]

Fiske, Nathan. *The Importance of Righteousness to the Happiness and the Tendency of Oppression to the Misery of a People; Illustrated in Two Discourses Delivered at Brookfield, July 14, 1774, Being a Day Observed by General Consent Through the Province, (at the Recommendation of the Late House of Representatives) as a Day of Fasting and Prayer, an Account of the Threatening Aspect of Our Public Affairs.* Boston: John Kneeland, 1774. [Evans, 13278]

Hancock, John. *An Oration: Delivered March 5, 1774, at the Request of the Inhabitants of the Town of Boston: to Commemorate the Bloody Tragedy of the Fifth of March, 1770.* Boston: Edes and Gill, 1774. [Evans, 13314]

Hitchcock, Gad. *A Sermon Preached Before His Excellency Thomas Gage, Esq.: Governor: The Honorable His Majesty's Council, and the Honorable House of Representatives of the Province of the Massachusetts-Bay in New-England, May 25th, 1774. Being the Anniversary of the Election of His Majesty's Council for Said Province.* Boston: Edes and Gill, 1774. [Evans, 13330]

Lathrop, John. *A Sermon Preached to the Ancient and Honorable Artillery-Company in Boston, New-England, June 6th, 1774. Being the Anniversary of their Election of Officers.* Boston: Kneeland and Davis, 1774. [Evans, 13371]

Maccarty, Thaddeus. *Reformation of Manners, of Absolute Necessity in Order to Conciliate the Divine Favour, in Times of Public Evil and Distress, Shewn in Two Sermons, Preached at Worcester, Upon A Special Fast Observed There, as Well as in Many Other Towns, July 14th, 1774. On Account of the Public Difficulties of the Present Day.* Boston: William M'Alpine, 1774. [Evans, 13388]

Niles, Nathaniel. *Two Discourses on Liberty; Delivered at the North Church, in Newbury-Port, on Lord's Day, June 5, 1774, and Published at the General Desire of the Hearers.* Newbury-Port: I. Thomas and H. W. Tinges, 1774. [Evans, 13502]

Parsons, Jonathan. *Freedom From Civil and Ecclesiastical Slavery the Purchase of Christ. A Discourse Offered to a Numerous Assembly on March the fifth, 1774, at the Presbyterian Meeting House in New Bury-Port.* New Bury-Port: I. Thomas and H. W. Tinges, 1774. [Evans, 13503]

Prescott, Benjamin. *A Free and Calm Consideration of the Unhappy Misunderstandings and Debates, Which have of Late Years Arisen, and yet Subsist, Between the Parliament of Great-Britain, and these American Colonies. Contained, in Eight Letters, Six Whereof, Directed to a Gentleman of Distinction in England, Formerly Printed in the Essex Gazette. The Other Two, Directed to a Friend. Written by One Who was Born in the Colony of the Massachusetts-Bay, Before King William III. and Queen Mary II. of Blessed and Glorious Memory Ascended the Throne of England, Scotland, France and Ireland.* Salem: S. and E. Hall, 1774. [Evans, 13553]

Priestly, Joseph. *An Address to Protestant Dissenters of all Denominations on the Approaching Election of Members of Parliament, With Respect to the State of Public Liberty in General, and of American Affairs in Particular.* Boston: Thomas and John Fleet, 1774. [Evans, 13555]

Quincy, Josiah Junior. *Observations on the Act of Parliament Commonly*

Called the Boston Port-Bill; With Thoughts on Civil Society and Standing Armies. Boston: Edes and Gill, 1774. [Evans, 13561]

Sharp, Granville. *A Declaration of the People's Natural Right to a Share in the Legislature, Which is the Fundamental Principle of the British Constitution of State.* Boston: Edes and Gill, 1774. [Evans, 13609]

Skillman, Issac. *An Oration on the Beauties of Liberty, or the Essential Rights of the Americans. Delivered at the Second Baptist-Church in Boston. Upon the Last Annual Thanksgiving, December 3, 1772. Humbly Dedicated to the Right Honorable the Earl of Dartmouth. Published by the Request of Many. By a British Bostonian.* Hartford: Ebenezer Watson, 1774. [Evans, 13627]

Story, Isaac. *The Love of Our Country Recommended and Enforced. In a Sermon From Psalm CXXII.7, Delivered on a Day of Public Thanksgiving, December 15, 1774.* Boston: John Boyle, 1774. [Evans, 13643]

Tucker, John. *Remarks on a Discourse of the Rev. Jonathan Parsons, of Newbury-Port, Delivered on the Fifth of March, and Entitled, Freedom From Civil and Ecclesiastical Slavery the Purchase of Christ.* Boston: 1774. [Evans, 13753]

Webster, Samuel. *The Misery and Duty of an Oppress'd and Enslav'd People, Represented in a Sermon Delivered at Salisbury July 14, 1774. On a Day Set Apart for Fasting and Prayer, on Account of the Approaching Public Calamities. Published by Request.* Boston: Edes and Gill, 1774. [Evans, 13758]

Whitney, Peter. *The Transgression of a Land Punished by a Multitude of Rulers. Considered in Two Discourses, Delivered July 14, 1774, Being Voluntarily Observed in Most of the Religious Assemblies Throughout the Province of Massachusetts-Bay, as a Day of Fasting and Prayer, on Account of the Dark Aspect of our Public Affairs. And Now Published at the Desire of the Hearers, to Whom they are Inscribed.* Boston: John Boyle, 1774. [Evans, 13769]

1775

Adams, Zabdiel. *The Grounds of Confidence; A Sermon Preached at Lunenberg to a Company of Militia.* Boston, 1775. [Evans, 13789]

Barry, Henry. *The General Attacked by a Subaltern: or, the Strictures on the Friendly Address Examined and a Refutation of its Principals Attempted. Addressed to the People of America.* Boston: John Howe, 1775. [Evans, 13823]

———. *Remarks Upon a Discourse Preached December 15th, 1774. Being the Day Recommended by the Provincial Congress: and Afterwards at the Boston Lecture. By William Gordon, Pastor of the Third Church in Roxbury. In a Letter from a Gentleman in the Country to his Friend in Boston.* New York, 1775. [Evans, 13825]

Croswell, Andrew. *Mr. Murray Unmask'd. In which, among other things, is shown, that His Doctrine of Universal salvation is inimical to vertue, and Productive of a Church in Boston. With a Short Appendix, Containing the Address of Mr. Chandler, of Glocester, to the People of His Charge, with Regard to Mr. Murray.* Boston: J. Kneeland, 1775. [Evans, 13997]

Fish, Elisha. *A Discourse, Delivered at Worcester, March 28th, 1775, at the Desire of the Convention of Committees for the County of Worcester.* Worcester: Isaiah Thomas, 1775. [Evans, 14030]

Gordon, William. *A Discourse Preached December 15th, 1774 (in the afternoon). Being the Day Recommended by the Provincial Congress. And Afterwards at the Boston Lecture. By William Gordon, Pastor of the Third Church in Roxbury.* Boston: Thomas Leverett, 1775. [Evans, 14072]

——. *A Discourse Preached in the Morning of December 15th, 1774. Being the Day Recommended by the Provincial Congress.* Boston: Thomas Leverett, 1775. [Evans, 14070]

——. *A Sermon Preached Before the Honorable House of Representatives, [19 July, 1775] on the Day Intended for the Choice of Councellors, Agreeable to the Advice of the Continental Congress. By William Gordon, Pastor of the Third Church in Roxbury.* Watertown: Benjamin Edes, 1775. [Evans, 14073]

Hitchcock, Gad. *A Sermon Preached at Plymouth December 22d, 1774. Being the Anniversary Thanksgiving, in Commemoration of the First Landing of Our New-England Ancestors in that Place, Anno Dom. 1620.* Boston: Edes and Gill, 1775. [Evans, 14118]

Lee, Charles. *Strictures on a Pamphlet Entitled a "Friendly Address to all Reasonable Americans, on the Subject of Our Political Confusions." Addressed to the People of America.* Boston: Greenleaf's Printing Office, 1775. [Evans, 14151]

Leonard, Daniel. *Massachusettensis [Letters I, to XVII. To the Inhabitants of the Province of Massachusetts-Bay. 12 December, 1774–3 April, 1775.].* Boston: Mills and Hicks, 1775. [Evans, 14157]

Lyman, Joseph. *A Sermon Preached at Hatfield, December 15th, 1774, Being the Day Recommended by the Late Provincial Congress; to be Observed as a Day of Thanksgiving.* Boston: Edes and Gill, 1775. [Evans, 14172]

Mein, John. *Sagitarrius's Letters and Political Speculations Extracted from the Public Ledger. Humbly inscribed to the Very Loyal and Truly Pious Doctor Samuel Cooper, Pastor of the Congregational Church in Brattle Street.* Boston: by order of the Select Men, 1775. [Evans, 14255]

Noble, Oliver. *Some Strictures Upon the Sacred Story Recorded in the Book of Esther, Showing the Power and Oppression of State Ministers Tending to the Ruin and Destruction of God's People and* the Remarkable Interpositions of Divine Providence, in favour of the Oppressed; in a Discourse, Delivered at Newbury-Port, North Meeting-House, March 8th, 1775. In Commemoration of the Massacre at Boston, March the Fifth, 1770. By Oliver Noble, M.A. and Pastor of a Church in Newbury. Preached at the Request of a Number of Respectable Gentlemen of Said Town; and Now Published at the General Desire of the Hearers. Newbury-Port: E. Lunt and H. W. Tinges, 1775. [Evans, 14352]

Stearns, William. A View of the Controversy subsisting between Great-Britain and the American Colonies. A Sermon Preached at a Fast in Marlborough in Massachusetts-Bay, on Thursday, May 11, 1775. Agreeable to a Recommendation of the Provincial Congress. Watertown: Benjamin Edes, 1775. [Evans, 14474]

Warren, Joseph. An Oration; Delivered March 6th, 1775. At the Request of the Inhabitants of the Town of Boston; to Commemorate the Bloody Tragedy of the Fifth of March, 1770. By Dr. Joseph Warren. Boston: Edes and Gill, 1775. [Evans, 14608]

West, Samuel. A Sermon Preached at the Ordination of the Rev'd Jonathan Newell, to the Pastoral Care of the Church of Christ in Stow, October 11, 1774. By Samuel West, A.M. Pastor of the Church of Christ in Needham. Boston: Edes and Gill, 1775. [Evans, 14621]

Williams, Samuel. A Discourse on the Love of Our Country; Delivered on a Day of Thanksgiving, December 15, 1774. Salem: Samuel and Ebenezer Hall, 1775. [Evans, 14627]

1776

Adams, John. Thoughts on Government: Applicable to the Present State of the American Colonies. In a Letter from a Gentlemen to His Friend. Boston: John Gill, 1776. [Evans, 14640]

Baldwin, Samuel. A Sermon Preached at Plymouth, December 22, 1775. Being the Anniversary Thanksgiving, in Commemoration of the First Landing of the Fathers of New-England, there; Anno Domini 1620. Boston: Powars and Wills, 1776. [Evans, 14627]

Clarke, Jonas. The Fate of Blood-Thirsty Oppressors, and God's Tender Care for his Distressed People. A Sermon, Preached at Lexington, April 19, 1776. To Commemorate the Murder, Bloodshed and Commencement of Hostilities, between Great-Britain and America, in that Town, by a Brigade of Troops of George III, Under Command of Lieutenant-Colonel Smith, on the Nineteenth of April, 1775. To Which is Added a Brief Narrative of the Principal Transactions of that Day. By Jonas Clarke, A.M. Pastor of the Church in Lexington. Boston: Powars and Wills, 1776. [Evans, 14679]

Essex County, Massachusetts. A Broadside Calling for Equal Representation and Proposing a County Convention. Salem: Ezekiel Russell, 1776. [Evans, 14749]

Fitch, Elijah. *A Discourse, the Substance of which was Delivered at Hopkinton, on the Lord's-Day, March 24th, 1776, Being the Next Sabbath Following the Precipitate Flight of the British Troops from Boston. Published at the Request of the Hearers.* Boston: John Boyle, 1776. [Evans, 14755]

Langdon, Samuel. *The Co-incidence of Natural with Revealed Religion. A Sermon at the Annual Lecture Instituted in Harvard College by the Last Will and Testament of the Honorable Paul Dudley, Esq.; Delivered November 1, 1775. By Samuel Langdon, D.D. President of Harvard College.* Boston: Samuel Hall, 1776. [Evans, 14822]

Maccarty, Thaddeus. *Praise to God, a Duty of Continual Obligation. A Sermon, Preached at Worcester, Thursday, November 23d, 1775. Being a Day of Public Thanksgiving by the Appointment of the Central Assembly. By Thaddeus Maccarty, A.M. Pastor of the Church in Worcester.* Worcester: I. Thomas, 1776. [Evans, 14830]

Mansfield, Issac Jr. *A Sermon, Preached in the Camp at Roxbury, November 23, 1775; being the Day Appointed by Authority for Thanksgiving Through the Province. By Issac Mansfield, Jun. A.M. Chaplain to General Thomas's Regiment, in the Continental Army. Published at the Request of the Officers in Said Regiment.* Boston: S. Hall, 1776. [Evans, 14831]

West, Samuel. *A Sermon Preached before the Honorable Council, and the Honorable House of Representatives, of the Colony of the Massachusetts-Bay, in New-England. May 29th, 1776. Being the Anniversary for the Election of the Honorable Council for the Colony. By Samuel West, A.M. Pastor of a Church in Dartmouth.* Boston: John Gill, 1776. [Evans, 15217]

1777

Conant, Sylvanus. *An Anniversary Sermon Preached at Plymouth, December 23, 1776. In Grateful Memory of the First Landing of Our Worthy Ancestors in that Place, An. Dom. 1620. By Sylvanus Conant, Pastor or* [sic.] *the First Church in Middlesborough.* Boston: Thomas and John Fleet, 1777. [Evans, 15256]

Cooke, Samuel. *The Violent Destroyed: and Oppressed Delivered. A Sermon Preached at Lexington, April 19, 1777. A Memorial of the Bloody Tragedy, Barbarously Acted by a Party of British Troops, in that Town and the Adjacent, April 19, 1775.* Boston: Draper and Phillips, 1777. [Evans, 15279]

Gordon, William. *The Separation of the Jewish Tribes, After the Death of Solomon, Accounted for, and Applied to the Present Days in a Sermon Preached Before the General Court, on Friday, July the 4th, 1777. Being the Anniversary of the Declaration of Independency. By William Gordon. Pastor of the Third Church in Roxbury.* Boston: J. Gill, 1777. [Evans, 15317]

Hitchborn, Benjamin. *An Oration, Delivered March 5th, 1777, at the Request of the Inhabitants of the Town of Boston; to Commemorate the Bloody Tragedy of the Fifth of March, 1770. By Benjamin Hitchborn, Esq.* Boston: Edes and Gill, 1777. [Evans, 15363]

Keteltas, Abraham. *God Arising and Pleading His People's Cause; or, the American War in Favor of Liberty, Against the Measures and Arms of Great-Britain, Shewn to be the Cause of God: In a Sermon Preached October 5th, 1777 at an Evening Lecture, in the Presbyterian Church in Newbury-Port. By Abraham Keteltas, A.M.* Newbury-Port: John Mycall, 1777. [Evans, 15378]

Stearns, Josiah. *Two Sermons, Preached at Epping, in the State of New-Hampshire, January 30th, 1777, On a Public Fast, Appointed by Authority, on Account of the Unnatural and Distressing Year with Great-Britain, in Defence of Liberty.* Newbury-Port: John Mycall, 1777. [Evans, 15602]

Webster, Samuel. *A Sermon Preached before the Honorable Council, and the Honorable House of Representatives, of the State of the Massachusetts-Bay, in New-England, at Boston, May 28, 1777. Being the Anniversary for the Election of the Honorable Council. By Samuel Webster, A.M. Pastor of a Church in Salisbury.* Boston: Edes and Gill, 1777. [Evans, 15703]

Whitney, Peter. *American Independence Vindicated. A Sermon Delivered at Northborough, Massachusetts-Bay, September 12, 1776, at a Lecture Appointed for Publishing the Declaration of Independence, passed July 4, 1776.* Boston: Powars and Willis, 1777. [Evans, 15710]

1778

Adams, Zabdiel. *Brotherly Love and Compassion, Described and Recommended, in a Sermon, Preached before a Society of the Most Ancient and Honourable Free and Accepted Masons, in Lancaster, New-England, On Wednesday, the Twenty Fourth of June, 1778. By Zabdiel Adams, Pastor of the Church in Lunenburgh.* Worcester: Isaiah Thomas, 1778. [Evans, 15716]

Backus, Isaac. *Government and Liberty Described: and Ecclesiastical Tyranny Exposed. By Isaac Backus, Pastor of a Church in Middleborough, September 19, 1778.* Boston: Powars and Willis, 1778. [Evans, 15727]

Bird, Jonathan. *Jesus Knocking—Sinners Opening. Jesus Entering—Sinners Saved. Opened and Applied in a Sermon from Revelations III. 20. By Jonathan Bird, Belonging to Hartford in Connecticut.* Worcester: Anthony Haswell, 1778. [Evans, 15745]

Cushing, Jacob. *Divine Judgement Upon Tyrants: and Compassion to the Oppressed. A Sermon Preached at Lexington, April 20th, 1778. In commemoration of the Murderous War and Rapine Inhumanely Per-*

petrated by Two Brigades of British Troops, in that Town and Neighborhood, on the Nineteenth of April, 1775. Boston: Powars and Willis, 1778. [Evans, 15776]

Ipswich, Massachusetts Convention. *Result of the Convention of Delegates Holden at Ipswich in the County of Essex, Who Were Deputed to Take into Consideration the Constitution and Form of Government, Proposed by the Convention of the State of Massachusetts-Bay. (By Theophilus Parsons).* Newbury-Port: John Mycall, 1778. [Evans, 15858]

Keteltas, Abraham. *Reflections on Extortion, Shewing the Nature, Malignity, and Fatal Tendency of that Sin, to Individuals and Communities, Displayed and Enforced in a Sermon Preached at Newbury-Port, on Lord's Day February 15th, 1778.* Newbury-Port: J. Mycall, 1778. [Evans, 15859]

Lathrop, John. *A Discourse Preached on March the Fifth, 1778 . . . Published at the Request of the Hearers. Together with some Marginal Notes.* Boston: Draper and Folsom, 1778. [Evans, 15866]

Maccarty, Thaddeus. *The Guilt of Innocent Blood Put Away. A Sermon, Preached at Worcester, July 2, 1778. On Occasion of the Execution of James Buchanan, William Brooks, Ezra Ross, and Bathshua Spooner, for the Murder of Mr. Joshua Spooner, at Brookfield, on the Evening of the First of March Preceeding. Together with an Appendix, Giving Some Account of Those Prisoners in their Last Stage. By Thaddeus Maccarty, A.M. Pastor of the Church in said Worcester.* Worcester: Isaiah Thomas, 1778. [Evans, 15872]

Payson, Phillips. *A Sermon Preached Before the Honorable Council, and the Honorable House of Representatives, of the State of Massachusetts-Bay, in New England, at Boston, May 27, 1778. Being the Anniversary for the Election of the Honorable Council. By Phillips Payson, A.M. Pastor of a Church in Chelsea.* Boston: John Gill, 1778. [Evans, 15956]

Powers, Peter. *Jesus Christ the True King and Head of Government. A Sermon Preached Before the General Assembly of the State of Vermont, on the Day of Their First Election, March 12, 1778, at Windsor. By Peter Powers, A.M. Pastor of the Church in Newbury.* Newbury-Port: John Mycall, 1778. [Evans, 16019]

Tucker, John. *The Validity of Presbyterian Ordination Argued, From Jesus Christ's Being the Founder, the Sole Legislator, and Supreme Head and Ruler of the Christian Church. A Discourse Delivered in the Chapel of Harvard-College in Cambridge, New-England, September 2, 1778. At the Lecture Founded by the Hon. Paul Dudley, Esq.; By John Tucker, A.M. Pastor of the First Church in Newbury.* Boston: Thomas and John Fleet, 1778. [Evans, 16069]

West, Samuel. *An Anniversary Sermon, Preached at Plymouth, December 22nd, 1777. In Grateful Memory of the First Landing of Our Pious*

New-England Ancestors in that Place, A.D. 1620. Boston: Draper
and Folsom, 1778. [Evans, 16169]

Wigglesworth, Edward. *The Authority of Tradition Considered, at the
Lecture Founded by the Hon. Judge Dudley, in Harvard College,
Nov. 5, 1777. By Edward Wigglesworth, M.A. Hollis-Professor of
Divinity.* Boston: Thomas and John Fleet, 1778. [Evans, 16171]

Whiting, William. *An Address to the Inhabitants of the County of Berkshire. Respecting Their Present Opposition to Civil Government.
By Impartial Reason.* Hartford: Watson and Goodwin, 1778. [Evans,
15717]

1779

Backus, Isaac. *Policy, as Well as Honesty, Forbids the Use of Secular Force
in Religious Affairs.* Boston: Draper and Folsom, 1779. [Evans,
16195]

Concord, Massachusetts. *Proceedings of the Convention Begun and Held
at Concord, in the County of Middlesex, in and for the State of
Massachusetts-Bay, on the 14th Day of July, 1779, for the Purpose
of Carrying into Effect the Several Interesting and Important Mes-
sages Recommended by Congress, to the Inhabitants of the United
States . . . [To check depreciation in the currency, by arrangement
of prices of necessary articles of consumption and commerce.].*
Boston: Benjamin Edes and Sons, 1779. [Evans, 16228]

Everett, Moses. *Early Piety Recommended. A Sermon Preached Lords'-
Day Eve, February 1st, 1778, to Two Religious Societies of Young
Men in Dorchester, Massachusetts.* Boston: 1779. [Evans, 16268]

Fiske, Nathan. *The Character and Blessedness of a Diligent and Faithful
Servant. A Sermon Delivered at Brookfield, October 19, 1779, at
the Funeral of the Honorable Jedediah Foster.* Providence: Bennett
Wheeler, 1779. [Evans, 16273]

Hitchcock, Gad. *Natural Religion Aided by Revelation and Perfected in
Christianity. A Discourse Delivered in the Chapel of the University
at Cambridge, in the State of Massachusetts-Bay. September 1, 1779.
At the Lecture Founded by the Hon. Paul Dudley, Esq.; by Gad
Hitchcock, A.M. Pastor of the Second Church in Pembroke.* Boston:
T. and J. Fleet, 1779. [Evans, 16303]

Howard, Simeon. *A Sermon on Brotherly Love, Preached at the Old Meeting House in Boston, December 28, 1778. Before the Most Ancient
and Honorable Society of Free-and-Accepted Masons.* Boston: Brother Thomas Fleet, 1779. [Evans, 16307]

Lesslie, George. *The Nature and Tendency of the Sin of Selfishness Considered. A Discourse Preached at Newbury Port, August 12, 1779.
Newbury: John My*call, 1779. [Evans, 16322]

Murray, John. *Nehemiah, on the Struggle for Liberty, Never in Vain, When*

Managed with Virtue and Perseverance. A Discourse Delivered at the Presbyterian Church in Newbury-Port, Nov. 4th, 1779. Being the Day Appointed by Government to be Observed as a Day of Solemn Fasting and Prayer Through-out the State of Massachusetts-Bay. Newbury: John Mycall, 1779. [Evans, 16379]

Stillman, Samuel. *A Sermon Preached Before the Honorable Council and House of Representatives of the State of Massachusetts-Bay, at Boston, May 26, 1779.* Boston: T. and J. Fleet, 1779. [Evans, 16537]

Tudor, William. *An Oration Delivered March 5th, 1779, at the Request of the Inhabitants of the Town of Boston; to Commemorate the Bloody Tragedy of the Fifth of March, 1770. By William Tudor, Esq.* Boston: Edes and Gill, 1779. [Evans, 16500]

Warren, Mercy Otis. *The Motley Assembly, A Farce. Published for the Entertainment of the Curious.* Boston: Nathaniel Coverly, 1779. [Evans, 16668]

1780

Backus, Isaac. *An Appeal to the People of the Massachusetts State, Against Arbitrary Power.* Boston: 1780. [Evans, 43766]

Bowdoin, James. *A Philosophical Discourse, Addressed to the American Academy of Arts and Sciences, in the Presence of a Respectable Audience, Assembled at the Meeting-House in Brattle-Street, in Boston, on the Eighth of November M,DCC,LXXX, After the Inauguration of the President into Office. By James Bowdoin, Esq.; President of the Said Academy.* Boston: Benjamin Edes and Sons, 1789. [Evans, 16720]

Cooper, Samuel. *A Sermon Preached Before His Excellency John Hancock, Esq.; Governor, The Honourable the Senate, and House of Representatives of the Commonwealth of Massachusetts, October 25, 1780. Being the Day of the Commencement of the Constitution, and the Inauguration of the New Government. By Samuel Cooper, D.D.* Boston: T. and J. Fleet, 1780. [Evans, 16753]

Howard, Simeon. *A Sermon Preached Before the Honorable Council and the Honorable House of Representatives of the State of Massachusetts-Bay, in New-England, May 31, 1780. Being the Anniversary for the Election of the Honorable Council. By Simeon Howard, A.M. Pastor of the West Church in Boston.* Boston: John Gill, 1780. [Evans, 16800]

Mason, Jonathan, Jr. *An Oration, Delivered March 6, 1780. At the Request of the Inhabitants of the Town of Boston, to Commemorate the Bloody Tragedy of the Fifth of March, 1770. By Jonathan Mason, Jr.* Boston: John Gill, 1780. [Evans, 13866]

Smith, William. *The Candid Retrospect; or the American War Examined by Whig Principles.* Charles Town: Robert Wells and Son, 1780. [Evans, 16728]

To the General Court of the Massachusetts, Assembled at Boston, October, 1780. We whose Names are hereunto subscribed . . . enter our PRO-TEST against the power claimed in the Third Article of the Declaration of Rights in the new plan of government now introduced among us. . . . (Broadside) Boston: 1780. [Evans, 17006]

Williams, Samuel. *The Influence of Christianity on Civil Society, Represented in a Discourse Delivered November 10, 1779, at the Ordination of the Reverand Mr. John Price, to the Pastoral Core of the First Church in Salem. By Samuel Williams, A.M. Pastor of the First Church in Bradford.* Boston: John Boyle, 1780. [Evans, 17073]

Index